Is Long-Term Psychotherapy Unethical?

· ·

Carol Shaw Austad

· ·

Foreword by
Nicholas A. Cummings

Is Long-Term Psychotherapy Unethical?

Toward a Social Ethic in an Era
of Managed Care

Jossey-Bass Publishers
San Francisco

The epigraph in the Introduction is adapted from *Health Affairs*, "An Interview with HMO Executive David Lawrence," John Iglehart. *Health Affairs, 13*, winter 1994, pp. 65–78. Copyright 1994 THE PEOPLE-TO-PEOPLE HEALTH FOUNDATION, INC.

The brief quotation used as an epigraph in Chapter Four is from *The Social Transformation of American Medicine* by Paul Starr. Copyright © 1982 by Paul Starr. Reprinted by permission of Basic Books, a division of HarperCollins Publishers, Inc.

The Churchill epigraph in Chapter Eight is reprinted from "The Doctor as Gatekeeper," Christine Meyer. *HMO Practice, 7*, 1993, pp. 12–14.

Substantial discounts on bulk quantities of Jossey-Bass books are available to corporations, professional associations, and other organizations. For details and discount information, contact the special sales department at Jossey-Bass Inc., Publishers (415) 433–1740; Fax (800) 605–2665.

For sales outside the United States, please contact your local Simon & Schuster International office.

 Manufactured in the United States of America on Lyons Falls Pathfinder Tradebook. This paper is acid-free and 100 percent totally chlorine-free.

Library of Congress Cataloging-in-Publication Data

Austad, Carol Shaw.
   Is long-term psychotherapy unethical? : toward a social ethic in an era of managed care / Carol Shaw Austad.
      p. cm.
   Includes bibliographical references and index.
   ISBN 0–7879–0218–7
   1. Brief psychotherapy—Moral and ethical aspects.   2. Managed mental health care—Moral and ethical aspects.   3. Psychotherapy—Social aspects.   I. Title.
RC480.55.A97   1996
616.89'14—dc20
                                                                      95–52113
                                                                      CIP

HB Printing   10 9 8 7 6 5 4 3 2 1   FIRST EDITION

Contents

Part Three: What Do We Need To Do?

Foreword

• •

Is Long-Term Psychotherapy Unethical? may well be the most important book of the managed care era. Austad has given us a scholarly work that assesses both the contributions and flaws of both managed care and the practice of psychotherapy. She demonstrates how both the health care industry and clinical professionals inadvertently have their own respective brands of rationing. And she asks hard questions about vested interests in the mental health profession who advocate long-term therapy despite growing evidence about what really works and what doesn't.

But she does not leave us there. Austad is a visionary whose conceptualization of a social ethic for the fair distribution of limited resources is at once pragmatic and compassionate. Ultimately she makes a convincing argument for brief intermittent therapy as the treatment of choice for most of the population.

The result is essential reading for everyone working in behavioral health care today: practitioners, managers, executives, policy makers. We can all benefit from its crucial message for these changing times for the delivery of mental health care in the United States.

Scottsdale, Arizona　　　　　　　　　　　　Nicholas A. Cummings
January 1996

To my grandfather, who predicted this book.

Love to my mother and father.

To all those who need some psychotherapy but get none.

Acknowledgments

* *

I am indebted to all of my managed care colleagues—those who participated in my research, worked with me in attempting to establish the Division of Psychologists and Managed Health Care within the American Psychological Association, and those who talked with me untiringly about the state of psychotherapy, long-term therapy, and managed care. I hope their interests and concerns are reflected in this book.

My thanks to all of the researchers, scholars, clinicians, and others whose research, work, and writing I have quoted or used as the basis of my arguments. So much of their thinking has inspired mine.

I am grateful to all my patients, from whom I have learned so much. They are my real teachers.

Special thanks to my editor, Alan Rinzler, who offered so much encouragement and expert comment and kept me on task. Without him, this book would have never been written. And my appreciation to all who worked in the production and distribution of the book.

Finally, a special appreciation to Arnold. And thanks to my family and friends, who have put up with my fixation on this topic for a number of years, but especially in the final six months of writing the book. Their love and patience have sustained me.

New Britain, Connecticut   Carol Shaw Austad
January 1996

Is Long-Term
Psychotherapy Unethical?

Introduction

> *Contrary to popular rhetoric, the quality of care now
> provided in the United States is uneven at best and
> mediocre in many instances. Consequently, our
> nation is spending too much money for too much
> unnecessary or even harmful care.*
>
> *David Lawrence*

In the best of all possible worlds, people would have access to
unlimited mental health care. But in today's world of dwindling
resources, choices must be made and limits must be set. Is it unethical to perform long-term psychotherapy in an era of diminishing
health care resources?

The recent profound transformation of our nation's health care
system is bringing issues to the surface that have seldom been
addressed before. With the future of psychotherapy and the fate of
the mental health professions hanging in the balance, we urgently
need to discuss matters that we hardly ever mention out loud.

My personal interest in health care and psychotherapy emerged
early in my career as a psychologist. In 1982, after interning for two
years in a public hospital for the indigent, the chronically ill, and

the severely disturbed, I took my first job as a full-fledged psychologist in a private psychiatric hospital. The contrast between the treatment of patients at that hospital was unsettling. The glaring inequities in the way the hospital dealt with those who could pay versus those who could not pay, between those who were insured and those who were not insured, appalled me. I knew I wanted to help, but I was at a loss as to how I could remedy problems that permeated the nation's mental health care delivery system.

In 1983 I left the private psychiatric hospital for a position in a health maintenance organization, or HMO, an integrated health care enterprise that employs salaried providers to give health care to its subscribers. Arriving as an enthusiastic long-term psychodynamic therapist, I knew absolutely nothing about managed care, and I certainly never intended for it to become the all-consuming passion it has been in my life.

Graduate school had not prepared me for working at the HMO. I learned "on the job" from experienced HMO clinicians. Staff meetings were microcosms of the mental health care universe. Our discussions centered around the professional, clinical, and social issues that were vexing all of American mental health care. Our interdisciplinary staff reflected the diversity of professions and problems within the field. We fought with one another over theory, practice, and even pay. Social workers complained that they ought to earn as much as psychologists. Psychologists argued that they ought to be at parity with psychiatrists. Nurse specialists believed that since they possessed limited prescription-writing credentials, they should be closer to psychiatrists in income. "Equal pay for equal work!" was the cry. This issue continues to be a source of conflict today.

Despite our disagreements, we struggled together to achieve our goal of delivering psychotherapy fairly and equitably to all our members. We were led by our chief, a psychologist with a progressive-socialist outlook. Our motto was "Our patient is not just the single individual but also the sociological matrix of the entire health plan membership." To take care of our patients, we needed to be creative in our clinical work and devise innovative ways of maintaining, improving, and repairing the mental health of the entire community. As a result of this atmosphere, I felt that my own practice was vibrant and alive.

In the HMO I learned new truths about psychotherapy that I would not have discovered for years in any other environment; I had a corrective emotional experience, which took place in a flash. As my caseload was building and I saw patient after patient, I noticed that a number of them came for only one or two sessions. Naturally, as a psychodynamically trained clinician, I agonized over these "treatment failures." Each made me doubt my therapeutic prowess and ponder what had gone awry. What had I done wrong? Why hadn't I broken through these patients' resistance? Why hadn't they returned? But after some time had passed, I began to receive an occasional call from some of these so-called treatment failures.

I remember the day that one such patient, Joyce, came back to see me after one year. As we sat face to face, her words jolted me: "I got so much from our conversation a year ago, I wanted to see you again to get a jump start." My whole body felt electrified. I remember telling myself at that moment to remain calm and not let my facial expression betray my utter amazement. I was experiencing a moment of truth. What I had interpreted as a treatment failure—a failure my supervisors would have attributed to a lack of therapeutic sophistication—had actually been a success. A single session could provide a powerful introjection for a patient, one that would have positive long-term effects. I saw Joyce for two more visits, after which she had again gotten what she needed. She told me she would call me again when necessary, and I knew she would. I was now filled with a great faith in patients' ability to judge what they did and did not require.

As more and more such incidents were repeated, I began to revise my thinking about psychotherapy. I combed the literature and discovered that others had shared similar experiences.

Nicholas Cummings, founder of Biodyne (a managed mental health care company that has evolved into a major force in mental health care delivery today) and formerly chief psychologist at Kaiser-Permanente Health Plan (a staff model HMO in northern California), had already published a substantial amount on what I had discovered for myself. He called it "intermittent psychotherapy throughout the life cycle." Others from Kaiser, including Michael Hoyt, Moshe Talmon, and Robert Rosenbaum, as well as mental health professionals from Harvard Community Health Plan, including Simon Budman, Michael Bennett, James Donovan, Steve Friedman, and Margot Fangor, had also written about brief therapy and the managed care setting.

My clinical experiences and reading helped me understand that patients do not always use psychotherapy in the way therapists think they ought to use it. Traditional therapists believe sessions should be held weekly, but patients tend to use it on a schedule that fits their own needs. Conceptualizing psychotherapy in this way made me happy; more people could enjoy the benefits of short-term interventions if therapists looked at how patients use psychotherapy more realistically.

After six years, I left full-time work at the HMO to teach at a university. I began a research program centered on how managed care has affected providers and patients and the evolution of psychotherapy. From my studies I learned that long-term therapists can work contentedly in some managed care environments if they acquire a new perspective and make some appropriate attitudinal adjustments. But after a year in academe, I found that I desperately missed my HMO patients. HMO therapy was in my blood. I returned on a part-time basis and have been there ever since as a frontline clinician and researcher for over thirteen years.

What incites my energy and attracts my attention about managed care is that it holds the potential to cure our sick health care system. Although we have the most expensive health care in the world, we can no longer say we have the best health care in the world. And the high cost of our health care affects every segment of our society. For example, U.S. auto companies must add $1,400 to the cost of each new car to cover their employee health insurance costs, thereby losing their competitive edge in the market. Moreover, the forty-one million or more uninsured Americans live with an uncertainty about their health care that most inhabitants of Third World countries don't have to tolerate. Many Americans go without basic services such as needed hospitalizations, medications, medical supplies, and emergency care. If a child of uninsured parents is born with a cleft palate, the family is required to finance the surgery; this means they must make many personal sacrifices, like having to eat low-quality food, drive a rundown car, or work a second job.

Myriad Americans suffer substantial physical, psychological, and economic hardship as a result of a lack of basic health care, let alone mental health care. When people are denied their basic right to health care, their mental health likewise suffers. A family struggling to pay for their child's surgery will hardly place a high priority on weekly $100 psychotherapy sessions. Moreover, many of our chronically mentally ill are homeless or poor and consequently unserved or underserved. It is a national outrage that we have neglected these vulnerable individuals, forcing them to live in a state of psychic suffering by not affording them basic health and mental health coverage.

In its early years, managed care (especially nonprofit HMOs like the one I worked for) reflected the desire of companies and unions to give their employees and members comprehensive, affordable health care. They originally held tremendous promise as a means of distributing health and mental health care fairly and equitably, allowing easy access to care, supplying appropriate care to a diverse array of patients, monitoring quality, and enhancing communication between providers and patients. Despite the complex economic realities of health care in the United States today, managed care has the potential to deliver the right care at the right time in the right way.

What saddens me, however, is that we seem to be losing sight of the humanitarian basis of health care. Instead of distributing health care through nonprofit, staff, or group HMOs, we seem to be headed in the direction of more huge, for-profit health care corporations created by merger after merger. Some of these corporations place too much emphasis on cost savings and profits and too little on caring for the sick, safeguarding their members' wellness, and providing good value for the energy and resources expended on health care.

Nevertheless, despite the shortcomings of managed care, any attempt to repair our health care system is better than no attempt. This is why it is so important for us, the stewards of psychotherapy, to keep in mind a fundamental fact—all managed care is not the same. I have found that when people discuss managed care they often concentrate on some particular aspect of it that they are familiar with—often an experience they did not like or agree with. The term "managed care" has many different meanings to different people, from nonprofit HMOs to huge for-profit health care corporations. Clarifying our definitions is an important step in engaging in constructive dialogue.

To add to the complexity of the situation, managed care is "in motion," changing day by day. Of course, such change is to be expected. We are in the midst of trying to remodel our health care system. New variables are introduced into the equation every day—new financial plans, new provider-patient-payer-employer relationships, new legal or regulatory demands. New challenges must be met. New rules, new risks, and new players appear daily. Managed care is growing so rapidly and becoming so complex that independent courses of study are now offered in newly formed "managed care institutes" to train new experts in the field.

In its ideal form, managed care offers a framework for distributing health care in a fair, equitable, and democratic manner; in its worst form, it fuels corporate greed, places cost above care, deprives patients of needed treatment, and robs providers of autonomy. A never-ending search for greater profits and cheaper products makes some managed care plans systems to be avoided.

How do psychotherapy and mental health professionals fit into the world of managed care? As it always has been, the role of psychotherapy will be very much influenced in the future by the fiscal paradigm under which it is delivered. So the activities of mental health professionals today have deep implications for the future of psychotherapy and what clinical prototypes will prevail. Will our future models be long-term or short-term? Will they be based in research and empirical findings? Will they emphasize the use of primary, secondary, or tertiary care?

Our professional codes of ethics invoke a sense of social responsibility. They ask us to mitigate the causes of human suffering and support social policies that serve the public interest. I believe that those of us who are fortunate enough to be members of the helping professions have a moral and ethical responsibility to be concerned about the welfare of society as well as the individual. Thus we must take appropriate action to solve the problems of our nation's mental health care system.

Just as the distribution of health care is not equitable in the United States, neither is the distribution of psychotherapy. Many who could benefit from psychotherapy do not receive it. Some who do not need it may get too much of it. Some groups may benefit at the expense of others. How can we make sure that everyone who needs psychotherapy gets his or her fair share?

This book is about this complex relationship between psychotherapy and the American health care environment. As I worked in various settings—public, private, managed—I began to see that psychotherapy is best studied and understood in the context within which it is delivered. It is an intricate entity that has its own social, economic, and cultural milieu. It occurred to me that just as medical sociology helps us understand medicine, a sociology of psychotherapy, in which we study its evolution, usefulness, and distribution, would likewise help us understand psychotherapy.

Developing a sociological perspective on psychotherapy is a complex task, requiring us to wander through a labyrinth of relevant issues and related matters. Hopefully this book will accomplish this, by examining controversies about psychotherapy, managed care, and ethics in an era of health care reform. Specifically, I want to pose the following questions related to psychotherapy and managed care:

- Does traditional psychotherapy contribute to inequity in the distribution of mental health care?

- Is managed care unfair in its distribution of mental health care?

- Is managed care destroying the practice of long-term psychotherapy?

- How does money affect the practice of psychotherapy? Can payment change clinical practice styles?

- How much of what long-term therapists do is based in myth versus empiricism?

- Is long-term or short-term therapy better? And for whom?

- How can current information about the epidemiology of psychotherapy improve psychotherapy services and techniques?

- Is it possible to provide adequate and appropriate mental health services to all Americans?

- Can we strike a balance between individual and societal needs to enable everyone to obtain his or her fair share of psychotherapy?

- How can mental health providers cope with the ethical and clinical demands of the changing health care environment?

Overview of the Contents

Part One examines the health care revolution, resistance to change, how profit influences care, and ethical issues in health care delivery. This discussion highlights how health care reform and the rise of managed care is affecting the individual practitioner, the practice of psychotherapy, and professional ethics.

Part Two focuses on specific differences between long- and short-term therapy, how today's patients use psychotherapy, and the empirical basis for determining the need for long- or short-term psychotherapy. Some sociological interpretations of how long-term psychotherapy became dominant and how managed care will affect its future are highlighted.

Part Three explores society's present need for psychotherapeutic revisionism. It looks at psychotherapy in the aggregate, exploring professional resistance to change, the need for revised ethics, and the importance of developing a sociology of psychotherapy. Wisdom is contributed from a variety of providers who are coping with these monumental changes.

I know this book will make some people feel uncomfortable, and I apologize for that in advance. But in order to find solutions to the problems discussed herein, we must begin to open a dialogue about them. All of us talk too little about the most pressing issues confronting the nation's health and mental health, and this threatens the very democratic fiber of our society.

Notes

p. 1, *"Contrary to popular rhetoric"*: Quoted by David Lawrence in Iglehart, J. K. (1994). Changing course in turbulent times: An interview with David Lawrence. *Health Affairs, 13*(5), 74.

p. 4, *Nicholas Cummings, founder of Biodyne*: Cummings, N., & Sayama, M. (1995). *Focused psychotherapy: A casebook of brief intermittent psychotherapy throughout the life cycle*. New York: Brunner Mazel.

Part I

· ·

The Current Transformation of Ethics
in Behavioral Health Care

The Therapist's Dilemma

Transformation of the Mental Health Care System

> If a hundred people sleep and dream, each of them
> will experience a different world in his dream. Every-
> one's dream might be said to be true, but it would be
> meaningless to ascertain that only one person's dream
> was the true world and others were fallacies.
>
> Kalu Rinpoche

D r. Anderson picked up a copy of the *New York Times* while drinking his morning coffee. The front page headline read "Managed Care Changing Practice of Psychotherapy." The article recounted the conflict raging between managed care companies and mental health professionals. It described disillusioned, disgruntled long-term therapists who indicted the managed care system for destroying the field of long-term psychotherapy. It quoted managed care proponents who accused long-term psychotherapists of keeping the "worried well" engaged in interminable talk with no measurable improvement.

Dr. Anderson, a seasoned clinician, realized that he, too, was caught in this current; it threatened to sweep away his three-decade-old practice. He knew that under this chaotic and unpredictable health care system, his profession was in crisis. He asked himself what was happening to the practice of long-term psychotherapy in this epoch of health care reform. He was not alone in asking this question.

Health Care Reform, Managed Care, and Psychotherapy

The curtain is closing on the era of fee-for-service practice covered by indemnity insurance. Under the fee-for-service system, health care providers were paid on the basis of services rendered. Most patients were covered by indemnity insurance, which reimbursed them for all covered expenses. This fiscal arrangement allowed health care providers to remain relatively autonomous, with third-party payers exercising little direct control over their practice. But gone are the days when a provider could render any service he or she thought fit, bill the patient's insurance company, and receive payment with no questions asked. Dr. Anderson's generation will be the last to remember giving and receiving health care in an unregulated, fee-for-service format.

American health care is undergoing a far-reaching paradigm shift, and mental health professionals are reacting in a way reminiscent of how resistant doctors reacted to analogous shifts in the past. In a 1912 editorial of the *Journal of the American Medical Association*, one physician objected vehemently to the institution of indemnity-style health insurance in the United States, citing dire potential consequences for the nation's health care. Before that time, patients had paid doctors directly, out of their own pocket. No third-party insurers existed. The medical profession was very protective, fearful of the potential of outside influences to infringe upon the sanctity of the doctor-patient relationship. Thus many doctors objected to health insurance, even if it was in the patient's best

interest and it lent patients peace of mind to know that a catastrophic illness would not bankrupt them. Anticipating the sentiments I hear today from many disconcerted colleagues, the 1912
editorialist wrote that the nation was witnessing "the beginning of
the end of the old system of individual practice . . . and of the old
relationship between patient and physician."

But despite physicians' fear and trepidation at the prospect of dealing with third-party payers, the doctor-patient relationship continued
to flourish. And indemnity insurance turned out to be very profitable
for health care providers. But now these arrangements no longer
receive strong support from payers. We are seeing a great shift away
from this well-established fiscal paradigm, toward managed care.

Catapulted into this sea of change, we mental health professionals must learn to navigate through an ocean of unfamiliar demands. Suddenly we must be experts on the interface between
financial and clinical aspects of mental health care. Suddenly we
must justify the cost of psychotherapy, demonstrate its effectiveness,
and ensure our patients' satisfaction. Suddenly patients are "customers" and payers are "reviewers."

Mental health care will not be practiced in the future as it has
been in the past. Power and control are slipping away from professionals and moving toward insurers, managed care administrators,
corporations, and conglomerates. The cottage industry that gave
many of us respected employment and provided us a comfortable
living is now teetering on the brink of becoming totally industrialized; managed care is the primary method being used to accomplish
this goal.

These changes have created an environment laden with dilemmas. Deep down inside, we know that if we fail to adapt to the
transformation of American health care, we run the risk of being
left behind. As our traditional roles and practices are jarred and
jolted, we find ourselves encountering predicaments we never
expected to face.

Four Case Examples

Let's look at some concrete examples. The following four vignettes summarize the kind of experiences and dilemmas many of us are struggling with today.

Dr. Jameson

Since 1968, Dr. Jameson has enjoyed a thriving private practice. He prides himself on his long-standing reputation as an excellent therapist. He has relished a life-style characterized by professional autonomy, high status, and a six-figure income.

Five years ago he detected the rumblings of change. A few patients informed him they could no longer retain his services because their insurance had switched from indemnity to managed care. Dr. Jameson saw more and more of what he calls "managed care patient kidnappings."

To add fuel to the fire, his income dropped by 30 percent in one year. When he applied to join the two large preferred provider organizations (PPOs) in his area, they turned him down. The panels in which he did participate reimbursed him at only 60 percent of his usual fee and demanded an inordinate amount of paperwork. His shrinking practice left him worried about his approaching retirement. Angry, he exclaimed, "If I would have known this, I would have sold my practice ten years ago. How will a new generation survive?"

Consequently, Dr. Jameson decided to get political. He is now active in state and national professional organizations lobbying against managed care. He prophesies that managed care is a passing fad and that as soon as people see it for what it is, it will fade away and dissolve.

Dr. Jones

Dr. Jones is a psychiatrist-turned-entrepreneur. Her eclectic style has proved to be quite compatible with the demands of managed care.

Employed for fifteen years in a staff model West Coast health maintenance organization (HMO), her firsthand knowledge of managed care helped her see the handwriting on the wall. Anticipating that many other parts of the country were turning toward managed care, she put together an innovative, multidisciplinary practice. Now, as CEO of her own managed mental health care company that insures a hundred thousand "heads," she is both a financial and a clinical success.

When Dr. Jones tried to organize a managed care–friendly committee within her professional organization so she could share her expertise and help others accommodate their practice to the reality of managed care, her efforts were met with anger and suspicion. Colleagues suddenly regarded her as "the enemy," hurling ad hominem attacks at her. Surprised by their attitude, she found solace in interacting with other managed care professionals. But she was distressed by the strong animosity of some of her peers, who accused her of selling out. She knew, however, that her colleagues would find out soon enough that she was right.

Dr. Moran

Dr. Moran was struggling to keep her practice alive. A newly minted doctor of psychology, or Psy.D., she found that getting enough patients was a virtual impossibility. Her income was much smaller than she had anticipated. She was enraged by accusations that she was overtreating and irritated with managed care reviewers who continually challenged her clinical decisions, denied payment for long-term treatment, and asked her to complete more paperwork.

She knew that many reviewers were uncredentialed and less qualified than she; on a few occasions, skirmishes with them had turned personal. She had even called one reviewer a "silly little bureaucrat who had the empathy and clinical acumen of Adolf Hitler"! Now she was worried she would be thrown off that company's panel.

Seeking guidance about what to do, she discovered that her national professional organization did not have any magic answers.

In fact, its leadership seemed divided in their opinions about managed care. While some insisted that it was unethical even to practice within a managed care system, others countered that long-term therapy was equally unethical. Floundering over how to deal with these matters, she did not know what direction to take. She hated politics! She simply wanted to treat her patients and practice her therapy.

Mr. Wilson

Mr. Wilson recently completed his social work degree. Ready to open a private practice, he asked his psychiatrist and psychologist friends for tips about how to launch a successful psychotherapy practice. They told him it was unlikely he would even survive, given the current climate. Established practitioners had lost 50 to 70 percent of their patients to managed care companies—and fees were dropping rapidly. Mr. Wilson asked if he should join as many managed care organizations as possible in order to ensure regular patient referrals. The reply was, "They only pay $30 per session!" The usual fee for psychologists and psychiatrists had been between $80 and $120 in the past.

Mr. Wilson said, "That was then and this is now. Thirty bucks a session is a lot of money. I'll work for that!" Taken aback, his friends realized that a new generation assumes new attitudes. Those who had not practiced in indemnity days would never experience the world they had known. In the space of one generation, private practice had been transformed from a high-status, high-income endeavor to one in which it can be difficult to scrape together a decent living.

. . . .

Although it is clear that today's rapidly changing health care system calls for rapidly changing attitudes, few, if any, guidelines exist to assist us in our struggle to resolve predicaments such as these.

Many of my colleagues feel they are adrift in an ocean of uncertainty, barely treading water in this sea of change. Doubt, disagreement, and dissension abound.

Sources of Variation and Therapist Characteristics

Until quite recently, most mental health professionals had limited exposure to managed care. Only a minority are well informed about its general history, structure, and philosophy or have worked within its confines for a period of years.

There is a great deal of variation in mental health professionals' reactions to managed care. We who deliver psychotherapy hail from a plethora of backgrounds and participate in a variety of professions. We come from psychiatry, psychology, social work, nursing, counseling, the clergy, and even various paraprofessions (such as chemical dependency counselors). Our training ranges from M.D. to doctoral, master's, or bachelor's degree programs or even life experience. We also embrace fundamentally different therapeutic approaches, including psychodynamic, biological, behavioral, eclectic, family systems, existential, and spiritual orientations, and techniques culled from other, less well known theoretical affiliations. We differ in the length and nature of our practice experience and in the settings in which we have practiced, such as outpatient, inpatient, private, public, community, and managed care. Our outlook also varies according to the guilds we belong to and the cohort we come from, not to mention our own personal experiences, profits, and losses.

Table 1.1 illustrates the "cohort effect." Practitioners are generally identified with the model of psychotherapy that was popular when they were educated. A psychiatrist who received his or her degree in the 1950s is much more likely to have been trained by psychoanalytic supervisors than one who went to school in the 1980s, when many more models of psychotherapy existed.

Table 1.1. The cohort effect.

Years in Practice	Year Graduated	Dominant Models
50	1945	Psychoanalytic/dynamic
40	1955	Psychoanalytic/dynamic
30	1965	Psychoanalytic/dynamic
		Biological
		Behavioral
20	1975	Psychoanalytic/dynamic
		Biological
		Behavioral
		Family and Systems
		Eclectic
10	1985	Psychoanalytic/dynamic
		Biological
		Behavioral
		Cognitive Behavioral
		Family and Systems
		Eclectic

Referring back to our vignettes, Dr. Jameson is a psychiatrist educated in New York in the late 1950s and early 1960s. Dr. Jones is a psychiatrist schooled in the 1980s in Wisconsin. Dr. Jameson is more likely to endorse a disease model of mental illness and long-term psychotherapy than Dr. Jones, who is more biological in her orientation and short-term in her approach.

Dr. Moran, a psychologist trained by a psychodynamic supervisor and also trained in biofeedback, is likely to take an eclectic approach, with psychodynamics as her theory of choice. Mr. Wilson, the social worker, is most likely to view patients from a systems approach and to see family therapy as an essential treatment of choice. Dr. Moran is more likely to see psychiatrists as dispensers of medication and not therapists. Dr. Jameson would take issue with her approach, but Dr. Jones would not.

In addition to such demographic and life factors, threats to autonomy, income, prestige, and life-style also affect how different psychotherapists perceive the changes in today's health care system. Naturally, those who are losing their practice feel differently about managed care than those for whom it represents new opportunities. Those who work in public health settings may find managed care to be less of a threat than do private practitioners.

Coping Styles and Patterns of Adaptation

I see a pattern in the way providers are responding to managed care. There seem to be four basic coping styles, each with its unique emotional, cognitive, behavioral, and demographic components.

1. *The old guard: opposition, denial, and anger.* When change involves loss, opposition follows. Providers who perceive managed care as precipitating a loss of autonomy, income, status, and prestige feel outraged and resentful. Those who react in this manner tend to be long-term, psychodynamic therapists with a private practice financed primarily by indemnity payments.

The old guard resists the present social and political climate and works toward maintaining the status quo. They think of themselves as "foes of managed care." Viewing managed care as a draconian enemy to be met with total opposition, they fight for the return of indemnity insurance. They conceptualize managed care as a temporary aberration and believe that once its pitfalls are exposed, everyone will come to their senses and it will dissolve. The stakes are high for this group—a good income and professional autonomy.

2. *The expert: a search for the silver lining.* When change represents opportunity, it is welcomed. Thus providers for whom managed care signals potential financial and clinical success anticipate it with enthusiasm and excitement. Those who react in this way are usually professionals with vision who are astute at anticipating the future and organizing profitable responses to changing social and business climates. They are able to take control of their destiny in

the face of adversity. Silver liners adapt their clinical and business behaviors to harvest the opportunities managed care presents. Some own or head successful managed care companies. Some integrate their own traditional practices into managed care frameworks, developing coordinated, integrated group practices—well-organized systems that respond to the needs of consumers, business, and payers. These experts can use their talents for purely personal profit or for altruistic ends.

Such individuals consider the old guard's ambition to preserve the status quo futile. Accepting the premise that nothing is permanent, they choose to "go with the flow." They see managed care as an inevitable step in the reorganization of a faulty American health care system.

3.   *The grassroots clinician: ambivalence and uncertainty.* When change heralds uncertainty, apprehension and uneasiness ensue. Grassroots clinicians dread the idea of becoming mere cogs in some huge managed care company's machine. For them, the changes brought about by managed care signal the potential for loss and thus engender anxiety or feelings of helplessness.

Grassroots clinicians are busy working long hours and depend on their practice for their income. They generally choose to concentrate on what directly affects their practice and ordinarily prefer not to be involved in the politics of their professional organizations. They pay their dues to get advice, information, or effective political lobbying. The dissension between the old guard and the experts only adds to their level of anxiety. The practice they dreamed about, that they went into debt to obtain, is becoming extinct. They feel betrayed. They "wait and see" and react after the fact. They are insecure about what the future holds.

4.   *The uninitiated: tabulae rasae.* When there appears to be no change, no reaction ensues. Beginners enter the health care arena free of the baggage that can obstruct new learning. Uncertain and unshaped, they are impressionable and flexible. Since they have little practice experience in general, they do not have strong opinions

about managed care. At this stage of development, their judgment is easily swayed by their mentors' worldview. Eventually, an outlook based on their own experience will prevail.

Master's-level providers, whose wages will not change drastically in the new health care system, may begin to dominate. They are the "tabulae rasae" of the practice world, those who are most likely to accept the new conditions without protest. The uninitiated, who will not lose prestige, status, or income, will not see the changes in the health care system as negatively as those who have already been around the block.

Grasping the Big Picture

Let's put aside subjective impressions for the moment and confront objective reality. To hope for the return of an indemnity system is unrealistic, especially in light of a few pertinent demographic facts.

According to current economic studies, one of the fastest-growing enterprises in the United States is the managed care business. Indemnity insurance was dominant until the 1980s, but this is no longer the case. The number of Americans enrolled in specialized behavioral health care insurance programs has grown from 86 million in 1992 to 92 million in 1994 and 107 million in 1995. More than 58 percent of people with health insurance are enrolled in some form of managed care. The pool of patients unencumbered by managed care insurance requirements is shrinking, and at the same time the number of mental health care providers is growing. In a recent meeting of the National Mental Health Congress, speakers on behavioral health care estimated that we have twice as many mental health providers as we need to cover necessary services. Since we have not definitively determined the number of providers needed, statements about the ideal number of providers is arbitrary; the important point is that many managed care companies perceive that there is a surplus of providers in our health care system. In the jargon of managed care, the mental health care system is heavy on the supply side and weak on demand. As a result, payers believe that providers are motivated by "case finding"—in other words, that they are actively *looking* for business and customers.

Providers and payers see health care through different lenses. Providers denounce managed care because it allegedly lowers quality, decreases patient choice, limits the quantity of care, and overwhelms them with paperwork. Payers see the escalating costs of health care ravaging local and national economies. They want lower costs, more manageable claims, better provider justifications for treatments, measurable outcomes, and a common understanding of the therapeutic process. Patients want universal coverage, good care, and protection from catastrophic costs.

As a result of these different worldviews, trust has diminished between payers, providers, and patients. What alarms many of the payers I have spoken with is that mental health costs have been and continue to be a fast-growing part of health care expenditures. Health care costs are rising much faster than the general rate of inflation. At a time when we should all be pulling together to find ways to stop spiraling costs, many mental health professionals are pressing for parity with medical services and reimbursement for their full range of services. In addition, all disciplines within the mental health care profession, except psychiatry, are proliferating at an unprecedented rate. Payers wonder why mental health professionals have not worked more collaboratively with them to help to curb out-of-control costs and reign in services.

While many providers believe payers are more attentive to profits than to patient welfare, payers see that the boundaries between self-interest, patient interest, and professional interest are often difficult to distinguish. Payers are angry at the experts for not policing these boundaries more strictly. Payers don't understand how providers can demand professional autonomy if they do not take the responsibility to manage their own escalating costs.

As Dacso and Dacso wrote in 1995, "Organized medicine was told twenty years ago to police itself with regard to pricing. It did not. Therefore, the promised external controls have been initiated. . . . [M]anaged care promises to place price controls in the market . . . to reduce cost or at least slow its growth by the application of market forces. . . . Managed care strategies tend to emphasize generic relationships and benefits . . . not the maintenance of an individual patient-physician affiliation. Society appears to be deciding that feature is dispensable in the face of the need for monetary savings."

Thus, when cost containment was not forthcoming from health care providers, payers turned to business-minded nonprofessionals to help them manage the professionals who would not manage themselves. A managed care subculture is firmly entrenched, replete with a new language and clinical arrangements based upon business concepts. The trend now is for a few managed care companies to become "mega" managed care companies as they become larger and stronger through merger after merger.

The old way of doing things will never return.

The Evolution of Psychotherapy

What does this shift in the fiscal framework of health care mean to the evolution of psychotherapy? Whereas long-term therapists prospered under the fee-for-service, indemnity insurance system, can they endure in the new, managed care environment? The practice of psychotherapy will be deeply affected by a "survival of the funded" mentality. Money will shape which psychotherapy models predominate. But hopefully, in the long run, so will true societal needs.

Raising our consciousness and grasping the big picture about these complex issues is very important at this point in time. The first step we need to take is to locate ourselves on the developmental lifeline of psychotherapy.

Seventy years ago, psychotherapy was a fledgling discipline. Freud fathered psychoanalysis in the hope of understanding and rectifying various pathologies of the human psyche. Since then, the number of different psychotherapies has proliferated to over four hundred!

Fifty years ago, American psychotherapy associated itself with the nation's medical health care system. As a result, instead of patients' paying their therapists out of their own pockets, more and more third-party payers began to reimburse for psychotherapy as a medical necessity. Payers entered the psychotherapeutic relationship as silent partners and remained that way—until recently.

Forty years ago, Hans Eysenck jolted the self-assurance of the psychotherapeutic community with his declaration that two-thirds of all patients improve significantly or recover within two years, whether they receive (nonbehavioral) psychotherapy or not! Psychotherapists scrambled to defend their profession against these very serious allegations. The avalanche of studies that followed, including metaanalytic works, demonstrated that psychotherapy can indeed be effective in relieving patients of symptoms of psychological distress.

In the 1980s, a "new Eysenck" arrived. There is no doubt that cost concerns are the motor that is beginning to drive specific inquiry into the effectiveness of psychotherapy. Payers are asking, How much is psychotherapy worth? How much psychotherapy is necessary?

To date, however, we have not been able to achieve a level of certainty about the effectiveness of our treatment methods comparable to that which exists within the medical profession, although some progress is being made. The type of outcome data that would enable us to use psychotherapy with the precision and certainty with which a physician operates to remove tonsils or gallstones simply does not exist. We cannot predict with great accuracy the likely length, course, prognosis, and cost of treatment for all mental health conditions, although inroads have been made for some forms of treatment for some conditions (for example, depression and anxiety). The search for data to conclusively demonstrate that one type of therapy is superior to another for a particular condition is under way, but there is still a long way to go.

In our materialistic society, where the almighty dollar reigns, the issues of the cost of care and determining responsibility for payment are breeding tension among payers, providers, and patients. Managed care is the primary agent of inquiry regarding these issues. So what will happen to the evolution of psychotherapy as a result?

A Sociology of Psychotherapy

What happens to the evolution of psychotherapy in the present health care system has great bearing on what will happen to our future as providers. Thus we must gain perspective, make sense out of relevant information, ease the transition in a constructive direction, and formulate constructive solutions to problems. We need to see psychotherapy as it is, as part of a sociological matrix—the millions of sessions conducted every year exert an aggregate effect upon our society. In short, a "sociology of psychotherapy" is required.

If we develop a sociological perspective on psychotherapy, it will help us develop a social ethic in addition to an individual ethic. We will think in terms of psychotherapy as an essential medical resource. After all, before we can articulate a micro ethic, we need to put a macro ethic into place. We must think deeply about the social matrix; we must regard societal needs as well as individual needs as matters of great importance.

Is psychotherapy evolving in a direction that will accommodate societal needs, so no American will have to go without adequate mental health care? Will managed care companies reimburse only short-term psychotherapy, making long-term psychotherapy unavailable to those who need it? Will psychotherapy remain an essential medical tool, or will it become a commodity whose future is shaped chiefly by economics?

To adapt to a changing health care environment, mental health professionals must restructure their perspective, flex their attitudes, and make a deliberate effort to see things differently. We will begin by examining provider resistance to change in Chapter Two.

Notes

p. 13, *"If a hundred people sleep and dream"*: Rinpoche, K. (1989). *Essence of the dharma* (p. 206). Delhi, India: Tibet House.

p. 13, *Dr. Anderson picked up a copy*: Managed care changing practice of psychotherapy. (1994, October 9). *The New York Times*, p. 1.

p. 14, *Under the fee-for-service system*: Dacso, S. T., & Dacso, C. C. (1995). *Managed care answer book* (pp. 1–8). New York: Aspen Publishers.

p. 14, *American health care is undergoing*: Starr, P. (1982). *The social transformation of American medicine* (pp. 235–265). New York: Basic Books.

p. 14, *In a 1912 editorial*: Socializing the British medical profession. (1912). *Journal of the American Medical Association, 59*(2), 1890.

p. 15, *The cottage industry that gave many of us respected employment*: Starr, P. (1982). *The social transformation of American medicine* (pp. 428–430). New York: Basic Books.

p. 16, *The following four vignettes*: The vignettes do not represent any specific practitioner but are a creative composite based on the clinical experience of the author.

p. 23, *According to current economic studies*: Himmelstein, D., & Woolhander, S. (1995). Care denied U.S. residents who are unable to obtain needed medical services. *American Journal of Public Health, 85*(3), 341–344.

p. 23, *The number of Americans enrolled*: Oss, M. (1995, April). *Trends in behavioral health care financing.* Paper presented at the National Managed Health Care Congress, Washington, DC.

p. 23, *In a recent meeting*: ibid.

p. 24, *Patients want universal coverage:* Navarro, V. (1992). *Dangerous to your health: Capitalism in health care.* New York: Cornerstone Books.

p. 24, *As Dacso and Dacso wrote in 1995:* Dacso, S. T., & Dacso, C. C. (1995). *Managed care answer book* (pp. 1–8). New York: Aspen Publishers.

p. 26, *Since then, the number of different psychotherapies:* Karasu, T. B. (1992). The worst of times, the best of times. *Journal of Psychotherapy Research, 1,* 2–15.

p. 26, *Forty years ago:* Glass, C., & Arnkoff, D. B. (1992). Beginnings of modern behavior therapy. In D. Freidheim (Ed.), *The history of psychotherapy* (pp. 594–595). Washington, DC: American Psychological Association.

. . . .

2

Resistance to Change

Status Quo, Biases, and Self-Interest

Make the mistakes of yesterday your lessons for today.

Long before managed care emerged, our health care system was in deep trouble and great disrepair. It would seem likely that mental health professionals—with their understanding of the human psyche, their need to nurture people and alleviate human suffering, and their codes of ethics obligating them to enrich society—would be eager to explore any means by which to achieve the admirable goal of reforming the health care system. Therefore it is difficult to understand how anti–managed care sentiments gained such a foothold within the professional mental health care community— especially in view of the fact that early in its development, when it was more a socialistic than a commercial enterprise, managed care represented a serious attempt to solve the maladies of the health care system.

Epigraph from *An Apple A Day*, Great Quotations, Inc.

The Experts' Warnings

Some visionaries have tried to prepare mental health professionals for the current change, but their advice has gone curiously unheeded. In 1986, Nick Cummings, past CEO and founder of Biodyne (now Medco), one of the largest managed mental health care companies in the United States, cautioned providers to develop strategies responsive to the current cost-containment climate, to use innovative models of mental health care, and to learn to market those models. If such action was not taken, Cummings stressed, providers would likely become poorly paid, little-respected employees of giant health corporations, which would then control most health care in the United States.

His message met with provider resistance and was ignored by the leadership of the American Psychological Association. Unfortunately, Cummings's words would later prove to be prophetic. Following up on his earlier remarks, Cummings wrote in 1995 that managed care has become the dominant force in health care delivery. He further reported that organized psychology has not kept pace with the rapid industrialization of health care, with the result that psychologists are often overlooked as participants in health-related economic decision making. Professional psychologists, he continued, must reexamine some of their most generally accepted attitudes and beliefs if they are to survive.

Monica Oss, editor of *Open Minds*, a publication about managed care, recommends that providers develop services that are both clinically sound (even innovative) and economically enticing, rather than assailing managed care. Oss says the only way to take back authority and control within the delivery system is to become more involved with and understanding of managed care administrators and third-party payers: "Practitioners need to respond more positively to health care payers. . . . Mental health providers are largely seen as opposed to everything. . . . There is a tremendous need to help people who are responsible for paying the benefits understand what it is you do, how you do it and what it costs."

Carl Zimet, a founding father of the *National Register,* also presented a strong admonition to mental health care professionals when he stated that failure to participate in shaping the quality of mental health care services amounts to social and professional irresponsibility. Zimet stresses that there is no standing still and no going back to the good old days of free choice and an independent market. He says it is essential to make a place for ourselves in the managed care marketplace rather than expend our energy trying to reverse the inevitable. The goal of mental health professionals is to help shape the managed care system and to put our talents and efforts toward ensuring quality.

Although these and a few other experts have offered hope, general guidance, and specific advice for dealing with managed care, the mental health care literature demonstrates a pervasive prejudice against managed care, as we'll see later in this chapter. The old guard mentality still prevails in many circles, and tremendous energy has been spent on opposing the inevitable. Anti–managed care rhetoric can reach such intensity that it blocks open-minded thinking and prevents free dialogue. How did such an adversarial situation develop? Why do some providers exhibit such hostility toward managed care?

Major Obstacles to Reform

Change is hard. Even when reframed as a challenge and an opportunity for growth, change is fraught with uncertainty and apprehension. Mental health providers, who are themselves agents of change, are as susceptible to the pitfalls associated with facing change as anyone else. The reorganization of the health care system is a source of stress for all who want to maintain the familiar comfort of the status quo. Providers are worried about their own personal and professional future—and with good reason, since the practice of psychotherapy is being turned upside down and inside out.

Two major obstacles encourage resistance to change. First, there is the desire to avoid the pain that accompanies loss, whether real or merely symbolic. Second, a number of culturally supported beliefs, deeply ingrained in our thinking, encourage health care professionals to expect certain entitlements.

Potential Provider Losses

Many psychotherapists, especially long-term therapists, face a loss of clinical autonomy, professional and personal status, and income. These threatened losses can be summarized as follows:

Clinical Losses

• Loss of traditional, long-term treatment models (especially psychoanalysis)

• Narrower choice of new models (that is, short-term, behavioral, cognitive)

• Less opportunity to apply long-term expertise

• Increased accountability to nonprofessionals

Financial

• Decreased fees and income

• Increased competition for patients

• Decreased pool of patients

• Increased work (from a larger bureaucracy) for no more financial return

Status

• Diminished public image

• Increased consumer scrutiny

• Diminished authority (the corporation is the boss)

In 1968, Irving Berlin, then president of the American Orthopsychiatric Association, discussed resistance to change among psychiatrists fighting the community mental health movement. His words are relevant today: "Personal satisfactions, contributions to the welfare of others, status and money have all been suggested as the reasons for entering, remaining in, and contributing to the mental health professions. I suspect that these are also the primary reasons for resistance to change and for the kinds of anxieties manifested by many when our rapidly changing society requires that we become more responsive to community work and to find more effective, innovative, and responsive models of theory and practice."

Providers who must learn new methods of working, especially methods that challenge established, familiar theoretical frameworks and practices, worry about an accompanying reduction in personal satisfaction, status, financial well-being, and feelings of competency. When asked to abandon well-known, safe models and use less-known, less-practiced techniques, we all feel imperiled. Relinquishing the familiar in exchange for the new is not easy. Changing our emphasis from long-term to short-term models of therapy means learning new skills, working harder, and tolerating decreased feelings of self-assurance.

It is only human to want to remain connected to our old ways of functioning. After all, there is great comfort attached to the familiar. For example, long-term, individual therapy for fifty minutes a session and a high hourly fee is a widely emulated, high-status model of practice. The fact that only a limited segment of the population has access to such therapy is less painful to endure and easier to ignore when we can satisfy our altruistic urges by engaging in one-on-one helping. This reinforcement is an immediate and satisfying part of the therapeutic dyad.

Concerns about our own potential losses can deter acceptance of change, promote resistance, and prevent practitioners from looking at the new and the unfamiliar. It is a force powerful enough to allow us to ignore that managed care "done the right way" offers the possibility of more help for more people with a wider range of problems and increased collaboration with other mental health professionals.

Providers' Underlying Beliefs and Assumptions

In addition to the resistance that comes from avoiding the pain of potential loss, certain underlying assumptions and belief systems can perpetuate resistance. Beneath practitioners' passionate objections to managed care is a set of assumptions that can stand in the way of open-minded analysis. These premises are familiar, but they are not necessarily correct. We at least need to evaluate them and ascertain whether they might be outdated or even irrelevant to practicing psychotherapy in today's changing health care landscape.

Not every provider regards every one of these beliefs as true. Not all of them are directly related to managed care, but they do all contribute to increased resistance to change. Each belief is described below and followed by a critical commentary.

1. *Managed care is destroying the practice of psychotherapy.* The following quotes represent a small sampling of the intense and impassioned anti–managed care rhetoric that is prominent in the current mental health literature. The most militant utterances come from the Coalition of Mental Health Professionals and Consumers, a national, interdisciplinary organization that has appointed itself to respond to the "damaging effects of managed care." On January 23, 1995, Dr. Karen Shore, a psychologist and a cofounder of the coalition, sent a letter to the American Psychological Association Council of Representatives which has been widely circulated among mental health professionals. The letter stated that managed care

> is destroying much of what our profession has built over the past 100 years and is defying the values we believe are essential for quality care. I, as many others, feel I cannot practice ethically or with any sense of personal dignity under a managed care system. Many good psychologists are being forced out of work because they refuse to under-treat people or to comply with the be-

trayal of their patient's trust. Others are already preparing to leave the field, demoralized and in utter despair because of what is happening to patients, treatment, morals, ethics, to themselves as human beings and as professionals. . . . We are working against great odds to try to stop a giant from destroying all we hold dear.

Other clinicians believe marketplace forces threaten to erode public confidence in mental health professionals: "We have exchanged a mere bloodsucking leech that sapped our strength for a ravenous carnivore that poses a much more fundamental threat to our very existence. . . . The wrongs that are being done in the name of saving money are simply unconscionable."

Some even contend that the principles of managed care are by nature incompatible with professional codes of ethics (such as the American Psychological Association's code): "Ignored at first, [managed care] has succeeded in clipping the wings of practitioners in all fields. . . . Managed care shortchanges patients and purchasers alike. . . . The demands of managed care are at variance with APA (professional) ethics."

Another practitioner postulates that managed care is inimical to therapeutic integrity because it blocks the therapist's empathy, neutrality, and authenticity. This integrity can only exist when a competent therapist establishes an environment that allows patients to reveal, define, and work on their problems until they feel comfortable continuing on their own. Managed care does not provide these conditions: "While brief therapy is a widely useful treatment modality, when it is mandated by a third party it violates the fundamental integrity of the therapeutic relationship."

In a recent edition of a well-respected psychological journal, the following words were published in an article, not an editorial: "Most often managed care contracts are sold on the basis of providing 20 sessions of psychotherapy a year. But data . . . indicate that this is not the most rational figure to establish on any basis, except the salesman's. Moreover, even the inadequate figure of 20 sessions is not really provided to the patients by the managed care systems. The therapists are explicitly told to get rid of the patients in six sessions."

The same journal published an article entitled "The Rape of Psychotherapy," in which the author concludes that market forces are placing psychotherapy under such unprecedented attack that public confidence in it could become completely eroded. The author adds that "it is in our best interests as professionals to see that long-term, intensive care does not disappear from the treatment landscape."

There is no doubt that some aspects of managed care pose a number of ethical dilemmas for practitioners, patients, and payers. These are discussed in greater detail in Chapter Three. Certainly criticism is deserved when wrongdoing can be demonstrated. But it does not help to vilify managed care, to lump all forms of it together, to treat proponents of managed care as adversaries, or to project onto managed care the inevitable frustrations, fears, and anger that accompany major change. We must be careful not to be blinded to the fact that managed care has the potential to be a positive force in American health care.

During times of change we are particularly susceptible to the pitfalls of jumping to conclusions and overgeneralizing. Since managed care has so many meanings to so many people, we need to clarify the definition of managed care, identify the specific practices we object to, distinguish good managed care from troubled managed care (as we do for fee-for-service care), not lose our objectivity, and analyze the assumptions underlying what people say about managed care. And—objectively speaking—it is not realistic to say that managed care is destroying the practice of psychotherapy.

First, most managed care plans, in order to be competitive, include some form of mental health benefits (including psychotherapy). Second, a mental health benefit that includes up to twenty outpatient sessions of psychotherapy per year may not be what we think of as generous, but it is certainly adequate for the needs of most plan members. There is a concern about the minority who need long-term therapy, and we must address how we will tend to the needs of the very disabled in this group. Third, if people are in need of care and their insurance company has promised it, the company is accountable to deliver that care. If it fails to deliver, there are procedures in place to appeal its decision to deny care. If more than twenty visits are necessary, an extension can often be negotiated. And if an in-company appeal process fails, the state insurance commissioner can be notified. Due process must be adhered to, just as it is in indemnity plans and fee-for-service practice.

Fourth, let me debunk the myth that *all* managed care plans do not provide long-term care. A good number do not, of course, but many do. At Community Health Care Plan in New Haven, Connecticut, we have a percentage of chronic patients who have received care for many years. Providers in managed care companies like Harvard Community Health Plan have worked very hard to maintain the mental health of their chronically ill patients. We do not treat these patients with traditional, long-term therapy; rather, we use intermittent brief therapy over the life cycle (discussed in Chapter Eight). We are committed to providing them with excellent mental health care for as long as they are with us.

Fifth, the term "psychotherapy" has many meanings. The psychotherapy marketplace is filled with a multitude of approaches. Any number of activities are carried out in the name of psychotherapy, ranging from cognitive behavioral therapy to primal scream therapy. Many managed mental health care firms have stimulated an interest in and been supportive of high-quality alternative treatments that help troubled individuals improve quickly. This both helps the patient and enhances company profits. Thus managed care can result in making sure that the most effective treatments are being utilized.

It is clear from this discussion that the accusation that managed care is destroying psychotherapy is simply not true. It may be changing it, shaping it, and influencing which models proliferate, but it is by no means destroying it. Now, it *is* accurate to say that the philosophies underlying managed care and those underlying long-term psychoanalytic therapy are basically at odds. I know of no managed care plan to date that will pay for psychoanalysis. Most CEOs of managed care companies would say that because there is no evidence that psychoanalysis is medically necessary or that it is even effective, it should be categorized as a form of personal improvement. A managed care plan will not pay for self-improvement anymore than it will pay for continuing education.

Is this unethical? Does an insurer have no right to limit the type of therapy it covers? Must it honor any ongoing therapeutic relationship? Although long-term, psychoanalytically oriented psychotherapy has been the principal, preferred paradigm governing psychotherapy for many years, just prior to the arrival of managed care there was a growing sense that the model of long-term psychodynamic psychotherapy had ceased to be useful for all patients. There are many other forms of psychotherapy that mesh well with managed care, and these psychotherapies are not being destroyed.

2. *A nonprofessional should never challenge the authority of the mental health expert.* A number of traditional mental health professionals believe that patients' welfare is best served by deferring to the authority of doctors or other qualified professionals. To many of those who endorse this view, any interference is unacceptable. They believe outsiders should not make demands on psychotherapists such as asking them to identify and justify their practice parameters. The fact that many managed care leaders are not mental health professionals but are from business, politics, and the insurance industry is disconcerting to these individuals.

Not only does interference from managed care administrators create tension for these professionals, so does the idea that laypersons who lack sufficient knowledge to define their own psychological needs ought to be part of decision making in medical matters. The following words express the outrage felt by one psychiatrist: "We must now contend with the regulatory influence of Geraldo, Oprah, Donahue and other tabloid vehicles, which compounds the organized antipsychiatry efforts of disaffected ex-patient groups, Scientology, and other special interests by debasing the level of discussion about ECT, antidepressants 'that kill,' psychostimulants, and other valuable treatment modalities. These developments are not occurring in a vacuum. They reflect anti-intellectual, unscientific, and antipsychiatric sentiments that are growing throughout our society. The outcome is regulation or regulatory-like influences that are controversial at best, unscientific, and even irrational at worst." Professional psychotherapists, skeptical that these nonprofessionals are driven by nonscientific objectives, policy goals, cost containment, or other special interests, believe that they must defend their position of authority for the sake of patient interests.

But is it really irreverent for patients, payers, and others to question the authority of the practitioner? Could it be possible that their concerns are not as outlandish as they may seem? Is it so unreasonable to have watchdog consumer groups measuring the performance of professionals?

The paternalism of our medical system is evident in traditional mental health circles, but Americans have begun to stop thinking of doctors as all-powerful authorities: "The bottom line is that the balance of power held by providers for many years has shifted to employers, third party payers, unions, and to a degree, consumers."

The patient rights movement, attention to patients' civil liberties, and patient consumerism are all on the increase. The erosion of deference to doctors' authority is evident in increased support for informed consent, the right to refuse treatment, the right to see one's medical records, and the right to participate in decision making concerning one's course of treatment. Furthermore, a number of factors have tarnished the image of psychiatry; lowered the credibility of the mental health professions with employers, insurance companies, and the general public; and resulted in increased outsider concerns and a desire for increased regulation of mental health practices. These include scandals associated with private psychiatric hospitals, violations of the civil rights of involuntary patients, and the occasionally unscientific nature of the psychotherapeutic process.

Our culture has endowed doctors with great authority, prestige, and status; now it is threatening to take these away. Managed care constitutes a very serious challenge to the remaining cultural authority, economic power, and political influence of the doctor of the soul.

3. *Cheaper providers with less credentials lower the quality of care.* A widely held belief, reinforced by payment schedules, is that the better the credentials, experience, and education, the better the psychotherapy. Some providers, particularly those high up within the hierarchy, equate the use of lesser trained providers, or "cheap labor," with a lowering of the quality of care: "And of course another cost-saving, profit enhancing mechanism is to drive down the hourly fees of therapists, forcing many experienced therapists (psychologists, social workers, and psychiatrists) off provider panels and replacing them with less experienced therapists or even with paraprofessionals."

The present hierarchy of mental health providers is based upon practitioners' training and skill. Each of the professions within the mental health field has a rank order and a distinct position within the health care economy. Psychiatrists are the preeminent and most highly paid mental health professionals because they have medical expertise and can therefore prescribe medication, admit patients to hospitals, and make diagnoses. Psychologists place second in this ranking. Although they are called doctors, their Ph.D.'s or Psy.D.'s do not give them the medical privileges psychiatrists enjoy. A third tier consists of professionals trained in master's degree programs (social workers, marriage and family therapists, master's-level psychologists and psychiatric nurses). A fourth rank consists of those with less than a master's degree, such as counselors, paraprofessionals, and chemical dependency workers. Clergy are in a league by themselves.

Does any one of these groups perform psychotherapy consistently better than the others? Robyn Dawes, in reviewing the literature on the effectiveness of therapy, eloquently argues (with supporting data) that "the credentials and the experience of the therapist don't matter" in the success of psychotherapy. Trained professionals do not demonstrate unique *therapeutic* effectiveness. Granted, there is a division of labor and expertise in regard to other matters. To prescribe medication, an M.D. or A.P.R.N. is required. But as far as psychotherapy is concerned, no single profession within the mental health field has demonstrated a consistently superior ability.

Interdisciplinary fighting among members of the mental health professions has continued over the years, with each profession spending untold dollars on lobbying efforts to protect their turf. Professional elitism, open hostilities, and competition, not cooperation, have prevailed, blocking the kind of constructive communication that would put the patient first and the provider second.

Payers would prefer a general pluralism within the field and hope that these groups come to terms with one another. They prefer to stay out of the battle. Claims made by the competing parties are difficult to believe or disbelieve.

4.   *Mental health professionals should earn a high income that is commensurate with their status.* Just as medical doctors in our society earn a high income, doctors of the mind expect to earn a better-than-average wage. They believe that since their work demands special training, expertise, and stamina, it should command very high wages.

Most medical specialists experience a decrease in pay when their practice takes in large numbers of managed care patients. A 1994 survey showed that when managed care patients made up 50 percent of a doctor's caseload, the doctor's annual income dropped.

Cardiologists' income decreased from $316,456 to $242,525; general surgeons' wages dropped from $201,769 to $190,500; and orthopedic surgeons' pay plummeted from $328,398 to $247,950.

Another survey showed a parallel drop in the earnings of some mental health professionals. In the New York area, where 20 percent of all therapists practice, fees ranged from $150 to $300 per hour for psychiatrists and from $40 to $150 per hour for social workers. Therapists complained that managed care companies would pay only 55 to 60 percent of these wages. One therapist reported that although he charges $160 a visit, managed care pays him only $80. Another stated that he has been asked to settle for only $40.

Annual earnings for New York psychiatrists ranged from $80,000 to $200,000, with some making far more. For social workers with a master's degree, income was upward of $50,000. Managed care companies reported savings during the period covered by the survey of 30 to 50 percent off therapists' usual fees; so, depending on how many managed care patients they carried, therapists' incomes were reduced by up to 25 percent. Therapists in California and Florida reported a drop in income as high as 50 percent.

In the United States, medical doctors earn seven times more than the average citizen. Mental health professionals, whether they are doctors or not, aspire to the same pinnacle of economic achievement. The collective power of the mental health professions has helped their members convert clinical authority into economic privilege. Is this fair? Does it have to be this way? In other countries, where doctors and mental health providers are part of a national health care system, doctors are paid fairly but much more modestly.

5.   *It is better to concentrate on gaining more benefits for the insured than on securing basic benefits for the 41 million Americans who lack insurance.* Some mental health providers are dedicated to fighting managed care and to fighting for the inclusion in health insurance packages of an outpatient psychotherapy benefit that promotes

unlimited individual psychotherapy and freedom of choice for sub-scribers and autonomy and high income for providers. Lobbying and political activism play an important role in this effort, aimed at pushing "open the door to the mental health market. . . . For the first time . . . the psychological community is in a proactive, rather than a reactive position to dictate what the mental health care delivery system should look like."

It is a disgrace that 41 million Americans remain uninsured for basic health and mental health care. While much professional lob-bying, fund-raising, and campaigning have been aimed at improv-ing the benefits of those who already have insurance, the need for universal coverage remains largely ignored. Shouldn't mental health professionals make a firm commitment to helping the uninsured before championing those who are merely underinsured?

6. *Psychotherapy is best practiced within a private practice or cot-tage industry setting.* Some psychotherapy providers believe it is wrong to impede their economic success by blocking the cottage industry of private practice. They look upon the industrialization of American health care with dread and terror.

One writer points out that Freud practiced psychotherapy in a way that was "individual, entrepreneurial, and unregulated by out-side agencies. Fees were for services rendered and came from the pocket of the patient or a family member. These conditions appear to have been very suitable for the development of the new disci-pline of psychoanalysis and subsequently its numerous derivatives."

Perhaps these conditions are optimal for the practice of psycho-analysis, but are they the best way to deliver psychotherapy to the American people today? Freud did not need to report to a third-party payer. In reality, the entrepreneurial, cottage industry of psy-chotherapy has failed U.S. citizens. We have the most expensive health care in the world and many uninsured citizens. We know we need to change. We might better serve our citizens by delivering health care in group practices within integrated systems.

Overcoming Provider Resistance

By calling attention to these underlying beliefs, I hope to encourage consideration of how they might further professionals' resistance to appropriate change. Mental health professionals from all disciplines have fought long and hard to become a part of the health care system, to become reimbursable, and to have the therapies they provide considered medical treatments. To lose this status and risk the humiliation and insult of being forced to work on contract for pitifully low fees is a fate we are all trying to avoid.

But we must search our souls and probe our motivations to be sure we are doing what is best for our patients rather than what is best for ourselves. What is wrong with using cost-saving techniques in a health care system characterized by high costs, inefficient delivery, and insufficient coverage? Can such techniques not be implemented ethically? What is wrong with giving providers incentives to control their use of resources? Is the alternative not to continue encouraging them to benefit from illness rather than health? What's so bad about cost-containment measures such as reducing hospital stays, eliminating unnecessary procedures, and rejecting inappropriate claims? What is inherently wrong with monitoring and reviewing treatment through prospective or retrospective reviews, preauthorization, or case management? What is it so troublesome about giving a case reviewer information when the patient has given his or her explicit permission via a signed release?

What is the problem with a case reviewer's asking that a therapist report a specific treatment plan to the payer or that he or she render a diagnosis, treatment plan, and prognosis? What is so terrible about insisting on outcome data, patient satisfaction data, and quality control measures? Are all reviewers monsters who have only profit in mind? Are reviewers not also practitioners? Why should it not be at the payer's discretion to contract with specific providers? Why should payers have to accept "any willing provider" when mental health professionals don't even have to accept "any willing patient"? What is so terrible about paying for brief treatment rather than long-term treatment when indemnity insurers have been doing it for years? Why is it despicable for a managed care company to make money but admirable for a private practitioner to do so?

None of these activities seem inherently evil in and of themselves; they become so only if they are abused. There are insurance laws in many states to protect people from abuses by managed care companies. Managed care is so new that there are few laws in place to govern it properly. It is changing, evolving, and developing as we speak. When a managed care company steps over its bounds and tries to behave unethically, many anti–managed care providers who are also lawyers will gladly contest their activities in court.

Managed care is not "the enemy." Had the nation's health care system not become riddled with grave inequities, had it not evolved into an unwieldy, resource-eating monster, it would not require management! The old system was good for many providers, and these individuals are understandably reluctant to give up the comforts they have become accustomed to. But these comforts are no longer the status quo. While change will be painful for some, it can also be positive. The best coping strategy is an active one—a restructured attitude that allows one to see things differently. Let's not succumb to this kind of forecast: "A new scientific truth does not triumph by convincing its opponents and making them see the light, but rather because its opponents eventually die, and a new generation grows up that is familiar with it."

Notes

p. 31, *"It is a familiar fact"*: Stern, S. (1993). Managed care, brief therapy, and therapeutic integrity. *Psychotherapy, 30*(1), 162–174.

p. 32, *In 1986, Nick Cummings:* Cummings, N. (1986). The dismantling of our health system. *American Psychologist, 41*(4), 426–431.

p. 32, *Following up on his earlier remarks, Cummings wrote:* Cummings, N. (1995). Impact of managed care on employment and training: A primer for survival. *Professional Psychology, Research and Practice, 26*(1), 10–15.

p. 32, *Oss says the only way:* quoted in Sleek, S. (1994). Chaos of reform has a silver lining for psychologists. *APA Monitor, 27*(10), 15–16.

p. 33, *Carl Zimet, a founding father of the* National Register: Zimet, C. (1989). The mental health care revolution: Will psychology survive? *American Psychologist, 44,* 703–708.

p. 33, *Two major obstacles encourage resistance to change:* Berlin, I. (1969). Therapists' resistance to change. *Journal of Orthomolecular Psychiatry,* 110–115.

p. 34, *In 1968, Irving Berlin:* ibid., pp. 110–115.

p. 37, *Other clinicians believe marketplace forces:* Fox, R. (1995). The rape of psychotherapy. *Professional Psychology: Research and Practice, 26*(1), 147–155.

p. 37, *Some even contend:* Saunders, R., & Ludwigsen, K. R. (1993). Special focus: Managed care and the delivery of psychological services. *The Independent Practitioner, 13*(4), 154.

p. 37, *Managed care does not provide these conditions:* Stern, S. (1993). Managed care, brief therapy, and therapeutic integrity. *Psychotherapy, 30*(1), 162–174.

p. 37, *In a recent edition of a well-respected psychological journal:* Karon, B. (1995). Provision of psychotherapy under managed health care: A growing crisis and national nightmare. *Professional Psychology: Research and Practice, 26*(2), 5–9.

p. 38, *The same journal published an article:* Fox, R. (1995). The rape of psychotherapy. *Professional Psychology: Research and Practice, 26*(2), 147–155.

p. 39, *At Community Health Care Plan in New Haven, Connecticut:* DeStefano, L., & Henault, K. (1991). The treatment of chronically mentally and emotionally disabled patients. In C. S. Austad & W. Berman (Eds.), *Psychotherapy in managed health care: The optimal use of time and resources* (pp. 138–152). Washington, DC: American Psychological Association.

p. 39, *Many managed mental health care firms:* Giles, T. (1991). Managed mental health care and effective psychotherapy: A step in the right direction. *Journal of Behavior Therapy and Experimental Psychiatry, 22*(2), 83–86.

p. 40, *Not only does interference from managed care administrators create tension:* Schwartz, H. (1994). The impact of cost-containment measures on somatic psychiatry. In H. Schwartz (Ed.), *Psychiatric practice under fire* (pp. 135–146). Washington, DC: American Psychiatric Press.

p. 41, *The following words express the outrage felt by one psychiatrist:* Schwartz, H. (Ed.). (1994). [Introduction]. *Psychiatric practice under fire* (pp. xvi–xviii). Washington, DC: American Psychiatric Press.

p. 41, *The paternalism of our medical system:* Zimet, C. (1989). The mental health care revolution: Will psychology survive? *American Psychologist, 44,* 703–708.

p. 42, *Some providers, particularly those high up within the hierarchy:* Barron, J. (1995). Hamlet, prince of Denmark: A parable of managed care. *Psychotherapy Bulletin, 31*(1), 52–54.

p. 43, *Robyn Dawes, in reviewing the literature on the effectiveness of therapy:* Dawes, R. (1994). *House of cards* (pp. 107–120). New York: Free Press.

p. 43, *A 1994 survey showed:* Insurance industry changing in the face of healthcare reform. (1994). *Group Practice, 9*(5), 1.

p. 44, *In the New York area:* Henneberger, M. (1994, October 9). Managed care changing practice of psychotherapy. *The New York Times,* p. 1.

p. 44, *In the United States, medical doctors earn:* Navarro, V. (1993). *Dangerous to your health: Capitalism in health care* (p. 71). New York: Monthly Review Press.

p. 45, *Lobbying and political activism play an important role in this effort:* Cantor, D. (1993). The challenge to psychotherapy: After managed care. *The Independent Practitioner, 13*(4), 162–163.

p. 45, *One writer points out that Freud:* Chodoff, P. (1987). Effects of the new economic climate on psychotherapy. *American Journal of Psychiatry, 144*(10), 1293–1297.

p. 47, *Let's not succumb to this kind of forecast:* Max Planck, quoted in Kuhn, T. S. (1971). *The structure of scientific revolutions* (2nd ed., p. 151). Chicago: University of Chicago Press.

3

Money Talks
Does Profit Influence Care?

*There are a handful of people whom money won't
spoil, and we count ourselves among them.*

Mignon McLaughlin

I magine you are a therapist with an established private practice.
Maureen is one of your patients. You've worked with her for a
total of twelve sessions over three months. You have diagnosed her
with adjustment disorder and anxiety disorder. Your mutually agreed
upon therapeutic goals are to help her improve her relationships
and her functioning at work. Maureen tends to become agitated and
anxious several times a month.

One day, Maureen telephones you to say she is upset and needs
to talk. She cannot identify any precipitant or particular reason for
her agitation. She asks to see you for an extra appointment this
week. Now, consider the following scenarios:

1.   Maureen has an excellent Blue Cross indemnity insurance
plan that covers 100 percent of her outpatient psychotherapy. It will

Epigraph from *Peter's Quotations: Ideas for Our Times*, published by Bantam Books.

cost her nothing to see you. You will charge her $110 on a fee-for-service basis. Your talking with her will calm her down. You have two hours open in the afternoon.

2.   Maureen is a member of a managed care plan of which you are a preferred provider. The plan has approved twenty sessions of treatment for her psychiatric episode. If her treatment expands beyond this limit, you must obtain permission from the case manager to extend her total number of sessions. You do not want to do this, because you are concerned that the managed care company will disapprove of your prolonging her treatment. You worry that if you make too many extension requests you could jeopardize your preferred provider status. You hesitate to see Maureen for this extra session.

3.   You have contracted with a managed care company to work with ten patients on a capitated basis, which means you must take care of all the mental health needs of these patients for the year for a single fixed price per patient. Maureen is one of these patients. You are at risk financially. No matter how great or how small the needs of your patients, no matter how many times you see them, whether they need one hundred sessions or two, you still receive the same amount of money. You have received $1,600 for each patient for the year.

How would you handle each of these situations? Would the different financial arrangements affect your decision making? Each major type of reimbursement—fee-for-service, preferred provider, and capitation—carries with it different financial incentives intended to shape clinical decision making. Would your own profit motive affect your choice of whether or not to see Maureen?

Business or Altruism?

Most psychotherapists are well-intentioned and dedicated to their patients. They see themselves as professionals who care more about their patients' welfare than about profit. They do not like to think that money could corrupt their clinical decisions. They presume it is patient need, not financial reward, that ultimately determines their clinical choices. Many are angry because they see managed care as an increasingly intrusive culprit that pits patient care against providers' financial well-being.

But the situation is more complicated than that. The unanswered question of whether providing health care is a business or an altruistic endeavor is the cause of considerable bewilderment.

Like medicine, psychotherapy is both a business and a helping profession. A constant tension between the profession's care ethic and its business ethic pulls and pushes providers. It is often difficult for providers to integrate their professional role with their business role and differentiate their professional motives from their profit motive. It is therefore easy for providers to blur boundaries and mix business and practice issues. The mental health professions have generally avoided looking at the very thorny issue of profit and practice. But even more than in physical medicine, the relationship between the doctor and the patient is the tool used to heal the patient; thus it is very important for mental health professionals to examine and clarify how business issues enter into that relationship. This chapter addresses this issue by examining the following points.

First, we establish the fact that profit does indeed influence practice. Second, we examine the incompatibility and conflicts between the business and professional aspects of psychotherapy practice. Third, we look at how profit seeking, whether under fee-for-service or managed care, has diminished public trust in the mental health professions. Fourth, we explore how insurance, or third-party payments, has woven itself into the therapist-patient relationship. Fifth, we identify and discuss inherent conflicts of interest between making a profit and practicing psychotherapy.

Profit Influences Practice: The HealthStop Docs Story

We begin not with a mental health practice but with the story of HealthStop, a major chain of for-profit, ambulatory medical care centers established in 1983. A study of this chain conducted between 1984 and 1986 provides an exceptionally clear illustration of how the profit motive operates within a medical practice. During the time of this study there were approximately twenty Health-Stop centers in operation. HealthStop physicians delivered basic primary care to their patients. At each HealthStop center at least two doctors worked full-time. The centers were designed to be user-friendly and to maximize patient access and convenience. Anyone could walk in without an appointment, at any time of the day and on any day of the year. Laboratory and X-ray facilities were located on-site.

In the middle of 1985, HealthStop decided to modify how it pays its doctors. Previously the chain had paid physicians a flat rate of $28 per hour. Under the new reimbursement system, doctors would be able to earn bonuses based on the gross revenue they brought into the clinic. They could either collect a flat hourly fee or a percentage of the gross monthly charges they generated, whichever was more. They could earn 21 percent of the first $24,000 of their charges and 15 percent thereafter.

A group of researchers seized this opportunity to study whether doctors' clinical behavior is affected by a change in fiscal incentives. Rarely does an opportunity present itself to observe such a real-life experiment. The researchers could study the practice habits of the same physicians, serving basically the same clinical population under two different payment systems! Each physician would serve as his or her own control.

The investigators compared the practice patterns of fifteen HealthStop doctors for an equal time period before and after the new fiscal arrangements began. The research revealed that the doctors adapted their clinical behavior in a way that increased revenues. The number of laboratory tests performed increased by 23 percent. The number of X-rays ordered went up 16 percent. The average number of patient visits per month grew by 12 percent. The overall charges per month rose by 20 percent. Physicians who earned bonuses augmented their wages by 19 percent.

The results of the HealthStop study clearly demonstrate that financial considerations had a direct impact on doctors' clinical decisions. And the HealthStop study is not the only evidence that money can influence clinical practice. A growing body of research shows that payment practices most certainly do affect physician behavior. There is compelling evidence to show that when doctors have a financial interest in increasing services, they do so. In the past and in the present, physicians have acted in an entrepreneurial role and engaged in practices such as fee-splitting and self-referral. Presently physicians have a financial stake in from 25 percent to 80 percent (depending on the geographical area) of accessory medical facilities such as laboratories, medical facilities, diagnostic services, hospitals, managed care companies, and drug companies. Ethicists are concerned that these conditions represent inherent conflicts of interest and will encourage providers to place their self-interest over that of the patient. And what is true for the relationship between medical doctor and patient may likewise be true for the relationship between doctor of the soul and patient.

A pivotal study published in 1993 provided definitive empirical support for the notion that mental health care is responsive to the profit motive via the changing insurance benefit structure. The authors examined and analyzed insurance claims from federal employees covered by Blue Cross–Blue Shield for two years, 1978 and 1983. In 1978 there were two plans available to these employees, the high-option plan and the low-option plan. The high-option plan contained a very generous benefit that paid 100 percent of inpatient mental health treatment for 365 days a year. The low-option plan paid 100 percent of inpatient costs for up to 90 days. By 1983 the high-option plan had substantially reduced its liberal benefit; it would now pay for 100 percent of inpatient care for up to 60 days a year, with a $50 deductible for each admission. The low-option plan had decreased its benefit to 100 percent of inpatient costs for up to 30 days a year, with a $100 deductible for each admission.

Between 1978 and 1983 there was a significant drop in the use of inpatient services and a 41 percent decrease in the length of hospital stays. In 1978 high-option patients stayed in the hospital for an average of 46.6 days; in 1983 they stayed for an average of 29.8 days. Low-option patients stayed an average of 32.3 days in 1978 but only 19.4 days in 1983. Overall there was a 22 percent drop in the use of inpatient services and a 41 percent drop in the mean number of days of hospitalization.

Mary Jane England, president of the Washington Business Group on Health, and Robert Cole, deputy director of a mental health services program for youth, wrote an emotionally charged commentary about this study, one that may not be easy for the mental health community to swallow. They concluded that the findings from the study definitively demonstrate what mental health professionals have been very reluctant to consider and acknowledge— that the use of psychiatric services is sensitive to the amount of available benefit dollars. They went on to make a highly controversial statement linking the rapid growth of managed care to previous unnecessary inpatient costs (which we can further generalize to include outpatient costs): "This study captures a period at the very beginning of that decade, when the use of psychiatric inpatient confinements was sensitive to the amount of the dollar benefits available. This will explain the rapid growth of 'managed care' products such as preadmission screening and concurrent review by insurers and benefits administrators that have dramatically controlled unnecessary inpatient costs and put the for-profit sector into eclipse." They added that if providers' willingness to prescribe mental health care that is restrictive and disruptive to a patient's life and well-being is susceptible to market pressures, then the way in which our present health care system is organized is obviously in great need of reform.

The unspoken secret is out. In essence, these studies show that the profit motive has caused providers to use services for their own economic advantage. It seems logical to assume that the behavior of mental health providers in outpatient settings is similar. Putting a brake on providers' profit-motivated behaviors has been the primary driving force behind the managed care movement. Thus the results of this large-scale, well-sampled, empirical research justifies the use of good managed mental health care techniques. It also seems likely that the behavior of mental health providers in an out-patient setting will be similar.

The Ethics of Psychotherapy Remuneration

The psychotherapist's duties are to care for those who are unfortunate enough to suffer from a sickness of the mind. By using the power of the therapeutic relationship, he or she helps diminish the patient's psychic discomfort and pain. This patient-therapist alliance, considered to be the primary therapeutic agent, is idealized, held sacred, and expected to be above corruption. But is it really possible to be sure that therapists are free from the contamination that comes from the profit motive, especially in the face of the above-mentioned empirical evidence?

Like medical doctors, psychotherapists in the United States are awarded special status and privileges in exchange for their altruistic dedication to serving the ill. The American public reveres doctors to such a degree that we see them as members of a helping profession rather than members of a business or trade. Our society has given its healers the autonomy to dictate not only how the sick are treated but also what they should pay for that treatment. The ability to dictate both the amount of goods sold and their price would be considered evidence of an illegal monopoly in other forms of business. Thus the remuneration of helping professionals has been exempt from the usual market forces, incentives, and competition that other businesses must typically endure. Jeffrey Goldsmith, noted health economist, points out that "health care is different from other services and goods in the U.S. economy. Both because of health care's intimate nature and critical importance to people's well-being, the demand for health services does not obey any of the conventional economic forces that animate markets. Because of the impact of illness and the patient's lack of knowledge as to its causes and the appropriate remedies . . . the patient is a pawn in a medical 'game' controlled almost entirely by the providers of care. The demand for care is provider-driven. Since providers of care are rewarded economically by a provider dominated payment system for delivering more care, the demand for care is effectively limitless."

In return for the advantages of suspending the rules of business as usual, the public expects its mental health professionals (like its physicians) to abide by a patient-centered ethos. Healers' first charge is to demonstrate absolute and undivided loyalty to their patients by looking out for their welfare, keeping their confidences, and placing their interests above those of anyone else, including themselves. Their second duty is to police their own profession. They must monitor the behaviors of their colleagues and identify and correct unethical activities and conflicts of interest.

Conflicts of Interest

Conflicts of interest come in two basic forms. First, there are clashes between a doctor's personal interests and the interests of his or her patients. Second, there are circumstances that divide a doctor's loyalty between two or more patients or between a patient and a third party. In the case of an ethical transgression, health professionals are expected to rectify the situation and make amends to patients who have been harmed.

Each mental health profession has its own code of ethics; all are centered around protecting and preserving the integrity of the sacred therapeutic alliance. A therapist who violates the sanctity of the patient-therapist relationship is subject to censorship by his or her peers. Depending on the severity of the breech of standards, punishments range from simple words of disapproval to temporary censorship to permanent expulsion from the profession.

In protecting the patient-therapist relationship, mental health professionals stress individual rather than societal ethics; thus they have tended to veer away from issues concerning money. When it comes to dealing with blatant and brazen breeches of ethics, such as having sex with patients, betraying a patient's confidentiality, neglecting or abandoning a patient, or making flagrantly fraudulent financial claims, professional codes of ethics are generally quite precise and certain. But when it comes to issues related to money, the guidelines fall short, failing to instruct either practitioners or the public about what to do.

The topics of money and profit making in mental health care were seldom mentioned in either the professional or popular literature until the late 1960s, and discussions after that time have been quite sparse. Asking questions that providers do not like to hear almost borders on a taboo. And yet, while most psychotherapists do not take advantage of their patients for the purpose of financial gain, they cannot help but have their judgment affected by money, as we have seen.

Not openly addressing these issues is detrimental to the effectiveness of the helping professions. I suspect that these arguments are not candidly discussed among mental health professionals because the dilemma is not solvable under our present health care system. As long as profits are not completely separate from medical service, they will influence the way that service is delivered. Some say it is impossible to totally divorce the costs of care from the rendering of care. To separate them will require a complete overthrow of the status quo.

The ambiguity of the role of money in mental health practice has reached great proportions, and some professionals are in crisis about their identity and that of their patients: Are they therapists or business owners? Do they treat patients or consumers? The psychotherapist of today exists in this untenable situation of definitional uncertainty and ambiguity.

Businessperson or Professional?

While it *is* possible to be a helpful businessperson, it is *not* possible to be both a "helping professional" and a "helping businessperson." And "the business of the helping professions" sounds like an oxymoron. The dictionary defines *business* as an activity with the objective of supplying commodities. The term *business* pertains broadly to all gainful activity, although it usually excludes the professions and farming. Professions are vocations requiring training in the liberal arts or science and advanced study in a specialized field. Some health professionals are accorded the entitlement and dispensations previously discussed. Thus, to be both in business and in a helping profession is to be divided between two inherently conflicting roles.

In the American health care system, therapists find themselves part of a financial structure in which patient welfare is constantly pitted against provider income. Can mental health care providers be left to choose what is best for their patients on their own when their own financial interests are at stake in that decision? Can the fox really be trusted to guard the henhouse? Can altruism consistently triumph over greed? Not unless we are all saints.

Is psychotherapy really a business? The term *medical industrial complex* was born in the 1980s and is increasingly used to describe today's American health care delivery system. We constantly hear that "the climate of health care is far more commercialized and profit-oriented than ever before" and that we are "halfway through the transition from a provider-driven market to a purchaser-driven market."

To see how much big business is involved, let's examine the figures for expenditures on psychotherapy in 1987. Americans made a total of 79.5 million outpatient psychotherapy visits at a cost of $4.2 billion. The majority of these visits were to mental health professionals, and the remainder were to primary care physicians. In 1987, psychotherapy accounted for approximately 8 percent of all outpatient medical care expenditures, 19 percent of Medicaid outpatient expenditures, 9.6 percent of self-paid outpatient expenditures, 2.1 percent of Medicare payments, and 5.7 percent of private insurance payments.

Psychotherapy is big business; to deny this fact is to distort reality, to believe that the naked emperor has beautiful clothes. Much money changes hands every year in the big business of psychotherapy and mental health. Entrepreneurs, venture capitalists, and money-minded tycoons from within and without the helping professions see that mental health care holds high income potential for some providers. Some observers suspect that some practitioners are milking the benefits as they see more and more "Mercedes-awarding practices" crop up. Since there is profit to plunder, they want a share. The sight of a "fat cat" practitioner makes them assume there must be a way to get some of the booty from this "garden of unlimited resources."

Prior to the rise of managed care, professional caregivers controlled the fate of health and mental health care. Exempting the business of medicine from the rules of competition gave these professionals a decided advantage. What health care providers call charging a "usual and customary" fee, businesspeople call price fixing; this practice has given medical professionals a monopolistic advantage in the health care marketplace, because they have not had to compete as other businesses do. Some business-minded people who believe competition is at the heart of good business practice in America feel there is a certain hypocrisy in using the Hippocratic oath to corner the health market. These people believe that since mental health professionals act like businesspeople, they ought to be treated as businesspeople.

Medicine and mental health kept growing until they were ripe for industrialization. Now the authority of the provider is in question, but is it the provider's professional authority or fiscal authority that is at stake? Or are these one and the same? Can there be professional authority without fiscal authority?

Only other helping professionals have the expertise to challenge a provider's clinical authority. But does anyone have the right to challenge a doctor's business authority? None of the businesspeople involved in managed care want to don white coats and perform appendectomies; they say they want to manage the business aspects of medicine so doctors can be free to concentrate on patients' welfare. Of course, the end result is that the doctors become their employees. This is repugnant to some, but since American health care has taken on the proportions of big business, it might be much more efficient to industrialize it.

When mental health care providers' fiscal autonomy is challenged, they quickly shed the role of businessperson and assume the role of helper, asserting that managed care violates the fundamental integrity of the therapeutic relationship. It seems that professionals use a double standard, allowing themselves to change from a business- to a patient-centered ethos at will.

The Public Trust

As mental health professionals precariously teeter between the demands of being in business and those of helping people, patient skepticism seems to be growing. The general feeling is that doctors used to care about patients but nowadays they care more about money. The image of the rich and successful therapist invokes resentment. While most psychotherapists see themselves as helping professionals motivated by altruism, others see them as being motivated by profit.

For example, mental health professionals have recently raised millions of dollars to lobby for generous mental health benefits in a national health insurance program. The Association for the Advancement of Psychology, an organization dominated by therapists who believe in long-term psychotherapy, was the eleventh-largest contributor among health industry political action committees during the 1992 election season, donating over $273,000 to various campaigns. (The American Medical Association ranked first, with nearly $3 million in contributions.)

Few causes have generated such passion for decades, even very pressing social problems. Mental health professionals, who have engaged in interdisciplinary wars for years, now find themselves allied in a collaborative effort to promote the inclusion of mental health benefits in national and private insurance plans. Coalitions are forming among psychiatrists, psychologists, social workers, marriage and family practitioners, psychiatric nurses, and many others—strange bedfellows indeed!

A common enemy—managed care—has unified these factions, ostensibly to fight for patients' rights. But as noted above, the line between therapists' interests and patients' interests is not always clear. While long-term therapists believe unlimited mental health benefits are in the best clinical interest of the patient, they are also in the best financial interest of the therapist.

At the same time that mental health providers have been complaining about managed care, they have been commercializing their practices and increasing their profit margins. We see advertisements for computer software designed to help mental health practitioners market their practice. Every day the mail brings yet another circular advertising a workshop that will transform your psychotherapy practice into a prosperous business. Such workshops teach therapists to become entrepreneurs and to sell their skills in the emerging managed care marketplace. They promise to help providers develop a mind for business, learn low-cost marketing techniques, develop sales strategies, and locate marketing resources. Marketing is the new buzzword of mental health practice.

I recall the look on the face of the parents of a schizophrenic boy when they read one of these marketing pitches on the back cover of a professional magazine in my waiting room. Lower-middle-class workers, they had spent their life savings to pay a psychiatrist for intensive, individual therapy in the hope that, against all odds, he could "cure" their son or at least keep him at home and working. They discovered that this professional possessed no special magic; he was unable to prevent their son's symptoms from growing worse. The inevitable occurred, and their son now resides in a state mental institution. They had put their trust—all too willingly—in the hands of the expert, and the expert was not at any financial risk whatsoever. The lesson they learned was costly, both in dollars and cents and in emotional turmoil. The drive to incorporate business principles into mental health practice is not likely to inspire such patients to have confidence in providers.

The dramatic changes taking place in American health care are bringing the economic underpinnings of the helping professions to the surface. Patients are becoming more observant and better informed about what they should expect from a therapist. They are increasingly willing to "shop around" for a therapist and to switch therapists if their needs are not met.

Indelibly imprinted in my memory are the words of one of my patients who transferred into my care after seeing a private psychiatrist for five years. Since she was a member of our HMO, she knew she had a benefit of twenty sessions of mental health care per year. When I asked her why she had decided to transfer, she replied that a dream had inspired her. In the dream she saw her therapist very clearly. He was extending one hand out to her in a helping gesture, as if to lift her up out of her psychic pain. As she reached out to grasp his helping hand, she turned her head far enough to the side to see that his other hand was in her pocket. She told her therapist the dream and terminated her treatment with him.

When I asked her what it meant to her, she said the dream had brought to the fore a feeling that had been nagging her unconsciously for almost a year but that she not been able to express overtly until she experienced her dream. At some level she had intuited that her therapist might be keeping her in therapy not so much because she needed treatment but because he needed her fees! When she spoke with him about it, he denied it completely. He even seemed to be annoyed with her. She decided on the spot that if they couldn't talk honestly about money, how good a relationship could it be? She said she decided right then and there to start a new therapy that was based upon truth—that psychotherapy is a business. She told me I was her consultant, not her "loving therapist."

The problem is that psychotherapists have never had a well-articulated policy concerning money. We must broach the unmentionable questions—are the helping professions really a business? Is it right or wrong to make money from people's sickness? To make a modest, comfortable living is all right, but to charge clients more than is reasonable or when they don't really need treatment is wrong. When psychotherapy is not fully a business and not fully a helping profession but it claims the rights and privileges of both domains, its ability to serve individual patients and society is diminished. If psychotherapists are primarily devoted members of a helping profession rather than businesspeople, they ought to fight for the welfare of their patients on a societal level. But if they are primarily entrepreneurs and owners of small businesses, they have no more right to expect society to abolish competition within their field than the owners of mom-and-pop convenience stores have to expect society to abolish supermarkets.

Providers' Ambivalence Toward Insurance

Another issue to be examined is how third-party payers have shaped doctors' and therapists' economic relationship with their patients and with society. The rise of managed care has raised society's consciousness about how the cost of health care has spiraled out of control. Why have providers until recently been spared from this awareness? I think it is because of the role played by health insurance prior to the advent of managed care. Ironically, insurance has been a prime tool in the ever-so-"discrete" evolution of psychotherapy into big business. As payments were made, one by one, to individual providers, few were able to estimate the enormity of the exchange, until recently, as national data bases have begun to reveal overall economic patterns.

No Questions Asked

Today's discord between providers and managed care can be seen as just one more battle in a long-standing scuffle between medical providers and payers. Up until now, providers have generally won. The active opposition of the medical profession has been instrumental in preventing the introduction of government-sponsored medical insurance. In the 1940s, in order to ward off an attempt to install such insurance, the AMA approved private health insurance—in a form that imposed no controls on doctors' or hospitals' decision making. According to Paul Starr, a medical historian, the rise of insurance plans such as Blue Cross (hospital coverage) and Blue Shield (medical service benefits) reflected a real accommodation of provider interests.

Before managed care, American medical insurance was dominated by indemnity benefits, which reimburse the subscriber directly, and service benefits, which guarantee direct payment to physicians and hospitals. Reimbursing third parties' only job was to pay the "usual and customary" fee, without questioning it; insurers abided by the wishes of the medical profession.

Up until the 1980s, qualified providers just mailed in a form to indemnity insurers and received payment, no questions asked, within thirty to sixty days. The general consensus among providers was that insurance was splendid. But when insurers began managing their payments, putting restrictions on them, asking for clinical justification for treatment, and requiring more paperwork, the reaction was very different.

From the time of its inception, indemnity health insurance acted as a buffer, protecting the doctor-patient relationship from lay interference and insulating both doctors and patients from the rules of business and the consequences of rising health care costs. Insured patients did not need to be sensitive to the costs of their care or calculate every charge, since fees did not come directly out of their pocket. Provider apprehension about interference from insurance companies in treatment decisions was quickly replaced by a sense of entitlement: insurers ought to simply pay out and shut up.

Whereas early health insurance plans generally provided no mental health coverage, in the 1970s mental health benefits—

particularly inpatient benefits—were added to many plans. Out-patient psychotherapy was generally reimbursed at a lower rate than medical benefits, with the patient having to make a copayment of 20 to 50 percent of the total cost.

Therapists could easily manipulate these plans, however. If a patient could not afford part or all of the copayment, therapists were sometimes willing to settle for what they could get from the insurance company. To collect, therapists would charge the highest allowable fee, say $120 per hour, collect $60 from the insurance company, and then forgive all or part of the balance. This seemed to be a fairly innocent breech of ethics, resulting in no real harm to anyone, especially when the insurance company is conceptualized as an anonymous profit-monger corporate entity based in some far-away state. So why not allow a needy patient to receive abundant treatment? The provider got a good payment, the patient received good treatment, and the insurance company wasn't any the wiser. But this action, multiplied many times, has a cumulative effect; and it enters into the realm of social ethics if you believe that in a world of limited resources what is used for one patient is thus denied to some other patient.

Although health insurance has made psychotherapy available to many more people, the inclusion of psychotherapy benefits in general medical insurance was initially met with trepidation and doubt on the part of mental health professionals—particularly psychiatrists, who worried that the insurance industry would try to regulate psychiatric practice and encroach on provider autonomy. Ambivalent feelings about the role of insurance in the doctor-patient relationship has been evident ever since.

Gratifying Wishes for Transference

In the 1970s, various analysts discussed the effect of health insurance on treatment. One analyst worried it would pay too much—if insurance pays all the fees, it is as if the patient is getting free therapy. What is wrong with free therapy? This analyst brought up the fact that even Freud discussed the pitfalls of receiving free therapy. Freud firmly believed that free treatment enormously increases the resistance of the neurotic; he stated that "the absence of the regulating effect offered by the payment of the fee to the doctor makes it very painfully felt; the whole relationship is removed from the real world, and the patient is deprived of a strong motive for endeavoring to bring treatment to an end."

This same analyst amplified Freud's beliefs by adding that insurance, like free treatment, could hurt the therapeutic alliance and prevent successful analysis: "Some patients . . . may not be amenable to psychoanalysis if full payment is [provided] by insurance. Certainly the possible gratification of transference wishes, via the use of insurance . . . indicates that the analytic task will probably be harder in all cases treated where the entire fee is paid by insurance."

Illustrating this point is a case in which a patient's resistance was increased by insurance payment:

> Insurance meant protection against castration and anal depletion. . . . I would speculate that, had this patient continued in treatment and had his fee been partially paid for by insurance, there would have been evidence of increased resistance. The anonymous third party, the insurance company, becomes like the anonymous therapist—a transference figure. But the insurance company, unlike the therapist gratifies transference wishes; it takes care of and protects the patient. For the patient presented, the insurance company would have gratified the following wishes to some extent: to have a bounteous breast to cling to; to have a slave girl cater to his wishes; to remove him from the reality of having to pay me and the feelings of depletion and rage which accompanied the payment; and to protect him from feeling close to or dependent on me. With these patients, these gratifications in the fantasy world would have made these core problems even less accessible to the work of treatment.

The Good Mother

Traditional therapists have also struggled with the potential for insurance to become a transference figure to the patient. Some analysts have alleged great similarities between the role of the good parent and that of the good insurance company. They believe both patient and therapist are strengthened when they feel supported. However, the effectiveness of therapy is diminished when external influences have a strong effect on the patient-therapist relationship.

In the golden era of mental health, insurance was like a "good mother" who granted generous benefits and gratified the transference wishes of the patient, fulfilling his or her need for unlimited nurturance. The benefits took care of both the patient and the therapist. Such was the case in the "Camelot era of psychotherapy reimbursement in the 1970s."

Today, long-term therapists are asking where that liberal, all-accepting, all-paying mother has gone. To therapists, the good mother has been transformed into an irate mother, a meddlesome, third-party mother. Managed care is a very unsatisfactory, ungiving mother who appoints case reviewers to act as her agents, individuals who confuse and hurt the patient. One writer described a patient in the clutches of the evil mother managed care this way: "When the patient was feeling better she became afraid that the case manager, upon discovering her improvement, would feel that she was cured and withdraw his treatment authorization. When she was feeling depressed and hopeless, which was often, she felt that the case manager, upon sensing her lack of progress, would refuse to underwrite any further treatment."

Mental health professionals are also worried that the outside pressures of insurance and managed care are more likely to make therapists treat only symptoms. One therapist worries that "the limits of treatment covered by an insurance company will gradually be registered in the mind of the therapist as 'This is all the patient needs.'"

Insurance coverage has played an important part in preventing therapists and patients from seeing how extravagant psychotherapy can be. Twice-weekly psychotherapy costs approximately $14,000 per year. Ironically, it is insurance that is now reminding the therapist and patient that the costs must be reduced.

It is interesting that initially, when therapists thought insurance would decrease their autonomy, they regarded it as a potential detriment to treatment. Gradually, as insurance became accepted and it became clear that it set no limits on providers, it was thought to be a good mother. The idea that it would block therapeutic progress somehow seemed to dissolve. But now that those who pay for care are setting limits and demanding accountability from those who provide it, insurance is again seen by providers as a very bad mother!

Views about insurance seem to be influenced by the profit motive. Before providers understood how helpful insurance would be in enhancing their income, some therapists plainly struggled with the question of whether insurance payments would be a detriment to treatment. Today, however, therapists struggle with the question of whether the *lack* of insurance payments is a detriment to treatment.

Removing the Profit Motive

The therapist cannot maintain neutrality when a fee is involved. If a condition of successful therapy is that the therapist remain neutral in order to be an effective therapeutic agent, then the fee becomes a means by which to have a real interaction. This interaction may not necessarily be transference, based on past childhood conflicts. Just as a cigar is sometimes just a cigar, sometimes a debate about a fee is just a debate about the worth of the goods being purchased. But the interaction about fees can contaminate therapeutic neutrality!

Furthermore, the patient's ability or inability to pay a fee can become a measure of his or her worth. This can cause problems when the therapist must give the patient unconditional positive regard and acceptance as a condition of successful psychotherapy. To be theoretically consistent, fees should not be directly paid to the therapist at all. If the patient's mental health is tied to the therapist's financial well-being, regardless of the particulars of the financial arrangement, there will be some built-in conflict of interest. Thus, collecting fees can interfere with the therapist's neutrality and unconditional acceptance of the patient.

Stephen Appelbaum's solution to the problem is simple and straightforward: "Some people argue that the ills of the health care system in general can only be solved by removing the profit motive, by establishing a national health service, as have all industrialized countries except the United States and South Africa. Such a health service is otherwise known to propagandized, indignant Americans as 'socialized medicine.' In such a system healers would be paid a salary and would thus be free to practice their trade with no other major motive than to do good works for their patients."

Appelbaum goes on to say that one (albeit draconian) solution to the evils of private practice is to lower fees to the point where financial interests play no part in therapeutic decisions, thereby freeing therapists from "medicine's high-flown financial demands" and reducing the "heady, luxurious aspirations and affectation that so often accompany exalted socioeconomic levels. Perhaps more humanistically and less materialistically inclined people would select the field."

Why Now?

The previous insulation of the doctor-patient relationship from the realities of the costs of therapy and the consequences to society created somewhat of a dream world. That world is now dead. Third-party intrusion into the practice of psychotherapy, particularly long-term psychotherapy, is reaching its height. The economic power and control that once belonged to the owners of a profitable cottage industry has begun to shift to new actors.

Therapists want to clarify the ethics of managed care, and rightfully so. But we have to ask ourselves a more basic question. If clinical practice can be so strongly affected by the profit motive, can our view of what is right and wrong likewise be affected by our financial self-interest? Chapter Four looks at the ethical dilemmas that face us as we enter the world of managed care and compare them to the ethical problems associated with the traditional fee-for-service system.

Notes

p. 53, *Like medicine, psychotherapy is:* Starr, P. (1982). *The social transformation of American medicine* (p. 4–55). New York: Basic Books.

p. 54, *A study of this chain:* Hemenway, D., Killen, A., Cashman, S. B., Parks, C. L., & Bicknell, W. J. (1990). Physician's responses to financial incentives. *New England Journal of Medicine, 322,* 1059–1063.

p. 55, *A growing body of research:* Epstein, A., Colin, B. B., & McNeil, B. J. (1986). The use of ambulatory testing in prepaid and fee-for-service group practices: Reaction to perceived profitability. *New England Journal of Medicine, 314,* 1089–1094; Hillman, P. M., & Kerstein, J. J. (1989). How do financial incentives affect physicians' clinical decisions and the financial performance of health maintenance organizations? *New England Journal of Medicine, 321,* 86–92; Woolhandler, S. & Himmelstein, D. V. (1995). Extreme risk: The new corporate proposition for physicians. *New England Journal of Medicine,* 1706–1708.

p. 55, *A pivotal study:* Patrick, C., Padgett, D., Burns, B., Schlesinger, H., & Cohen, J. (1993). Use of inpatient services by a national population: Do benefits make a difference? *Journal of the American Academy of Child and Adolescent Psychiatry, 32*(1), 144–152.

p. 56, *Mary Jane England, president of the Washington Business Group on Health:* England, M. J., & Cole, R. (1993). Discussion of "Use of inpatient service by a national population: Do benefits make a difference?" *Journal of the American Academy of Child and Adolescent Psychiatry, 32*(1), 153–154.

p. 57, *Jeffrey Goldsmith, noted health economist:* Goldsmith, J. (1984, Fall). Death of a paradigm: The challenge of competition. *Health Affairs,* pp. 12–14.

p. 58, *Conflicts of interest come:* Rodwin, M. (1993). *Medicine, money and morals* (p. 51). New York: Oxford University Press.

p. 59, *The topics of money and profit making:* ibid., pp. 2–9.

p. 60, *The dictionary defines* business: *The American Heritage dictionary of the English language* (New College Edition). (1979). Boston: Houghton Mifflin.

p. 60, *The term* medical industrial complex: Relman, A. (1980). The new medical-industrial complex. *The New England Journal of Medicine, 303*(17), 963–970.

p. 60, *We constantly hear that:* Relman, A. (1993). [Foreword]. In M. Rodwin, *Medicine, money and morals* (pp. 2–9). New York: Oxford University Press; Boland, P. (1988, March 9). Reposition now for the managed care market of the 1990s. *Trustee,* p. 9.

p. 60, *To see how much big business is involved:* Olfson, M., & Pincus, H. A. (1994). Outpatient psychotherapy in the United States. I: Volume costs and user characteristics. *American Journal of Psychiatry, 151,* 1281–1288.

p. 61, *Some observers suspect that some practitioners:* Appelbaum, S. (1992). Evils in private practice. *Bulletin of the Meninger Clinic, 56*(2), 141–149.

p. 62, *The Association for the Advancement of Psychology:* Navarro, V. (1993). *Dangerous to your health: Capitalism in health care* (p. 34). New York: Monthly Review Press.

p. 65, *Today's discord between providers and managed care:* Starr, P. (1982). *The social transformation of American medicine* (pp. 291–320). New York: Basic Books.

p. 66, *Before managed care, American medical insurance:* ibid.

p. 67, *But this action, multiplied many times:* Glasson, J., & Orentlicher, D. (1995). Managed care: Ethical issues. *Journal of the American Medical Association, 274*(8), 611.

p. 68, *Freud firmly believed:* Halpert, E. (1972). The effect of insurance on psychoanalytic treatment. *Journal of the American Psychoanalytic Association, 20,* 122–133.

p. 68, *This same analyst amplified Freud's beliefs:* Halpert, E. (1973). A meaning of insurance in psychotherapy. *International Journal of Psychoanalytic Psychotherapy, 1,* 62–68.

p. 68, *Illustrating this point:* ibid.

p. 69, *Such was the case:* Meyer, W. S. (1993). In defense of long-term treatment: On the vanishing holding environment. *Social Work, 38*(5), 571–578.

p. 69, *One writer described a patient:* ibid.

p. 69, *One therapist worries that:* Halpert, E. (1972). The effect of insurance on psychoanalytic treatment. *Journal of the American Psychoanalytic Association, 20,* 122–133.

p.70 *Twice-weekly psychotherapy:* Blackmon, W. D. (1993). Are psychoanalytic billing practices ethical? *American Journal of Psychotherapy, 47*(4), 613–620.

p. 70, *The therapist cannot maintain neutrality:* London, P. (1964). *The modes and morals of psychotherapy* (pp. 9–10). New York: Holt, Rhinehart & Winston.

p. 71, *Stephen Appelbaum's solution:* Appelbaum, S. (1992). Evils in private practice. *Bulletin of the Meninger Clinic, 56*(2), 141–149.

4

Ethical Abuses in Managed
and Unmanaged Care

Hearing from Both Sides

*Medicine and other professions have historically
distinguished themselves from business and trade by
claiming to be above the market and pure commer-
cialism. In justifying the public's trust, professionals
have set higher standards of conduct for themselves
than the minimal rules governing the marketplace.*

Paul Starr

As I made clear in Chapter Three, I believe that the fierce criticisms of managed care put forward by mental health professionals are sometimes clouded by self-interest. Although we strive
to rely on scientifically derived information when we make our judgments as professionals, we are often oblivious to the degree to which
our own belief systems, values, personal needs, and limitations color
our interpretations of world events. Therefore, before we discuss the
ethics of long- or short-term psychotherapy in an era of managed
care, it would be helpful if we analyzed some of the ethical dilemmas unique to each of the systems under which it is delivered.

The most rabid critics assert that managed care is a fertile
ground for serious violations of patient welfare, the likes of which
have never been seen under fee-for-service practice. This argument

implies that such indecencies hardly ever occur in mental health care delivered outside of managed care.

Is this accusation fair? Is it true that unethical treatment of patients is far more prevalent under one system than another? Obviously managed care is not a panacea for all the problems of American health care, and it has its share of horror stories. But before we condemn it, shouldn't we try to be objective and compare it with fee-for-service? Shouldn't we ask ourselves why there was a need for change? How was managed care able to gain such a major toehold?

In this chapter I describe ethical dilemmas that have arisen in both managed care and fee-for-service practice, using several case examples. My purpose is not to dwell upon the unpleasant and sordid details of various breeches of ethics but to heighten people's awareness that problems exist on both sides. Where there are people, there is both good and evil, compassion and greed—and a multitude of mistakes. As long as human beings are in charge of a system, it can never be free from transgressions.

Comparing the Systems

Comparing managed care with fee-for-service is not a simple task. We need to think about a number of variables that affect such a comparison. First, the indemnity system is the "incumbent," or old, familiar structure, under which the doctor was both the ultimate expert and the dictator of fees and treatment. Mental health professionals have grown up with the perception that we render care, we bill the customary and reasonable fee, and insurance pays. If the cost of treatment is not covered by insurance, the patient pays out of his or her own pocket. Doctors (and mental health professionals who assume a similar role) are not accustomed to having either their treatments or their fees challenged by anyone. An economic scheme that creates conditions as provider-friendly as indemnity insurance can engender quite a sense of entitlement in its beneficiaries. Who wouldn't be reluctant to relinquish a milieu as comfortable as this?

Second, managed care is in the unenviable position of being the newcomer, the harbinger of change. With change comes scrutiny and resistance. As an unfamiliar challenger to the status quo, it will be probed and examined with great intensity.

Third, we must also ask ourselves *who* is collecting information about managed care and ethics and *how* they are collecting it. As social scientists, we know that every experiment possesses unique demand characteristics that suggest how the subject should behave. Researchers can emit cues that influence their subjects' behavior and affect the outcome of their experiments. If we expert professionals solicit specific information, then a group of patients is likely to deliver exactly what we seek.

For example, the American Psychiatric Association established a "managed care hotline" with the express intent of gathering complaints from patients and providers. Creating an advocacy system is an admirable way to help patients and assist providers, but it is disconcerting that there is no parallel device such as a "fee-for-service hotline" that solicits patients to report problems such as unaffordable copayments, terminations due to lack of finances, or prohibitive fees.

Fourth, it is easier to complain about undertreatment than overtreatment. In cases of unnecessary surgery or excess chemotherapy, the result is obvious. But how can we establish that a patient has been "overtreated by talk"?

Fifth, it is easier to complain about unsatisfactory conditions under managed care than under indemnity care because dissatisfaction seems to be aimed at a depersonalized corporate entity rather than at a single provider.

With these variables in mind, I will identify and discuss the divergent points of view about the major ethical issues that exist under both systems.

Ethical Issues in Managed Care

Opponents of managed care say that it is inherently unethical because it gives providers a financial incentive to withhold care.

Capitation, for example, pays the provider a certain amount per year to take care of a patient's total mental health needs. Thus, the less care rendered, the greater the provider's profit. But while the practitioner profits from providing less care, the danger of undertreatment is palpable.

Opponents also contend that the financial incentives inherent in managed care tempt the provider and the payer to

- Deny and limit access to necessary care (such as long-term psychotherapy)

- Narrow patients' choice of provider

- Disrupt continuity of care

- Use less-qualified providers to render care

- Use less-qualified providers to review care

- Breach patient confidentiality by giving reviewers too many details about patients' personal lives

- Follow a business ethic instead of a professional ethic

To illustrate these issues, I will discuss background information and case examples that come from personal experience, word of mouth, insurance reports, hotline reports, consumer groups, legal cases, and the media.

Denying and Limiting Care

The American Psychiatric Association's managed care hotline received nearly eight thousand calls in its first three years of operation. The complaints fell into both clinical and administrative categories. The most common complaints from both providers and patients were as follows:

- Managed care companies deny necessary care as well as access to a full range of effective treatment modalities (for example, they limit treatment for depression to medication, denying psychotherapy).

• Certain diagnostic groups such as chronic schizophrenics, bipolar disorders, recurrent depressives, autistics, and patients with medically complex conditions are singled out and denied care.

• Authorization for care for patients with conditions such as eating disorders and chemical dependency is often made arbitrarily.

• The gatekeeper system blocks patients from easy access to care, particularly to long-term therapists.

• Inpatient care is very restricted. Often hospitalization is limited to those who are suicidal or homicidal.

• Prevention, early intervention, and appropriate maintenance of treatment is lacking.

Opponents also claim that managed care companies severely limit outpatient psychotherapy. Although a managed-care benefit package may give patients up to twenty sessions per year, providers claim that some treatment authorizations are limited to one, two, or three sessions at a time. Some companies try to exclude patients who have had prior therapy on the basis that they have a preexisting condition or that their condition is "chronic" and their benefit package does not include care for chronic conditions. By limiting treatment to this extent, opponents believe managed care is hurting both patients and the mental health professions.

The New Republic discussed a case of a suicide attributed to the denial of care by a managed care company.

• •

In April 1990, Larry Megge crashed his car into a highway barrier near Detroit, killing both himself and his wife. The Megge family is suing Larry's health plan and providers, claiming breach of contract and gross negligence because the patient was allegedly denied needed care. Mr. Megge had repeatedly sought treatment for his suicidal tendencies, delusions, sexual abnormalities, and depression. His medical records show that his managed care company had recently refused authorization for hospitalization three times. His therapist had told him to use a drop-in center and to keep in touch by telephone. Two days before he died, he called his managed care therapist; his phone call allegedly went unreturned.

Narrowing Patient Choice

Managed care patients can receive treatment only from approved providers, or they may pay higher rates to go outside the managed care network. Critics of managed care claim that decreasing patient choice is destructive to the quality of psychotherapy and the healing relationship. Not being able to choose one's own provider diminishes trust and therefore curtails the power of the therapeutic relationship.

. . . .

John

After much hesitation, John finally decided to seek professional help for his sexual dysfunction, which had been hurting his marriage for over two years. He heard that Dr. Croter was an excellent therapist. When he asked for authorization for treatment, the gatekeeper informed him that since Dr. Croter was not on the company's panel of approved therapists, he could not be reimbursed for his services.

John was angry. He said that he needed help now. Why couldn't he get what he wanted? The managed care plan referred him to another provider; John attended the appointment but remained dissatisfied and insisted that he be allowed to see Dr. Croter. He complained again, and the managed care plan gave him a second referral to an alternate provider. John felt his plan was not giving him the help he needed. Discouraged, he sought no additional therapy and attempted to handle his problems on his own. A year later, John's wife filed for divorce, and he blamed the managed care company for his problems.

Disrupting Continuity of Care

When a patient involved in psychotherapy is switched from fee-for-service insurance coverage to managed care, the patient may suffer the loss of his or her familiar therapist if that therapist is not on the managed care company's panel of approved providers. Opponents contend that managed care companies have little or no regard for the sanctity of established therapist-patient relationships. The vulnerable patient is faced with the difficult choice of either paying for therapy out of his or her own pocket, terminating therapy, or transferring to an approved therapist.

Marie

Marie had been seeing Dr. Daley for over five years when her employer changed her health coverage. Although she petitioned to continue with Dr. Daley, she quickly found that she could no longer see him unless she paid out of pocket, which she really could not afford. Since finances had to dictate her treatment, she transferred to an approved provider.

When she met with her new therapist, he told her that he did not think it was necessary for her to be in psychotherapy at all, let alone on a weekly basis. She called customer relations and complained. Although they listened politely, they did nothing. She complained to her employer, who in turn contacted the managed care plan.

Marie was allowed to see another therapist, who judged that she needed about ten sessions over the next six months. Again she was very discouraged. She wanted weekly appointments, but no one would approve it. She decided she would get a part-time job so she could go back to Dr. Daley and pay him out of pocket.

Using Less-Qualified Providers

Critics of managed care state that training and credentials are very important to the success of psychotherapy: the most experienced therapist is the best therapist. Companies that do not employ such practitioners are not only not providing the highest quality care, they may actually be providing incompetent care. Psychiatrists complain that managed care is replacing them with psychologists. Psychologists complain that master's-level providers will soon take over because managed care wants "cheap labor." Opponents of managed care say that the corporate motivation for profit is so strong that it supplants the desire to offer providers with advanced training and high educational standards.

Added to this list of objections is that gatekeeping is performed by unqualified primary care providers and others who are not trained in the correct techniques for detecting mental illness and referring mentally ill patients for appropriate care. Consequently, patients are not receiving the level of care appropriate to their needs.

Su

Su is a ten-year-old girl who was traumatized by an accident in which a parent and sibling were killed. She was brought to the mental health department of her family's HMO because she had become increasingly depressed and mute. After the ninth session, Su's mother discovered Su as she was attempting suicide. The HMO therapist treating Su had less than a master's degree. She determined that by the tenth session Su should be finished with therapy, even though she was still mute and suicidal. Su's parents had enough money to take her to an outside psychiatrist, who saw her three times a week for eighteen months. Su started talking again only after twelve months.

Using Less-Qualified Reviewers

A frequent complaint is that case reviewers who are less qualified and credentialed than the providers they evaluate frequently dictate the parameters of treatment. Often a case manager and therapist will subscribe to disparate definitions of medical necessity and use widely divergent criteria for determining the proper level and course of care. Case managers may force providers to use treatment protocols they do not agree with. Critics claim that reviewers shackle provider creativity when they adhere to case review guidelines and prescribed treatment protocols. They also claim that the use of computer-generated guidelines and algorithms can damage the unique nature of the therapeutic relationship by emphasizing technique over relationship. Moreover, they say, such devices are dehumanizing and degrading.

Joan

A managed care psychiatrist reported that he wanted authorization to hospitalize Joan, a borderline patient who was expressing passive wishes to die but who was covered under another managed care plan. The psychiatrist claimed the patient's depression was so great that she could not function at work or at home. A psychiatric nurse from the patient's managed care company demanded that she be allowed to interview the patient. When the nurse finished, she insisted that Joan did not need to be hospitalized. Instead, intensive intervention consisting of three psychotherapy sessions a week, medication, and phone contact would be implemented until the patient stabilized. The nurse stated that she would perform the work herself.

Joan was frightened about having an unfamiliar provider work with her, and she called her psychiatrist to let him know. He lodged a complaint against the company. The patient was eventually admitted for an inpatient stay. She claims that she was put through unnecessary harm by the managed care nurse who disagreed with her psychiatrist. She stated that she had much more faith in her psychiatrist because he was much better qualified than the nurse to make treatment decisions.

Breaking Confidentiality

Critics say that if managed care prevails, privacy in psychotherapy will be a thing of the past. Providers complain that reviewers and case managers often want to know too many personal details about their patients. The presence of case managers interferes with patients' trust in the therapeutic relationship. Although patients sign a release form to allow for communication between their provider and a managed care case reviewer or manager, opponents believe that the patient may not fully understand how dangerous such breaches of confidentiality can be.

George

George went for psychotherapy to Ms. Kaplan, M.S.W. He discussed his alcoholism and his history of hospitalization. George was making considerable progress in therapy. He had remained abstinent, and he wanted to apply for a promotion that would nearly double his salary. He was concerned that if the therapist were to record a diagnosis of alcoholism and his employer found out, his chances for promotion might be harmed.

The case reviewer called Ms. Kaplan, insisting that she be told details of the treatment plan in order to estimate how long it would take for George to improve. Ms. Kaplan was in a quandary. In her judgment, George was doing well and needed to continue in treatment—with no interference from any outside source such as his insurer. The reviewer reminded her that George had signed a release form. Afraid she would lose her place on the managed care panel of approved therapists, she succumbed to the case reviewer's pressures and informed her about George's alcoholism. Afterward she felt unsettled and guilty, as if she had betrayed her patient.

She decided to tell George about every detail of the conversation and the exchange of information. George, disgruntled and angry, told Ms. Kaplan he could no longer continue to work with her and walked out of the therapy session. Despite efforts to get George back in therapy, his trust had been broken, and he would not return even to another therapist.

Two months later, George called Ms. Kaplan and apologized for being "hotheaded." He informed her that he did get the promotion he had been seeking. But he made it very clear that he did not want to return for any psychotherapy sessions, since his last experience had caused him such distress.

Following a Business Ethic

Giant corporations now own much of the mental or behavioral health care industry. The managed care concept is even being adopted by the public health system, as each state accepts bids and contracts with some of the giant behavioral health corporations that are cornering the mental health care market.

Critics of managed care believe that the corporate mentality will take the heart and soul out of psychotherapy and turn it into big business. The great and real fear engendered by the trend toward the corporatization of mental health care is that business ethics rather than bioethics will prevail.

Opponents add that the assumptions underlying managed behavioral health care are unfounded. Is it really true that insurance companies are better at controlling costs and quality of care than anyone else? After all, despite the fact that managed care is gaining control, the costs of general health care remain overwhelming. The costs of mental health care are a concern to payers because they have continued to grow at a rate faster than general health care. At the same time, managed care companies are making huge windfall profits. What is happening to the money that is being saved by preventing unnecessary care and reducing practitioners' fees? Is it going from the pockets of patients and providers into the pockets of well-paid administrators and entrepreneurs? If so, what is the point of saving? Who is reaping the benefits? And is it right for greedy entrepreneurs to make so much money from the sickness of others?

Critics also object to the assumption that patients are not cost conscious because they do not pay for their own health care. Americans pay more out of their own pockets for mental health care than citizens of any other industrialized nation—approximately 45 to 48 percent of psychotherapy in the United States is paid for out of pocket, whereas private insurance pays for 26 percent, Medicaid and Medicare pay for 19 percent, and various other sources pay for the remainder.

Ethical Issues in Unmanaged Care

Proponents of managed care argue that the fee-for-service system produced an insulated industry in which practitioners used their status in society to gain the privileges of high income and clinical autonomy. Providers not only set their own fees, they also determined the volume of service they provided. The greater the fees a patient paid for care, the greater the provider's incentive to render services. The larger the practice, the larger the profit. Where was the impetus to deliver cost-effective care? Support for these accusations of unbridled greed and opportunism lies in the fact that under the fee-for-service system, in which providers policed their own spending, out-of-control costs were never curbed.

The profit motive under fee-for-service arrangements make it easy for mental health providers to

- Create, inflate, and extend the need for care (such as long-term psychotherapy)

- Maximize individual care

- Artificially multiply and politicize diagnoses

- Overuse services

- Ignore societal needs

- Fail to develop a system that provides continuity and coordination of care

- Narrow patient choice based on ability to pay

- Fail to establish universal standards of care

- Protect the providers' financial interests through professional guilds, at the consumer's expense

- Focus on illness, not wellness

To illustrate these issues, I will discuss some background information and some examples that come from personal experience, insurance reports, consumer groups, legal cases, and the media.

Creating, Inflating, and Extending the Need for Care

Payers worry that in a system under which mental health providers can concoct a never-ending supply of patient problems for which services can be provided, no amount of mental health treatment will ever be enough. They suspect that providers may expand or even fabricate diagnoses and prescribe unnecessary treatments to maximize their own financial gain, rather than treat their patients effectively.

Are payers wrong? Over the past decade, hospital scandals, insurance fraud, and inflated and faddish diagnoses have lent credence to payers' suspicions of abuse. In the early 1980s, many health insurance policies had liberal mental health benefits. Private psychiatric hospitals doubled in number, from 220 in 1984 to 444 in 1988, and earned windfall profits. By the late 1980s insurance plans began limiting psychiatric hospital stays, so more patients were needed in order to fill the same number of beds.

Newsweek publicized a case of a fourteen-year-old boy who was literally abducted by a private psychiatric hospital in order to exploit his insurance benefits.

. . . .

Jeremy

Jeremy was committed to a private psychiatric facility in San Antonio, Texas. A psychiatrist who had never seen him committed him based upon what Jeremy's brother, an inpatient at the facility, had said about him. Arriving unannounced at his home, two private security guards took Jeremy to the facility, despite strong protests from his guardians. It took a court order to secure his release five days later.

- -

Was this case an exceptional or isolated incident? It stimulated other patients with similar stories to come forward in Texas, Florida, Alabama, and New Jersey.

- -

Kyle

Kyle Williams, a forty-one-year-old carpenter, was committed to the same San Antonio hospital. Pressured by staff to sign voluntary-admission papers, he finally hired a lawyer to help him to leave. He was billed for half the hospital charges, $4,800. He sued.

Georgette

Georgette Hinson, upset about her grandfather's death a few years before, signed up for a counseling program at her high school. She told the counselor about her depression, and the counselor suggested that she and her mother visit a hospital. By the time mother and daughter arrived, the counselor had informed the hospital that Georgette was suicidal. She was placed in the hospital. The bill for her stay was $12,000.

"Free Counseling"

A newspaper reported the case of a thirty-seven-year-old depressed woman who decided to answer an ad for "free counseling." Once the phone screener determined that she was insured, she was given an address. Upon her arrival, she was committed to a ward filled with seriously disturbed patients. She called on an attorney, who helped her be released the next day. The hospital billed her $1,700 for her coerced stay and charged her for a visit with a doctor she never saw.

- -

Cases such as these inspired a large-scale investigation into insurance fraud and psychiatric treatment by the federal government and six states. In 1991 the *New York Times* published a series of articles on the problem, including "Paying for Fraud—A Special Report: Mental Health Chains Accused of Much Cheating on Insurance." The articles described abuse after abuse uncovered by a team of federal and state officials. Their findings stigmatized private mental health practice in the eyes of many payers and the public: "Widespread fraud related to the filing of insurance claims is present in the industry, a circumstance they blame for exorbitant medical costs nationwide. . . . Insurance fraud and abuse may permeate the entire medical field and contribute to the country's soaring health care costs."

Maximizing Individual Care

What is known in the insurance industry as gaming—the use of diagnoses to maximize reimbursement—is a well-documented phenomena. The *New England Journal of Medicine* has published studies showing evidence of "DRG creep." The Medicare system pays a set fee for treatment of specific medical conditions, called diagnostic related groups, or DRGs. It has been demonstrated that providers manipulate diagnoses in a way that increases their revenues. For example, one study showed that when Medicare limits the length of a hospital stay for a given diagnosis, providers tend to substitute a more serious, better-paying diagnosis associated with a longer stay.

As a staff member at various private psychiatric facilities, I followed an unspoken but tacitly understood protocol that pegged the length of suggested treatment for a patient to the limits of his or her insurance benefits. None of us intended to defraud the insurance companies; we simply based our treatment plans on an unshakable—but unfounded—belief that more is better. Whether the insurance benefit was for thirty days or a full year, we genuinely believed the best plan was to use up the entire benefit in order to give the patient as much care as possible.

Even hospital slang reflects how much insurance benefits impact treatment. I remember the first time I asked what an "IMG discharge" is and received the smiling reply, "Insurance Money Gone."

George

George Pally filed suit against a hospital in Boca Raton, Florida, that had billed him and his insurance company over $70,000 for unwanted care for his three children. He and his wife were embroiled in divorce proceedings, and she accused him of sexually abusing their children, aged three, eight, and nine. The hospital claimed that since it had reasonably believed that the father had abused the children, it was justified in holding them over their father's protests. But one day before the children's insurance benefits were exhausted, they were discharged.

Cinde

Cinde Allen testified at a public hearing in Palm Beach County, Florida, that her thirteen-year-old daughter had been misdiagnosed and mistreated in order for a hospital to get the most out of her insurance policy. Ms. Allen complained that although her daughter obviously had a drug problem—she admitted to smoking six marijuana cigarettes daily as well as taking PCP, LSD, and alcohol—she was diagnosed as having depression and treated in the hospital's psychiatric unit. Ms. Allen stated that while her daughter's insurance policy paid out only $10,000 for substance abuse, it paid $1 million for psychiatric diagnoses. The hospital bill was $82,000.

Artificially Multiplying and Politicizing Diagnoses

Skeptics ask if there is any correlation between the increasing numbers of psychiatric diagnoses seen today and the fact that a disorder must now be officially listed in the American Psychiatric Association's *Diagnostic and Statistical Manual* (DSM) in order to be insurance reimbursable. The newest revision of the manual, DSM-IV, includes over three hundred mental disorders, more than three times the number listed in the 1952 edition. Furthermore, critics contend, the diagnostic inflation evidenced by DSM-IV is not necessarily based on empirical data but upon expert consensus and political processes. For example, Vietnam veterans actively lobbied for the inclusion of posttraumatic stress disorder in the manual. Gay activists protested the manual's classifying homosexuality as a disorder, and to resolve the issue, ad hoc procedures based on strategic political negotiation rather than valid and reliable scientific information were used. DSM-IV's diagnostic categories seem to have been decided more by politics and plebiscites than by science.

Opponents of fee-for-service plans accuse mental health professionals of generating business by reframing what used to be seen as lamentable or inauspicious personal problems as insurable medical conditions. The promise of solving such problems through mental health care has resulted in a boom for some providers.

A number of trendy psychological conditions have given birth to a multimillion-dollar industry. Many mental health professionals now specialize in treating victims of satanic ritual abuse, adult children of alcoholics, codependent individuals, "women who love too much," "the child within," and people with multiple personalities. Long-term psychotherapy and lengthy inpatient stays are often considered to be the treatment of choice for these conditions. But the justification for such treatment frequently comes from unreliable, nonscientific sources. For example, Bass and Davis's book *The Courage to Heal* is touted as the incest survivor's bible. The book abounds with scientifically unfounded statements such as if you think you were the victim of incest, then you were, or it is "natural" for incest survivors to "self-mutilate."

Adolescent acting-out behaviors have also been added to the list of conditions for which people now seek professional treatment. Over the years I have received many calls from parents asking me to hospitalize their "out-of-control" adolescents. When I ask them to describe the behaviors that they believe merit confinement, they generally mention things like having sex, breaking curfews, skip-ping classes, flunking out of school, smoking marijuana, talking back to authority figures, or fighting with siblings. Often, frustrated but well-meaning parents hear advertisements for private psychiatric hospitals and become convinced that such hospitals can "cure" their adolescent of these unwanted behaviors. It is becoming increasingly difficult to differentiate between what is normal but annoying behavior and what is a treatable psychiatric condition.

While I am not denying that incest, dysfunctional relationships, dissociative disorders, and seriously impaired adolescents in need of intensive treatment do exist, can we justify this explosion of ques-tionable diagnoses? Can we blame payers for demanding to know whether or not treatment decisions are empirically based?

Dr. Maura

Dr. Maura called a major managed care company asking for autho-rization for treatment. Her patient, a thirty-two-year-old secretary who had been in intensive psychotherapy with her for three years, was suddenly faced with the trauma of recovering memories of childhood incest and abuse. Her patient also had a long history of codepen-dency. Dr. Maura recommended that the patient travel one thousand miles to attend a 90- to 180-day program that specialized in code-pendency and incest treatment. The cost of the care would be $780 per day. Upon discharge, she would return to Dr. Maura for twice-weekly therapy.

When the reviewer asked how she arrived at this treatment plan, the therapist referred the reviewer to a workbook from the codepen-dency literature and an advertisement that read, "Only one mental health facility provides this specialized combination of care for the codependent and the sexually abused."

Dr. Goldstein

Dr. Goldstein began billing for ten to fifteen sessions a week for a patient with multiple personality disorder. The reviewer called to find out how this could be, and Dr. Goldstein informed the reviewer that he was submitting a separate claim *for each personality* that appeared in his therapy sessions. The reviewer denied the claim, informing the therapist that if he wanted the company to honor each of the claims he submitted, "Each of these personalities needs his or her own insurance policy."

Overusing Services

Overuse of services is now considered a form of fraud. Insurance companies hire review companies like Mental Health Programs Corporation to monitor use. Officers of this company say that "the overuse of tests, services or drugs is extremely widespread at psychiatric hospitals across the nation. Doctors . . . often prescribe thousands of dollars in expensive but uncalled-for tests, like Magnetic Resonance Imaging at $600 to $1,000 a test. Another form of overuse is keeping patients in the hospital longer than necessary."

Ignoring Societal Needs

Those in favor of managed care argue that fee-for-service arrangements focus on individual care to the neglect of societal needs. They say that professionals have convinced the public that the highest-quality care is continuous, uninterrupted, long-term psychotherapy with no end point other than the patient's sense of satisfaction and contentment. Private practitioners spend millions aggressively recruiting monied patients into therapy and marketing their private practices to the well-insured. Furthermore, mental health professionals prefer to work with patients who have mild disorders and cater to young, attractive, verbal, intelligent, successful (YAVIS) individuals rather than the severely and chronically mentally ill, who are more troublesome to deal with and are generally poor.

Critics note that providers who are vocal about protecting the benefits of their insured patients have not been as outspoken about the socially marginalized, impoverished patients who are deprived under the fee-for-service system. Rationing of care appears to be based upon the patient's financial well-being. While many practitioners concentrate on giving long-term psychotherapy to the "worried well," needy patients are denied treatment because they have no insurance, are not covered by a social program, or cannot pay out of pocket. Patients who lose or use up their insurance benefits are often refused care by private practitioners or "dumped" onto the public sector.

Dwight

A malpractice suit was launched against Dr. John Felber by the family of one of his patients, Dwight Pink, a man who allegedly went on a crime spree due to Dr. Felber's negligence. Pink had asked Felber for help, saying that he was beginning a manic episode. Allegedly Felber refused to treat him because he owed $750 on a $1,500 bill. Shortly after making this request for help, Pink became very agitated. He shot a car salesman and then hijacked a school van. He was fatally wounded by police during the rescue attempt.

Although some professionals have made an effort to create a more socially responsive clinical network, there is a crisis in public mental health care today. Jails and prisons are replacing mental hospitals. One-third of the three million homeless in the United States are thought to be mentally disturbed, and those subject to the most deplorable conditions in terms of mental health care are often the poor.

Joan

Joan is a thirty-two-year-old female who did not complete high school. She is hoping to get her GED someday. Her two children, aged two and seven, receive no support from their fathers. Struggling with how to be a good mother, Joan works full-time as a health aid at a hospital. The job has no insurance benefits, and she has no other form of insurance.

She recognizes that she has been suffering from racing thoughts and euphoric moods. She knows that her father, who committed suicide years ago, was manic-depressive. From the reading she has done and conversations with friends, she thinks she might have the beginnings of the same illness. She is afraid that if she goes off into a real manic episode, her children won't be taken care of. She wants to get into therapy and prevent any episodes of mania before her symptoms cause her any problems. She is on the waiting list at a free clinic.

When health care costs are inflated, they harm everyone. They are passed along to everyone in the form of higher premiums or increased expenses for employers, which in turn results in reduced income for employees or lowered profits for shareholders. And exploitation of the system is on the rise: "In the past, estimates have put fraud and abuse at about 10 percent of the nation's health care costs, between $60 billion and $80 billion. But law enforcement officials and fraud specialists like Edward J. Kuriansky, New York State Deputy Attorney General, say the percentage is probably much higher because the accumulating evidence, including Medicaid-fraud cases, indicates that fraud is growing and that much abuse goes undetected or unreported."

Neglecting Continuity, Coordination, and Follow-Up

Under the fee-for-service system, care is fragmented, uncoordinated, and subject to the vicissitudes of idiosyncratic private practice or social programs. If a fee-for-service patient can no longer pay for private treatment, the therapist's responsibility is limited to making appropriate referrals. The public system is then responsible for the patient.

Martha

Martha is a twenty-eight-year-old woman who suffered her first schizophrenic episode when she was twenty. Hospitalized two times, she must take Melaril daily or she hears voices. She is in outpatient therapy now, and as long as she sees her therapist once to twice a week and attends group therapy she is able to maintain herself outside the hospital.

When her mother was laid off from her job, Martha's family could no longer afford her insurance coverage. Her therapist saw her pro bono for several months but eventually transferred her to a community mental health center. Due to a staff shortage she was seen only once per month by a therapist. She tended to be noncompliant with her medications when she was not closely supervised, as she had been in private therapy. Her family was quite concerned because staff turnover was high at the community mental health center. She never seemed to have the same therapist for more than six months.

Eventually she stopped taking her medications and was hospitalized for several months. The only place to send her was the state hospital, where she became even more frightened and upset.

Narrowing Patient Choice

Managed care proponents point out that although managed care narrows provider choice for the insured, the uninsured have even less choice. While these marginalized people have had limited options for years, there were few protests from private practitioners. Many fee-for-service providers have in the past refused to take on Medicare and Medicaid patients because the fees are low and the paperwork is inconvenient; therefore these patients have been repeatedly shifted onto the public system.

Beth

Beth found herself at the emergency room after inflicting superficial wounds on her wrists when her boyfriend broke up with her. The on-call therapist diagnosed her with borderline personality disorder and alcohol dependence. After a two-week stay in the hospital, she was discharged. She was set up with a private psychologist. When she arrived at the office, she found out that he did not accept Medicaid payment and insisted on being paid out of pocket.

Beth told him she would find another practitioner. In search of stable care, she phoned five other private mental health providers, but not one of them would take on a Medicaid patient. Discouraged, she stopped seeing any therapist. In six months she made a more serious suicide attempt and wound up back in the emergency room. She finally returned to a community agency that welcomed her Medicaid payments.

Critics point out that while one of the major objections to managed care is the use of "cheap labor" in the form of master's-level providers, for years many interns and paraprofessionals worked as staff members at community mental health clinics under the supervision of higher-level professionals. Until recently there has been no outcry about the use of less than optimally qualified providers to treat public patients. Interestingly, now that the care of these patients is going out to bid to managed care companies, there is a surge of interest in working with the indigent and the seriously mentally ill.

Failing to Establish Universal Standards

One of the major arguments of managed care advocates is that psychotherapists need to be held accountable for the services they render. Providers have resisted such accountability, claiming that the special nature of psychotherapy makes it impossible to quantify. Nevertheless, managed care companies continue to pressure providers to supply objective measures of how well their treatments work as well as how valuable they are to the patient in terms of their functioning and satisfaction.

A lack of standards is at the root of many problems between therapists and reviewers. As one reviewer described it,

I have had [a psychologist] request 3–5 more years of weekly therapy for a client he has already been seeing for eight years, treating her for Generalized Anxiety Disorder. I have had a psychologist bill $3,000 for comprehensive testing for an individual needing detox. . . . I have seen an adolescent who didn't want to go to school be diagnosed with 'addicted to skipping school' and admitted to the chemical dependency unit for thirty days of treatment because they were the 'addiction experts.' I have seen psychologists take functioning individuals and put them into 'memory recover' therapy and turn them into debilitated human beings with massive debts to hospitals for their repeated suicide attempts. . . . I have seen a 54-year-old woman die because the psychiatrist failed to identify her cardiac failure, diagnosing her as suffering from major depression.

Good managed care's mission includes defining standards of practice, decreasing variation in treatment among different patients, developing a common language among providers, ensuring that patient satisfaction is factored into the assessment of good care, and monitoring the cost, utilization, and quality of care and using that information to help providers improve care. As a result, behavioral health outcomes research has developed. Instruments such as the Health Plan Employer Data Information Set represent attempts by managed care administrators to codify health care quality and establish universal data banks to accumulate provider and patient treatment information.

Practice parameters—patient care strategies developed to assist providers in their clinical decision making—are used by good managed care administrators and providers to judge the appropriateness and quality of care. There are three levels of practice parameters: standards, guidelines, and options. Standards are set techniques that providers should execute each time they encounter a given situation, with no deviations (for example, making an appropriate referral to an M.D. to make sure a panic or anxiety disorder does not have an organic base). Guidelines spell out why a particular treatment technique might be selected from among others for a specific patient in a specific setting (for example, Becks's cognitive therapy for depression over Jungian analysis). And options are treatments that can be used with no clear recommendations concerning which option is preferable (for example, the use of Jungian analysis over Adlerian). Managed care advocates claim that the creation of practice parameters will help society assess its needs and avoid wasting scarce health care resources.

Protecting One's Own

Although public dissatisfaction with the cost and quality of mental health care continues to increase, there is still little recourse for consumers damaged by poor-quality, impaired, or out-of-date practitioners other than costly, time-consuming litigation. Malpractice cases brought against psychotherapists generally revolve around fee disputes, breaches of confidentiality, sexual abuse of patients, suicides caused by negligent administration, documented fraud and charlatanry, inadequate supervision, premature release, release of a dangerous patient, wrongful commitment, or inadequate supervision.

By maintaining that self-regulation is the only appropriate method for policing the professions (because the public supposedly does not have the ability to judge clinical competence), professional associations have given their members tremendous power. This enables professionals to sweep many of their transgressions under the carpet, keeping them "all in the family" and out of the public view. Yet, many ethics cases really are the consumer's business. Managed care gives patients more consumer protection and provider accountability. It is a vehicle through which their care is monitored for necessity, appropriateness, and effectiveness. Insurance executives say it is hard for insurance companies to police fraud. It is difficult because laws make it hard to prosecute and "public licensing agencies and medical societies are reticent about punishing medical professionals who cheat the system."

Managed care proponents contend that mental health professionals have confused ethics with guild interests. Turf battles are often disguised as efforts to protect the consumer. For example, both the National Association of Social Workers and the American Psychological Association have lobbied for laws granting their members the exclusive right to practice psychotherapy. The American Psychiatric Association urges that psychotherapy should be practiced only under medical supervision. Many believe that such regulations help professionals protect their turf more than they help patients. In *House of Cards*, Robyn Dawes mounts a searing attack on the whole notion of credentialing. He claims that a thorough review of the literature reveals "no positive evidence supporting one profession's proficiency over another. . . . There are anecdotes, there is plausibility, there are common beliefs, yes—but there is no good evidence. . . . The training, credentials, and experience of psychotherapists are irrelevant, or at least that is what all the evidence indicates."

Focusing on Illness, Not Wellness

Another criticism of fee-for-service mental health practice is that it focuses on illness, whereas good managed care emphasizes health maintenance, prevention, and wellness. Proponents of managed care point out that fee-for-service, by its very nature, is antithetical to community-based and prevention services. Yet, if the best possible mental health care is primary prevention and not secondary and tertiary care, why is so much emphasis placed on pathology and not on prevention?

Proponents of managed care claim that many of today's private practitioners would be put out of business if they emphasized primary health care (which is what is best for the patient)! Managed care has encouraged practitioners to change from a long-term, individual perspective to a primary care, holistic, integrated orientation. Managed care therapists are invested in maintaining the good health of their patients and encourage the development of short-term therapy that can prevent overutilization of medical services, iatrogenic effects, deterioration effects, and low-quality care.

The debate over which form of health care delivery is better rages on. Proponents of fee-for-service care and advocates of managed care have both identified matters of importance to the ethical treatment of patients and the social good. One system is not inherently evil while the other is all good. In reality, both fee-for-service and managed care can promote both ethical and unethical behavior. Any system will offer opportunities for ethical violations. All human beings falter. People make mistakes, violate ethical principles, and commit crimes. It is those who run the system that behave ethically or unethically.

The question that is begging to be answered is this: Which system—fee-for-service, managed care, or some other system—is most likely to maximize high-quality, effective mental health care? We must weigh the pros and cons of each option. In the same way, we must also weigh the helpfulness of various models of psychotherapy, no matter the health care system. Which model—long-term psychotherapy, short-term psychotherapy, or some other model—provides the patient and society with the most effective and appropriate mental health care? We will discuss these issues in the next several chapters.

Notes

p. 75, *"Medicine and other professions"*: Starr, P. (1982). *The social transformation of American medicine* (p. 23). New York: Basic Books.

p. 77, *For example, the American Psychiatric Association established:* Hanin, E. (1994). The regulatory effect of the managed care movement. In H. Schwartz (Ed.), *Psychiatric practice under fire* (pp. 147–172). Washington, DC: American Psychiatric Association Press.

p. 78, *The American Psychiatric Association's managed care hotline:* ibid.

p. 79, The New Republic *discussed a case:* Kuttner, R. (1991, December 2). Sick joke. *The New Republic,* pp. 20–22.

p. 80, *After much hesitation, John finally decided to seek professional help:* This and the following clinical vignettes (unless otherwise referenced) do not represent any specific client but are a creative composite based on the clinical experience of the author. They are used here to demonstrate specific problems and interventions.

p. 82, *Su is a ten-year-old girl:* Su's case was described in a January 1995 letter from Karen Shore to the American Psychological Association Council of Representatives.

p. 85, *Americans pay more out of their own pockets:* Olfson, M., & Pincus, H. A. (1994). Outpatient psychotherapy in the United States. II: Patterns of utilization. *American Journal of Psychiatry, 151*(9), 1289–1294.

p. 87, Newsweek *publicized a case:* Gentile, B. (1991, November 4). Money madness. *Newseek,* pp. 50–52.

p. 88, *Georgette Hinson, upset about:* ibid.

p. 88, *A newspaper reported:* Cited in Moffit, S. (1992, February 2). Healing patients or profit? *The Los Angeles Times,* pp. A24–A25.

p. 89, *Their findings stigmatized private mental health practice:* Kerr, P. (1991, October 22). Paying for fraud—A special report: Mental hospital chains accused of much cheating on insurance. The *New York Times,* Section 1, Pt. 1, p. 1; Kerr, P. (1991, November 24). Paying for fraud—A special report: Mental hospital chains accused of much cheating on insurance. The *New York Times,* Section 1, Pt. 2, p. 1; Moffit, S. (1992, February 2). Healing patients or profit? The *Los Angeles Times,* pp. A24–A25.

p. 91, *Vietnam veterans actively lobbied:* Kirk, S., & Kutchins, H. (1992). *The selling of DSM: The rhetoric of science in psychiatry* (pp. 77–121). New York: Aldine de Gruyter.

p. 91, *For example, Bass and Davis's book:* Bass, E., & Davis, L. (1994). *The courage to heal: A guide for women survivors of child sexual abuse* (3rd ed). New York: HarperPerennial.

p. 93, *Insurance companies hire review companies:* Kerr, P. (1991, October 22). Paying for fraud—A special report: Mental hospital chains accused of much cheating on insurance. The *New York Times,* Section 1, Pt. 1, p. 1; Kerr, P. (1991, November 24). Paying for fraud—A special report: Mental hospital chains accused of much cheating on insurance. The *New York Times,* Section 1, Pt. 1, p. 1.

p. 95, *In the past:* ibid.

p. 97, *A lack of standards:* Mould, D. E. (1994). A call to arms: But is managed care really the dragon? *Psychotherapy Bulletin, 29*(4), 42–44.

p. 98, *Good managed care's mission includes:* Talbott, J. A. (1990). Developing practice parameters: An interview with John McIntyre. *Hospital and Community Psychiatry, 41*(10), 1103–1105.

p. 98, *Instruments such as:* Migdail, K. (Ed.). (1995). *The 1995 behavioral outcomes and guidelines sourcebook.* New York: Faulkner and Gray.

p. 98, *Practice parameters:* Talbott, J. A. (1990). Developing practice parameters: An interview with John McIntyre. *Hospital and Community Psychiatry, 41*(10), 1103–1105.

p. 99, *Managed care advocates claim:* ibid; Migdail, K. (Ed.). (1995). *The 1995 behavioral outcomes and guidelines sourcebook.* New York: Faulkner and Gray.

p. 99, *It is difficult because:* Kerr, P. (1991, October 22). Paying for fraud—A special report: Mental hospital chains accused of much cheating on insurance. The *New York Times,* Section 1, Pt. 1, p. 1.

p. 100, *He claims that a thorough review:* Dawes, R. (1994). *House of cards* (pp. 58–62). New York: Free Press.

Part II

Psychotherapy Today

5

The Myth of Long-Term Psychotherapy
Research Ignored and Neglected

*Man's judgments of value follow directly his wishes
for happiness—they are an attempt to support his
illusions with arguments.*

Sigmund Freud

In Part Two we will explore what I call "long-term bias," or a partiality on the part of providers toward long-term therapy, despite the lack of any substantial empirical evidence to support this preference. Long-term bias grows from two commonly held beliefs about psychotherapy: long-term psychotherapy is superior to short-term therapy, and most patients in "real" therapy are in long-term or extended therapy. These two credos reached nearly mythical proportions as modern psychotherapy evolved.

Although providers are beginning to reverse these assumptions, and respect for brief therapies is growing, long-term bias lingers today, permeating the practice of psychotherapy and, I believe, delaying psychotherapy's full integration into the health care system. As Bernard Bloom writes in his classic book *Planned Short-Term*

Therapy, the belief that intensive long-term therapy is the most desirable treatment persists, despite the fact that the overwhelming majority of cases are brief; research clearly shows that planned short-term therapy, or therapy that is short-term by design rather than by default, is effective; more people can be reached, served, and helped by short-term therapy; and brief work is more cost-effective.

This chapter clarifies the basic values and underlying assumptions of both long- and short-term therapy. It then examines the dominance of long-term models and reviews the empirical evidence to support the belief that long-term therapy is more effective than short-term therapy.

Chapter Six examines how patients *really* use psychotherapy, in contrast to how long-term therapists believe they use it. It then discusses the "clinician's illusion," one explanation for the discrepancy between fact and fantasy. Chapter Seven explores undebunked myths, professional conditioning, and social circumstances that have allowed long-term therapy to overshadow brief therapy and discusses the importance of understanding psychotherapy within its sociocultural context. Conceiving of a "sociology of psychotherapy" can help us think more globally in what is fast becoming a worldwide community; this in turn can help us better control the destiny of psychotherapy as a health care commodity.

Long-Term Versus Short-Term

Psychotherapists tend to identify themselves as either long- or short-term clinicians. Short- and long-term clinicians hold different values about how both time and psychotherapy affect attitudes, choices, and beliefs about what treatment is best for their patients. And their beliefs about how patients ought to use psychotherapy are strikingly different.

Hopefully, the more we discuss and learn about how time affects psychotherapy, the sooner we will develop a "temporal eclecticism"— an ability to work in both long- and short-term modalities and the wisdom to know when to apply each method in a way that maximizes the effectiveness of necessary and appropriate therapy.

The literature is replete with books and articles that compare and contrast long- and short-term therapy and therapists. Considerable overlap can occur between the two methods, but a growing number of authors describe how each is associated with a distinct set of ideologies and values that bear some relationship to time. The major differences between them are summarized below.

What Long-Term Therapists Value

Most long-term practitioners use models of therapy derived from Freudian thinking. Their basic belief system assigns considerable weight to the following core tenets:

1. *The goal of therapy is character change, a "reerecting" of the personality.* An undertaking this ambitious can take many years, so in general "good therapy is long therapy." (There can be exceptions to the rule, of course. For example, Freud treated Mahler, the composer, of impotency with a very abbreviated course of therapy.)

2. *The past molds the present.* Exploring early childhood development is a seminal component of bringing about change. Its effects are critical to what is happening in the patient's present life.

3. *Presenting problems are not to be taken at face value.* The patient initiates therapy with a "cover story"; the therapist's job is to uncover its hidden, unconscious meaning. Symptoms are manifestations of underlying, unconscious conflicts. Insight into their origins is required for their resolution. Consequently, the therapist's primary responsibility is to learn as much as possible about a patient's psychodynamic functioning. This information is essential to therapeutic success.

4. *The role of the therapist is that of an authority and transference figure—nondirective, passive, encouraging transference and dependence.* The therapist, knowing that the relationship accounts for a

significant percentage of change, believes that a strong therapeutic alliance is established slowly, over time.

5.   *The patient-therapist relationship is sacred.* Secrecy allows it to remain inviolable. Confidentiality is so important that the patient-therapist relationship should not be subject to outside scrutiny, lest it become contaminated.

6.   *Therapeutic interventions are generally interpretive, confrontational, transferential, cathartic, nondirective, and reflective, and they are possibly regressive.* The processes of uncovering unconscious conflicts, building a therapeutic alliance, and achieving transference must unfold slowly, even painstakingly.

7.   *Psychotherapy is almost always a help and seldom a hindrance.* If a little therapy is good, then more therapy is even better. It is so valued that being in therapy is seen as a momentous event in a patient's life, into which he or she must invest much psychic energy, time, and money.

8.   *Therapy-induced character changes represent a cure and are relatively permanent.* Most long-term therapy is based upon the concept that, like a cancer patient, the mental health patient should stay in treatment until all dangerous pathology has been eliminated. A thorough job of analyzing and eliminating unconscious conflicts must be accomplished. The end result is character restructuring. If a patient returns for additional therapy, it means the previous therapy was imperfect and the work that needed to be done was obviously not completed.

9.   *Time has no boundaries.* Freud finally concluded late in his career what long-term therapists believe today—that psychoanalytic psychotherapy is a lengthy business. Long-term therapy is "timeless." Both therapist and patient act as if time and resources are unlimited. The patient cannot rush the analyst, and the analyst cannot rush the patient. The process of uncovering the patient's psyche has a time frame of its own. Liberation from neurotic symptoms and abnormalities of character is a process that cannot be hurried. Insight occurs in a flash or at a slow and steady tempo.

When these nine tenets inform a therapist's practice, it can be difficult to establish a standard for length of treatment, since there is no way to know for certain when symptoms will remit and just how much character change can be expected.

A Very Long-Term Case

A seventy-one-year-old woman who entered treatment with a new long-term therapist after her previous therapist, a psychoanalyst with a respected reputation in psychoanalytic circles, died. She had been in therapy with him for two decades. When she first saw her new therapist, she was suffering from "mild to moderate feelings of depression, which seemed consistent with the loss of the analyst she had so esteemed. . . . She also reported some irritation with her dead therapist for having abandoned her at this late stage of her life without having cured her of the symptom that had brought her into treatment with him . . . a lifelong feeling, of near delusional intensity, that her son (a man in his late 40s) had been fathered by a black man."

Although it took two or three more years, the patient was able to successfully work through her irrational belief of five decades. She was able to express the rage she felt toward her former therapist for having failed to cure her and work through the guilt associated with choosing to visit her former therapist "on the day her husband had died, instead of going to visit him at the hospital." The new therapist judged the treatment outcome a success because the patient was able to gain a greater degree of sexual gratification and improve her interpersonal relationships.

The long-term therapist's attitude about time is summed up in this story about Bruno Bettleheim, a well-known and revered psychiatrist. He described the case of a boy in analysis who sat in his waiting room each week and plucked and chewed leaves from a cactus plant. One day Bettleheim asked the child why, after two full years of analysis, he continued to act so bizarrely. Listening to the child's reply, Bettleheim arrived at a great realization about time and therapy: "He . . . spoke his first sentence to me saying disdainfully, 'What are two years when compared with eternity?' Johnny's comment about time permitted me to grasp that neither I nor anybody else can put a limit on the amount of time one needs to become able to cope or to change, and that hurrying up the process has more to do with one's own anxieties than with anything else. Only people themselves can judge when they are ready to change."

A long time is of the essence to long-term therapy! Long-term therapists see brief therapy as a "threat undermining the apex of [the long-term] system of values" and warn enthusiasts of brief therapy not to be led astray by the prospect of quicker results.

What Short-Term Therapists Value

Brief therapy comes in hundreds of forms. There are a number of ways in which they can be classified, but research experts generally agree that they can be sorted into five broad orientations: psychoanalytic-psychodynamic, cognitive-behavioral, eclectic, crisis intervention, and other verbal behavioral therapies (such as hypnosis, emotional catharsis, and problem solving). Not all short-term therapists endorse each of the following key ingredients of brief psychotherapy, but they do sanction some combination of them:

1. *The goals of therapy are circumscribed and limited.* The responsibilities of both the patient and the therapist are clear and overtly articulated. Negotiating a clear contract between therapist and patient for defined, specific, achievable goals and outcomes that are quantifiable and measurable is essential to therapeutic success.

2. *The past is addressed primarily in relation to the present.* The focus of the work is in the here and now. Childhood is not considered to be the most significant determinant of a person's present character. A total-life-span, developmental perspective is presumed, and maturation is seen as a lifelong process, not a reaction to child-

hood events. The problems of the present are more important than events in the past.

3. *Presenting problems are taken at face value.* The therapist accepts what the patient says and does not interpret its meaning at a level that impedes taking immediate action. Symptom relief and a return to an adaptive level of functioning (if needed) are often the major goals of treatment.

4. *The therapist's role is authoritative but not authoritarian.* The therapist is active and directive and does not limit his or her therapeutic role to that of a transference figure. When appropriate, the therapist assumes the added role of coach and consultant in a pragmatic alliance. The nature of the work is practical, concrete, and realistic. Since a positive therapeutic relationship plays a powerful role in bringing about change, a strong therapeutic alliance is rapidly established. The therapist encourages autonomy and independence rather than transference and dependence, and the patient assumes a high degree of responsibility for the results of therapy. Homework is assigned for outside the therapy session, and patient follow-through on these assignments is stressed.

5. *The patient-therapist dyad is demystified and viewed pragmatically as a psychoeducational relationship.* Outside scrutiny such as case reviews and progress reports are not seen as threatening if the requests are conducted in an ethical way and the patient gives informed consent. (Scrutiny is less likely to be accepted by psychodynamically oriented therapists, however.)

6. *Therapeutic interventions are generally eclectic and flexible.* This is the case unless a very specific form of therapy is conducted that uses a manual with prescribed outlines to guide specific therapist behaviors.

7. *Psychotherapy is not always seen as helpful.* The therapist is aware of the potential for negative effects from psychotherapy for some people in some situations. Careful consideration is given to whether or not the patient truly needs to be in psychotherapy. The short-term therapist worries about the potential for iatrogenic effects

that might cause the patient to develop problems even worse than the ones he or she presented with. Therapy is seen from the perspective of temporal realism—it is helpful for the patient, but it represents only a small portion of his or her life. While the patient lives 168 hours every week, therapy lasts only an hour or so per week and most likely involves only several hours of thinking and homework at a maximum.

8. *Change occurs naturally during a person's life, in or out of therapy.* The change inspired by therapy is just one of many that will occur. No change is permanent. A "cure" never takes place, because it is not possible to heal life's problems; rather, symptom remission and better adaptation to those problems can occur with therapy.

9. *Time is precious.* Short-term therapists tend to exercise therapeutic minimalism; in other words, they choose to use the least amount of time possible to achieve their therapeutic goals. This is accomplished by employing efficient schedules that make the best use of the frequency, length, and timing of treatment. Sessions are often intermittent and staggered.

When the above tenets inform a psychotherapy practice, it is possible to establish standards for estimating length of treatment. Both therapist and patient accept that time and resources are limited.

The short-term therapist is convinced that pivotal and meaningful work can be accomplished in a fleeting moment because therapy sets a process in motion that can be long-lasting and can influence the future. Even a single session can have a lifelong impact.

. . . .

Mr. Bremer

Mr. Bremer came in for an evaluation. His spouse had told him she was very dissatisfied with their relationship of five years. Shocked when his therapist told him he was an alcoholic, he left without making a second appointment. A long-term therapist might have construed this departure to be indicative of his own underdeveloped clinical skills or of a weak character structure on the part of Mr. Bremer that prevented him from engaging in long-term psychodynamic work. But Mr. Bremer's therapist saw it differently.

When Mr. Bremer was confronted, he was simply not ready to change. Seven years later, when he was in a more mature developmental stage and his alcoholism had finally disrupted his family to the point where his wife had initiated divorce proceedings, he recalled the therapist's words and sought help from Alcoholics Anonymous. Consequently, he became an avid member and a sober man. Although it was hard for him to hear the therapist's words earlier, the message always remained in the back of his mind, until he was ready to use it. He always remained appreciative of the honesty and directness he received in that single therapy session.

The short-term therapist's basic belief about time is similar to the view expressed earlier by Bruno Bettleheim that only people themselves can judge when they are ready to change. Thus brief therapists do not keep people in therapy if treatment is not essential. Rather they let the patient go free after making an appropriate intervention, trusting that the process that has been set in motion will evoke change when the patient is ready for it, even if that change occurs outside of therapy. As Charles Darwin once said, "A man who dares to waste one hour of time has not discovered the value of life."

The Dominance of Long-Term Therapy

Since its inception by Freud, the traditional, psychodynamic model has dominated the practice, theory, and research of psychotherapy. As surveys of practicing clinicians have shown, only recently have more psychotherapists (especially psychologists) begun calling themselves eclectic rather than psychodynamic practitioners. To be eclectic, however, means to bear no allegiance to any one model of therapy but to mix and match a hodgepodge of techniques without any unifying theory to guide one's work.

Although eclecticism is on the rise, psychodynamic therapy remains the most popular single therapeutic model. Even though behaviorists and humanists have in the past challenged the legitimacy of its sovereignty, no one has thus far been able to overthrow this reigning monarch.

As a consequence of this prominence of the psychodynamic model in psychotherapeutic thinking, the belief that psychoanalysis is the purest, most unadulterated, most desirable form of psychotherapy has permeated the field of psychotherapy throughout this century. All other forms of psychotherapy are seen as watered down or inferior, superficial, less intense, and less capable of effecting true change.

Long-term therapists believe little can compete with what Freud called the "pure gold of analysis." Real therapy is analytic, and to be good, it must be long. Like fine wine, good therapy must age. If the pure gold is unattainable, then the next best substitute is psychodynamic psychotherapy, but the more closely therapy approximates analysis, the better. There is an implicit belief that although abbreviated forms of therapy do have a place within mental health treatment, they ought to "stay in their place"—a position of inferiority and low status. In the immortal words of Sigmund Freud, "the application of our therapy to numbers will compel us to alloy the pure gold of analysis plentifully with the copper of direct suggestion."

While long-term therapists have seldom questioned these convictions, outside forces—payers and patients—are beginning to challenge their veracity. In the past third-party payers endured the financial consequences of long-term bias, but today they will no longer tolerate it. Many managed care companies will reimburse only cost-effective, brief mental health treatment. This state of affairs imposed from without is causing internal stresses within the profession, rekindling some of the conflicts and antagonisms that have historically arisen between those who endorse long- versus short-term therapy. But the mental health community cannot afford to be blinded by biases or to hold sacred any misguided beliefs that can jeopardize its survival in this crucial developmental period.

The Current State of Psychotherapy Research

Definitive evidence has never been produced to prove the claim that long-term therapy is superior to short-term therapy. Let's take a quick glimpse at the state of psychotherapy research today. In this section I draw heavily from the rich information contained in the fourth edition of *The Handbook of Psychotherapy and Behavior Change*, which serves as the standard psychotherapy reference throughout the world. It is the definitive work on psychotherapy research, with 864 pages devoted to summaries of empirical investigations.

First, as most mental health professionals already know, the good news is that the vast majority of accumulated research on adult outpatients clearly shows that, in general, psychotherapy is beneficial. Not every patient gains to a clinically meaningful extent. Some even deteriorate and are actually hurt by inept applications of treatments, negative therapist characteristics, or mismatches between their problems and therapeutic techniques. And some people—a substantial number—improve without formal intervention. The causes of "spontaneous improvement" are not well understood, but the likelihood of such improvement occurring is affected by the nature, seriousness, and persistence of the patient's disorder and the strength of his or her social supports.

The many therapies that have been studied have positive effects on a wide variety of patients and produce appreciable gains. Psychotherapy seems to work because it expedites the natural healing process, helps relieve the patient's symptoms, and helps people learn new coping strategies.

Once researchers established that psychotherapy does help, they posed the question of which type was most effective. Although investigators have invested tremendous time and effort in conducting hundreds of comparison studies, no one has been able to demonstrate beyond a shadow of a doubt that one type of therapy is consistently superior to another.

For example, Thomas Giles, a therapy researcher involved in outcomes research and review, recently asserted that in the last twenty years research has shown that superior short-term treatments have arisen for schizophrenia, unipolar depression, panic disorder, obsessive-compulsive disorder, simple and social phobias, bulimia, autism, conduct disturbances, enuresis, and others.

He concludes that "although a substantial body of literature exists that [supports the contention that] specialized treatments, usually of a behavioral nature, are available with comparatively superior outcome, much of this information is clinically underutilized across a wide range of disorders."

He adds that the practice community needs to make use of these preferred practices which have demonstrated superior treatment outcomes.

Traditional researchers, however, say that massive evidence exists which attests to the fact that psychotherapy techniques do not have specific effects. For example, different approaches to treating depression show little difference in efficacy. They argue that the equivalence of therapies, or the notion that all forms of psychological treatment yield comparable results, is a well-documented, scientifically respectable, generally accepted finding. The highly revered researchers Allen Bergin and Sol Garfield have concluded that the results from outcome studies of various forms of therapy have not been pronounced enough to draw any general conclusions. Although some forms of cognitive therapy, behavioral therapy, and eclectic therapy have demonstrated better outcomes than traditional verbal therapies for specific conditions in some investigations, relatively minor statistical advantages do not mean that cognitive and behavioral therapies are clinically superior in real practice settings. Therefore these findings cannot be seen as the "general case," as psychotherapy researchers Michael Lambert and Allen Bergin point out: "The results have been attributed to the bias of researchers and the selectivity in criteria of change. Although there is little evidence of clinically meaningful superiority of one form of psychotherapy over another with respect to moderate outpatient disorders, behavioral and cognitive methods appear to add a significant increment of efficacy with regard to a number of difficult problems (e.g., panic, phobias, and compulsion) and to provide useful methods with a number of non-neurotic problems with which traditional therapies have shown little effectiveness (e.g., childhood aggression, psychotic behavior, and health-related behaviors)."

Bergin and Garfield also remark that the "equal outcomes phenomena" seems to be difficult to conceptualize. Tremendous resistance to accepting it pervades the field, and they speculate that the reasons for this hesitation may be "to preserve the role of special theories, the status of leaders of such approaches, the technical training programs for therapists, the professional legitimacy of psychotherapy, and the rewards that come with having supposed curative powers."

Research Comparing Long- and Short-Term Therapy

If the mental health community disagrees about whether or not most therapies are equivalent in their effectiveness, will it resist research findings that say long-term therapy is no more effective than short-term therapy?

Mary Koss and Julie Shiang, in their fastidious review of comparisons between short- and long-term therapy, point out that brief therapies are effective in treating a wide range of psychological and health-related problems, including anxiety disorders, depression, grief reactions, posttraumatic stress disorders brought on by experiences such as rape and earthquakes, and poor interpersonal relationships.

The literature comparing short- and long-term therapies shows essentially no differences in results, so it is safe to conclude that brief therapies have the same success rate as longer-term treatments. Despite the major differences in values, short-term therapies achieve results and render outcomes that are equal to those of longer-term therapies.

The dearth of data supporting the superiority of long-term over short-term therapy has prompted Lambert and Bergin to comment that this state of affairs "certainly raises questions about the general necessity of long-term treatments for the majority of patients and has clear implications for the practice of psychotherapy. Long-term therapy cannot easily be justified on the basis of research."

Although much of the theory, research, and practice of psychotherapy has been subjugated to many of the core beliefs of traditional therapists, the fact of the matter is that these claims have little or no foundation in empirical research. Whether traditional researchers are correct or the new breed of researchers prove to be more accurate in their interpretation of the literature, the point is that there is little evidence to show that long-term therapy is superior to short-term therapy. If either form of therapy has had a slight edge until now, the evidence is in favor of short-term therapy's outdoing longer-term models.

However, the debate will continue at a fever pitch. Just recently, *Consumer Reports* published a survey that Martin Seligman, a noted psychologist, called the "most extensive study of psychotherapy effectiveness on record." Patient improvement was measured by summing the answers from three questions: How much had therapy helped patients with the problems for which they entered therapy? How satisfied were patients with their therapist? How much had patients improved at the time of the survey, compared to when they started therapy? The study showed that no specific modality of psychotherapy was any better than another, and all mental health professionals (except for marriage counselors) did equally well. Patients limited in length of therapy or choice of therapists did worse. The longer people stayed in therapy, the more they improved. This is the first large-scale study to lend credence to the claims of long-term therapy. But there are many who say the *Consumer Reports* study is very flawed. Their criticisms are that the survey was retrospective, used overly gross measures of outcome, and lacked a control group. Some say that the survey is little more than a patient satisfaction inventory. One of the most relevant concerns is about the nature of the sample. The sample represented mostly educated, middle-class people and may not give us the broad vista from which we need to view psychotherapy. In Chapter Six, we will be discussing the characteristics of patient populations and the clinician's tendency to attribute the characteristics of limited groups to entire populations.

So, in light of these facts, why should long-term therapy be used when brief interventions can save the patient a great deal of time, effort, and money? Furthermore, short-term therapists can potentially touch greater numbers of people. Therefore, researchers recommend that the treatment of choice be short-term therapy. It is a well-recognized fact that, unfortunately, there is a huge gap between psychotherapy research and practice. For many years practitioners have veered away from putting research into practice.

Psychotropic Medications

Psychotropic medications present a substantial challenge to the dominance of long-term therapy, especially since the pressure is on for therapists to find treatments that alleviate psychological distress as quickly as possible. Whenever mental health professionals attempt to develop standards and guidelines for effective treatments, they always include medications and some forms of brief therapy, but they seldom refer to long-term psychotherapy. Medications have stood the test of systematic study in controlled clinical trials.

The Senate Subcommittee on Appropriations requested the National Advisory Mental Health Council to prepare a report on the feasibility of covering comprehensive treatments for individuals with severe mental disorders such as schizophrenia, schizoaffective disorder, manic-depressive disorder, autism, severe depression, panic disorder, and obsessive-compulsive disorder.

The council issued a report that reads much like a pharmacopeia. Short-term therapies are included on the list of effective treatments primarily as adjunctive aids. The report mentioned that a growing body of research has verified the efficacy of

1. Antipsychotics for schizophrenia, especially recent drugs such as Clozapine and Risperidone, coupled with psycho-educational treatment programs

2. Lithium for management of manic-depressive illness (takes effect within ten days of administration), or valproate and carbamazepine for nonresponders (either can be combined with psychosocial interventions that emphasize compliance to medications)

3. Antidepressants for major depression, especially the recent drugs known as selective serotonin re-uptake inhibitors, and depression-specific therapies—cognitive, behavioral, interpersonal, and brief dynamic—as adjunctive aids in severe cases or as the primary treatment for less severe forms of depression

4. For panic disorders, antidepressants such as tricyclics, MAOIs, high-potency antianxiety benzodiazepines, and Panic Control Treatment, a new behavioral approach

5. Clomipramine, serotonin re-uptake inhibitors, and behavioral treatments for obsessive-compulsive disorders, with the addition of behavioral therapy and booster sessions.

The council did not include long-term traditional therapy as an essential ingredient in the armamentarium of rational and effective mental health treatments. This document, delivered to Congress, will have a significant impact on the body that will eventually decide which health care delivery system will be supported by the nation's health care policy.

How have medications affected "time" in psychotherapy? With psychotropic medications, therapists can treat targeted symptoms effectively and rapidly. Appropriate pharmacology can decrease the length of treatment, provided therapists focus on specific problems rather than character reformation. In light of the research findings about what medications and some forms of short-term therapy can do, it is difficult to justify the use of long-term therapy as anything more than discretionary care for many users.

Neglected Research

The old saying, "Of all sad words of tongue or pen the saddest are these—it could have been" applies to the fact that the mental health community has not stressed research into three areas—medical offset, behavioral medicine, and practice variation—that could have put psychotherapy on the health care map. Mainstream psychology has curiously neglected these approaches until recently. Had we invested as much energy into studying these areas as we did learning about psychodynamics, psychotherapy would be far more advanced, and arguments for keeping psychotherapy as a necessary, reimbursable form of basic health care would be strong. Some professional organizations have come to their senses, reviewed the relevant information, and begun to educate their memberships about medical offset and behavioral medicine. Better late than never.

Medical Offset

When mental health treatment results in general health care savings, "medical offset" occurs. In the 1960s, researchers at Kaiser-Permanente Health Plan in California began to conduct pioneering medical offset studies. These early findings showed that

1. Patients in emotional distress are significantly higher users of both inpatient and outpatient medical facilities as compared to the health plan average.

2. Significant decreases in medical utilization occurred among emotionally distressed individuals who received targeted short-term psychotherapy as compared to an untreated control group of matched emotionally distressed health plan members.

3. The declines remained constant for five years after termination, but the most significant declines occurred in the second year after the initial session of therapy.

Numerous studies have since produced similar findings.

Today we know that 11 to 36 percent of visits to general care doctors involve mental health problems. As much as 50 to 70 percent of a physician's caseload involves patients whose medical problems are related to psychological factors. Patients in emotional distress who seek psychological services tend to be higher users of all general medical services before they receive psychological intervention. Patients with mental illness use medical services heavily; but if they are given appropriate therapy, their medical utilization will decrease. Patients with serious mental illnesses and physical illnesses can realize an offset if they receive appropriate psychotherapy. The medical offset effect shows that mental health services can increase the effectiveness of medical care and decrease medical costs if appropriate forms of therapy are used.

Skeptics contend that early studies of medical offset had methodological flaws and biases and that more carefully designed studies have produced mixed results. The complex phenomena must be considered in light of the severity of a patient's psychiatric disorder, how the offset is measured, and the length of the offset. We must cautiously interpret findings of offset studies before definitive claims can be made.

In 1994, results from the Hawaii Medicaid study, a randomized prospective design involving some sixteen thousand Medicaid recipients, clearly indicated that short-term therapy delivered within the context of managed mental health care was both clinically productive and cost-effective, "reducing medical services costs and utilization by 23 to 40 percent relative to control groups. For enrollees with chronic medical diagnoses, managed treatment reduced medical costs by 28 to 47 percent, while medical costs for fee-for-service enrollees increased by 17 percent. For enrollees without chronic medical diagnoses, traditional fee-for-service also reduced medical costs by about 20 percent but used three times as many outpatient visits. Costs of managed treatment were recovered in 6 to 24 months, suggesting that managed mental health treatment should be incorporated in health reform initiatives."

The authors of the study point out that the costs for traditional therapy would have been recovered in approximately two years with sessions at $48. However, fee-for-service treatment had little effect on medical costs when patients with chronic medical diagnoses were treated.

A way to make psychotherapy a welcome part of health care is to demonstrate a "total offset" that proves psychotherapy results in an overall health care savings. Medical offset provides an economic in addition to a humanitarian rationale for including psychotherapy as a basic health benefit. Medical offset studies can serve as tools to reassure payers that an increased demand for psychotherapy does not have to financially endanger a health care system—if appropriate, brief therapy is used. It is not the number of referrals that brings up costs but the way in which psychotherapy is delivered that determines expenditures. On the other hand, if therapists used intensive, long-term psychotherapy to treat high medical utilizers, increased costs could result.

Behavioral Health Care

Awareness of the fact that psychological and physical health reciprocally influence each other is growing. Short-term psychotherapy can effectively decrease stress, which contributes to such conditions as hypertension, diabetes, cardiac disorders, gastrointestinal disorders, infertility, migraines, and chronic pain. Even patients with life-threatening diseases can improve their quality of life if they are encouraged to alter damaging life-styles. Behavioral medicine techniques can aid in patients' physical recovery, pain management, smoking cessation, weight control, medication and diet compliance, and recovery from or adaptation to surgery and chronic illness. A medical patient's psychological well-being impacts the length of his or her hospital stay, potential complications, and the cost of care.

Therapists should be jumping on the bandwagon of behavioral health care. These treatment models hold promise for helping relieve both physical and mental suffering, integrating mental health services into the general health care system, promoting collaboration and integration of care, and bringing therapists great professional satisfaction. Yet most graduate training programs do not even include a course on behavioral medicine.

Practice Variation

About two decades ago the medical profession was taken aback when a groundbreaking study showed that widespread variations existed in medical treatment. Medical experts concluded that 17 to 32 percent of all surgical procedures were unnecessary. Practice variations are defined as detectable, even obvious, patterns of practice differences that are evident in medical decision making. Investigators have reported significant variations in the use of various medical specialties and surgical procedures among patients with the same medical conditions. These variations were confirmed by a method called small-area analysis, which shows that the chances of an American's having a surgical procedure for a given condition is greatly influenced by where he or she lives.

For example, in Iowa in 1984, the chances that men aged eighty-five had had prostrate surgery ranged from 15 to 60 percent, depending on the hospital market. In Maine, by the time a woman reached seventy the likelihood of her having had a hysterectomy was 20 percent in one hospital market and 70 percent in another. In Vermont the probability that a child would undergo a tonsillectomy ranged from 8 percent to 70 percent, depending on the hospital market.

What impact did these findings have? Variations in the use of medical services quickly became a target for cost containment in medicine. Why? Because nearly everyone—providers, patients, payers, and policy makers—had believed that the amount of medical care provided to a population was proportional to the amount of disease present in that population. No one had suspected that a provider could control the demand for medical services. Practice variation studies clearly showed that rates of hospital admission were not related to incidence of disease or even to factors such as patient age or income but were strongly associated with providers' practice style and the available supply of medical resources (hospital beds, number of physicians, hospital employees per capita, and so on).

Interestingly, variation was not widespread for some conditions, including hernias, hip fractures, cancer of the bowel, and appendicitis, but variation was prevalent for certain procedures, including hysterectomies, tonsillectomies, and prostrate surgery. One national study looked at procedures carried out on Medicare beneficiaries in thirteen areas of the United States. For 123 different procedures, 67 showed at least a threefold difference between the highest and lowest rate of use.

Researchers confirmed that variation occurs when physicians lack consensus regarding diagnosis, treatment, and outcomes of medical procedures. When disagreement within the medical profession increases, so do provider practice patterns. Analyzing the rate, pattern, and distribution of utilization has helped the medical profession identify overuse, underuse, and unnecessary use and differentiate discretionary services from necessary services (many medical decisions involve discretionary judgments on the part of physicians). As a result of these variation studies, most physician organizations began to develop practice standards, guidelines, and outcome measures to discourage variation that could result in unnecessary care for patients as well as unnecessary costs for payers.

If variations in use are evident in general medicine, where diagnoses are primarily based upon concrete, physical, observable symptoms, then how susceptible to variation is mental health care? Most of us know the answer to this question without even having to think. Psychotherapy is a field filled with practice variation, especially concerning the length of treatment. A psychodynamic therapist might treat a borderline personality disorder for ten years in individual therapy, while a cognitive therapist might assign her to group therapy for six to twelve months. And these two therapists would argue interminably over which treatment was best!

How do we justify such marked differences? We have not yet effectively resolved these issues, and such a lack of practice standards should be a matter of great concern to the mental health community. It is of the utmost importance that patients receive needed treatment, but we must demonstrate the effectiveness of that treatment with outcome data. Studying practice variations allows us to look at our clinical behavior and discover differences arising from our profession, training, and practice style.

Studies of practice variation have contributed much to our understanding of how general medical services are used and distributed. Now that the demand for demonstrated effectiveness has reached the mental health field, professional organizations such as the American Psychiatric Association have pressed to institute standards that establish uniform treatment protocols and time frames. Hopefully, the more we discuss and educate ourselves about time in psychotherapy and length of treatment, the sooner we will develop an attitude of temporal eclecticism.

One last point regarding practice variation: small-area analyses have been used to yield what are called "medical care signatures," or practice profiles, characteristic of particular hospitals and individual providers. It is becoming increasingly easy to see how any one provider's practice pattern compares to that of any other provider or group. In the future these profiles will be readily available, and they will likely be used as report cards to evaluate providers.

Mental health professionals will either take these matters into their own hands or watch others do it for them. The July 1995 issue of *The Nation's Health*, the newspaper of the American Public Health Association, included a want ad for a director of a practice pattern research unit. The position had the job goal of "studying the relationship between the organization and the financing of mental health systems and the clinical and cost effectiveness of services." The studies to be performed will compare patterns of service delivery, outcomes, and cost of mental health care in diverse mental health settings.

Who will employ this director? Who will own the research information that comes from such studies of practice variation? How will this knowledge be used? For fiscal reasons? To cut costs so corporations can make greater profits? To aid in devising practice standards for both length and effectiveness of psychotherapy? Will the information help patients and therapists engage in better psychotherapy? Mental health professionals are at a crossroads. They must take control of the future of psychotherapy, lest business interests prevail. Mental health professionals must demonstrate the effectiveness of their psychotherapeutic treatments, long- or short-term. And if it is true that long-term psychotherapy is superior to short-term therapy, it is time for its advocates to come forward and produce the empirical evidence to back up their beliefs.

Notes

p. 107, *"Man's judgments of value"*: Peter's quotations: Ideas for our time. (1977, p. 507). New York: Bantam Books.

p. 107, *Although providers are beginning to reverse these assumptions*: Bergin, A. E., & Garfield, S. L. (1994). [Introduction]. In A. E. Bergin & S. L. Garfield (Eds.), *Handbook of psychotherapy and behavior change*. (4th ed., pp. 1–18). New York: Wiley.

p. 107, *As Bernard Bloom writes:* Bloom, B. (1992). *Planned short-term therapy: A clinical handbook* (pp. 4–28). Boston: Allyn & Bacon.

p. 109, *The literature is replete with:* Budman, S., & Gurman, A. (1988). *Theory and practice of brief therapy* (pp. 1–21). New York: Guilford; Bloom, B. (1992). *Planned short-term therapy: A clinical handbook* (p. 4–15). Boston: Allyn & Bacon; Hoyt, M. F. (1995). *Brief therapy and managed care.* San Francisco: Jossey-Bass.

p. 110, *Most long-term therapy is based upon the concept:* Cummings, N. A. (1991). Brief intermittent psychotherapy throughout the life cycle. In C. S. Austad & W. Berman (Eds.), *Psychotherapy in managed health care: The optimal use of time and resources* (pp. 35–45). Washington, DC: American Psychological Association; Hoyt, M. F. (1994). Characteristics of brief psychotherapy under managed health care. In M. F. Hoyt (Ed.), *Brief therapy and managed care: Readings for contemporary practice* (pp. 1–8). San Francisco: Jossey-Bass.

p. 110, *Freud finally concluded late in his career:* Bauer, G., & Kobos, J. C. (1987). *Brief therapy.* Northvale, NJ: Jason Aronson.

p. 111, *A seventy-one-year-old woman:* Myers, W. A. (1984). *Dynamic therapy of the older patient* (pp. 145–146). New York: Jason Aronson.

p. 111, *The long-term therapist's attitude:* Meyer, W. S. (1993). In defense of long-term treatment: On the vanishing holding environment. *Social Work, 38*(5), 571–578.

p. 112, *Long-term therapists see brief therapy:* Parad, L. G. (1971). Short-term treatment: An overview of historical trends, issues, and potentials. *Smith College Studies in Social Work, 41,* 119–146.

p. 112, *Brief therapy comes in hundreds of forms:* Koss, M., & Shiang, J. (1994). Research on brief psychotherapy. In A. E. Bergin & S. L. Garfield (Eds.), *Handbook of psychotherapy and behavior change.* (4th ed., pp. 664–700) New York: Wiley.

p. 114, *Even a single session:* Talmon, M. (1993). *Single session solutions.* Reading, MA: Addison-Wesley.

p. 115, *As surveys of practicing clinicians have shown:* Norcross, J., & Prochaska, J. O. (1983). Psychotherapists in independent practice: Some findings and issues. *Professional Psychology: Research and Practice, 6*(14), 869–881.

p. 116, *In the immortal words of Sigmund Freud:* Freud, S. (1933). Turnings in the ways of psychoanalysis. In *Collected Papers* (standard edition) (p. 402). London, England: Hogarth Press.

p. 117, *First, as most mental health professionals:* Lambert, M. J., Shapiro, D. A., & Bergin, A. E. (1986). The effectiveness of psychotherapy. In S. L. Garfield & A. E. Bergin (Eds.), *Handbook of psychotherapy and behavior change* (3rd ed., pp. 157–211). New York: Wiley.

p. 118, *Although investigators have invested tremendous time and effort:* ibid.

p. 118, *Others maintain that:* Norcross, J. C. (1995). Dispelling the dodo bird verdict and the exclusivity myth in psychotherapy. *Psychotherapy, 32*(3), 500–503.

p. 118, *Thomas Giles, a therapy researcher:* Giles, T. (1991). Managed mental health care and effective psychotherapy: A step in the right direction. *Journal of Behavior Therapy and Experimental Psychiatry, 22*(2), 83–86.

p. 118, *The highly revered researchers:* Bergin, A. E., & Garfield, S. L. (1994). Overview, trends and future issues. In A. E. Bergin & S. L. Garfield (Eds.), *Handbook of psychotherapy and behavior change.* (4th ed., pp. 821–830). New York: Wiley.

p. 119, *Therefore these findings cannot be seen:* Lambert, M. J., & Bergin, A. E. (1994) *Handbook of psychotherapy and behavior change.* (4th ed., p. 181) New York: Wiley.

p. 119, *Tremendous resistance to accepting it:* Bergin, A. E., & Garfield, S. L. (1994). Overview, trends and future issues. In A. E. Bergin & S. L. Garfield (Eds.), *Handbook of psychotherapy and behavior change.* (4th ed., pp. 823). New York: Wiley.

p. 119, *Mary Koss and Julie Shiang, in their fastidious review:* Koss, M., & Shiang, J. (1994). Research on brief psychotherapy. In A. E. Bergin & S. L. Garfield (Eds.), *Handbook of psychotherapy and behavior change.* (4th ed., pp. 664–700). New York: Wiley.

p. 120, *The dearth of data:* Lambert, M. J., & Bergin, A. E. (1992). Achievements and limitations of psychotherapy research. In Friedheim, D. (Ed.), *History of Psychotherapy* (p. 377). Washington, DC: American Psychological Association.

p. 120, *However, the debate:* Vessey, J., Howard, K., Luegar, R., Kachele, H., & Mergenthaler, E. (1994). The clinician's illusion and the psychotherapy practice: An application of stochastic modeling. *Journal of Consulting and Clinical Psychology, 62*(4), 679–685.

p. 120, Consumer Reports *published a survey:* Mental health: Does therapy work? (1995, November). *Consumer Reports*, pp. 734–739; Seligman, M. (1995). The effectiveness of psychotherapy: The Consumer Reports study. *American Psychologist, 50*(12), 969.

p. 121, *It is a well-recognized fact:* Beutler, L., & Clarkin, J. (1991). Future research directions. In L. Beutler & M. Crago (Eds.), *Psychotherapy Research* (pp. 329–334). Washington, DC: American Psychological Association.

p. 121, *Psychotropic medications present a substantial challenge:* Klerman, G., Weissmena, M., Markowitz, J., Glick, I., Wilmer, P. J., Mason, B., & Shear, K. (1994). Medication and psychotherapy. In A. E. Bergin & S. L. Garfield (Eds.), *Handbook of psychotherapy and behavior change.* (4th ed., pp. 734–782). New York: Wiley.

p. 121, *The Senate Subcommittee on Appropriations:* U.S. Congress. Senate. National Advisory Mental Health Council. (1993). Health care reform for Americans with severe mental illness. *American Journal of Psychiatry, 150*(10), 1447–1463.

p. 123, *Some professional organizations:* The APA now has a partial review of the literature on medical offset available to its members by fax.

p. 123, *In the 1960s, researchers at Kaiser-Permanente Health Plan:* Follette, W. T., & Cummings, N. (1967). Psychiatric services and medical utilization in a prepaid health care setting. Part I. *Medical Care, 5,* 25–35; Cummings, N. A., & Follette, W. T. (1968). Psychiatric services and medical utilization in a prepaid health care setting: Part II. *Medical Care, 6,* 331–341.

p. 124, *The medical offset effect:* Cummings, N. A., & Follette, W. T. (1968). Psychiatric services and medical utilization in a prepaid health care setting: Part II. *Medical Care, 6*(1), 31–41; Cummings, N. A., & VandenBos, G. R. (1981). The twenty-year Kaiser-Permanente experience with psychotherapy and medical utilization: Implications for national health policy and national health insurance. *Health Policy Quarterly, 1*(2), 159–175.

p. 124, *In 1994, results from the Hawaii Medicaid study:* Pallak, M. S., Cummings, N. A., Dorken, H. D., & Henke, C. J. (1994). Medical costs, Medicaid, and managed mental health treatment: The Hawaii Study. *Managed Care Quarterly, 2*(2), 64–70; Cummings, N. A. (1991). Arguments for the financial efficacy of psychological services in health care settings. In J. J. Sweet (Ed.), *Handbook of clinical psychology in medical settings.* New York: Plenum.

p. 126, *Behavioral medicine techniques:* Benson, H., & Proctor, W. (1987). *Your maximum mind.* New York: Times Books; VandenBos, G., & DeLeon, P. (1988). The use of psychotherapy to improve physical health. *Psychotherapy, 25,* 335–343.

p. 126, *About two decades ago:* Wennberg, J., & Gittelsohn, A. (1973). Variations in medical care among small areas. *Scientific American, 246*(1), 120–134.

p. 126, *Practice variations are defined:* Caper, P. (1987). The epidemiological surveillance of medical care. *American Journal of Public Health, 77*(6), 669–670.

p. 126, *For example, in Iowa in 1984:* Caper, P., & Zuboff, M. (1984, September). Managing medical costs through small area analysis. *Business and Health,* pp. 20–25.

p. 127, *Practice variation studies:* Smits, H. L. (1986, Fall). Medical practice variation revisited. *Health Affairs,* pp. 91–96; Chassin, M. R., Brook, R., Park, R. E., Keesey, J., Fink, A., Kosecoff, J., Kahn, K., Merrick, N., & Solomon, D. H. (1986). Variations in the use of medical and surgical services by the Medicare population. *New England Journal of Medicine, 314,* 285–290; Kopta, S., Newman, F., McGovern, M., & Sandrock, D. (1988). Psychotherapeutic orientations: A comparison of conceptualizations, interventions, and treatment plan costs. *Journal of Consulting and Clinical Psychology, 54*(3), 369–374; Lawler, F. H., & Hosokawa, M. C. (1987). Evaluation of standards of practice for primary care physicians using 12 hypothetical cases. *The Journal of Family Practice, 4*(4), 377–383; Modest, G. (1990). Financial incentives and performance of health maintenance organizations. *The New England Journal of Medicine, 322*(1), 62–63.

p. 128, *Now that the demand for demonstrated effectiveness has reached the mental health field:* Talbott, J. A. (1990). Developing practice parameters: An interview with John McIntyre. *Hospital and Community Psychiatry, 41*(10), 1103–1105.

p. 128, *One last point regarding practice variation:* Smits, H. L. (1986, Fall). Medical practice variations revisited. *Health Affairs,* pp. 91–96.

. . . .

6

How Patients Really Use Psychotherapy

The Clinician's Illusion

*Do not let what you cannot do interfere with what
you can do.*

John Wooden

Long-term therapists have various names for patients who do not remain in extended therapy— "dropouts," "early terminators," "premature terminators," "refusers." Are these descriptors accurate? Are people who leave psychotherapy after a few sessions not really "in" psychotherapy? Do most people who enter therapy stay for long-term therapy? The answer to that question is most definitely no.

Patients in long-term treatment represent only a very small percentage of those who seek psychotherapy. Epidemiological research shows that patients in long-term treatment are simply not representative of most patients in psychotherapy.

Epigraph from *An Apple A Day*, Great Quotations, Inc.

An Epidemiological View

Recent advances in computer technology that allow us to collect and analyze large amounts of information have provided a depth to our understanding of psychotherapy that we could not have imagined only thirty years ago. Philip Caper, a professor of public policy, points out that not very long ago researchers could only analyze large data bases using mainframe computers. But rapidly evolving technology "has now made techniques for large database manipulation almost completely portable and infinitely more responsive to the needs of the analyst for use either in research or management. . . . The results . . . [are] accessible to private and public policy makers who are not statisticians and [are] much more useful for routine management purposes. Medical care epidemiology is a powerful approach for posing the right questions about the use and effectiveness of medical services and their relationship to the rates and distribution of illness."

Just as epidemiological information has advanced our understanding of medical diseases, so has it enhanced our understanding of psychotherapy. Epidemiology is the study of the frequency and distribution of a disease or disorder—mental or physical—in a population. Epidemiologists study "prevalence" samples, consisting of individuals who are all suffering from a disease or condition at some specified point or period of time, and "incidence" samples, consisting of individuals who all represent new cases of a disease or condition at some specified period of time.

Working with epidemiological data bases enables us to keep track of the psychotherapy encounters of entire populations. Never before have researchers captured such a holistic view of psychotherapy use. We now see what therapists and patients actually do, and it does not fit the stereotype of how traditional therapists *think* people seeking psychotherapy behave. The reality is nothing like the assumptions about utilization implicit in long-term models of psychotherapy.

Researchers have been gathering very specific information in a number of national data bases relevant to our knowledge about short- and long-term therapy. This includes information on patient demographics and on the prevalence and incidence of attrition and dose response to psychotherapy. I will discuss the findings from three major sources:

1. The National Medical Care Utilization and Expenditure Survey (NMCUES), conducted in 1980 and 1987, consists of three parts—the National Household Survey, the State Medicaid Household Survey, and the Administrative Records Survey. The NMCUES summarizes information about all medical visits made in 1980 and 1987, including the date, the reason the patient sought treatment, the charge, the type of provider, the payment source, and which medications were prescribed.

2. The Epidemiological Catchment Area Study (ECA), sponsored by the National Institute of Mental Health, ran from 1980 to 1985. It represented an attempt to obtain reliable national estimates of discrete diagnostic disorders as well as to gather information about utilization of mental health services. Researchers looking for estimates of the prevalence of DSM diagnoses used the Diagnostic Interview Scale (DIS) at five universities—Yale, Johns Hopkins, Washington University, Duke University, and the University of California at Los Angeles. The ECA used a more liberal definition of psychotherapy than the NMCUES, and it estimated that 10.7 percent of the population used mental health services each year during the period studied.

3. A number of research institutes and universities are also conducting large-scale studies. The Northwestern-Chicago University collaborative project and a study sponsored by George Washington University have provided data pertaining to patient demographics, utilization patterns, and the effectiveness of therapy. This information has augmented our understanding of the psychotherapy delivery system.

How Patients Really Use Psychotherapy

Based on NMCUES data, 4.3 percent of the U.S. population made at least one visit for mental health care in 1980. Of those who made mental health outpatient visits in 1980,

- 8.2 was the average number of visits per person.

- Two visits was the median number for all patients.

- 34.7 percent appeared for only one session.

- 57.4 percent appeared for three or fewer sessions.

- 15.5 percent appeared for fifteen or more sessions.

- 9.4 percent appeared for over twenty-four sessions.

- The 9.4 percent that appeared for over twenty-four sessions was responsible for nearly 50 percent of all mental health care expenditures for the year.

In 1987,

- 3.1 percent of the outpatient population went for a psychotherapy session.

- 79.5 million outpatient psychotherapy visits were made.

- 33.9 percent of all patients appeared for one or two visits (very short-term users).

- 37.0 percent appeared for three to ten visits (short-term users).

- 13.4 percent appeared for eleven to twenty visits (intermediate users).

- 15.7 percent appeared for twenty-one or more visits (long-term users).

- The 15.7 percent that made twenty-one or more visits was responsible for 62.9 percent of total mental health care expenditures for the year.

Although these studies report a slightly different usage break-down in 1980 and 1987, a very consistent pattern emerges—a high proportion of individuals with one, two, or three visits; a gradual drop-off in the number of clients as the number of visits increases from four to ten, and the small concentrations of heavy users.

The evidence is compelling—the majority of people who seek outpatient mental health care in the United States expect, receive, and get short-term psychotherapy. The median duration of psychotherapy in these years was four to eight sessions. Most patients had only one session! While most outpatients engaged in relatively few sessions, a small number of patients accounted for the bulk of psychotherapy visits and costs or expenditures.

The Attrition Curve

Lakein Phillips, a pioneer in the study of psychotherapy, was the first to strongly advocate the idea that to understand psychotherapy we need to understand its delivery system. Phillips invented the term "attrition curve" to describe the naturally occurring pattern of utilization by large groups of individuals.

This explorer of the topography of the psychotherapy delivery system has spent many years examining international, national, and local data bases. His combined samples total over a million cases. Plotting the number of sessions of psychotherapy on the X axis of a graph and the number of patients remaining after each session on the Y axis, he pictorially illustrated the topography of a psychotherapy delivery system. He has determined that a characteristic curve develops, with the properties of a "negatively accelerating, declining, attrition . . . decay curve with approximately equal mean and standard deviation values with the median being smaller than the mean and the asymptote extending several standard deviations beyond the mean."

The attrition curve shows that regardless of practice setting or the therapist's theoretical orientation, the average number of psychotherapy visits is four to eight. Between one-third and one-half of patients who come for psychotherapy do not return after a single session. As time goes on, fewer and fewer clients remain in psychotherapy. By the fifth or sixth session, about 60 to 70 percent of those who began therapy no longer remain. Only about 8 to 10 percent continue in therapy beyond ten or fifteen sessions. Phillips's attrition curve is consistent with information from the ECA and NMCUES studies.

Phillips cautions that much of our existing information about psychotherapy is based on an understanding of long-term patients. Ultimately we may have to face the fact that we hold a distorted view of the therapy process. Some of our most cherished beliefs may be based on information from atypical populations (the few patients who remain in therapy past fifteen sessions). Furthermore, as part of their methodology, many research studies eliminate patients from the data analysis who have attended fewer than some specified number of sessions. But those so eliminated represent the majority who enter into the psychotherapy delivery system.

We can take this reasoning one step further: isn't it possible that we may be letting the successes get away? We may be investigating only the difficult-to-treat patients, or even the treatment failures, when we concentrate on long-term patients. What if the most potent effects of psychotherapy occur in the earliest stages? (This idea is supported by dose-response data, which I will discuss shortly.) We might be thwarting our own enlightenment about the potency of the early effects of psychotherapy.

If a patient is not responding well early in therapy, perhaps we need to reconsider the appropriateness of the treatment itself. If after a six-week trial on Elavil a depressed patient does not respond favorably, would the physician insist that the patient was resistant

to the drug? Would the doctor advise the patient to continue taking the ineffective substance because it will ultimately result in
improvement? No, the physician would assume that the Elavil and
the patient are not a good match. A change to some other class of
antidepressant, such as Zoloft or Prozac, would be in order.

Patients who do not respond well within the first twenty-six
sessions may be a poor match for the model of therapy being used—
or the therapist. Unfortunately, some patients will continue to
participate in ineffective treatments because of the ingrained beliefs that "the doctor knows best" and that if they just cooperate
with the doctor's prescribed treatment, it will ultimately lead to
improvement.

Unfortunately, information about why patients leave after short-
term encounters is presently unavailable on a large-scale basis. So
the belief that those who leave are treatment failures is an unproven
assumption. It is also frequently presumed that those who drop out
are dissatisfied. One analyst among the handful of authors who have
investigated length of treatment and patient reaction after "premature termination" concluded that "there . . . appears to be no support for the clinical assumption that patients who unilaterally
terminate treatment are dissatisfied with their care and there is little support for the notion that they are functioning more poorly
than patients whose terminations from therapy were mutually
agreed upon ahead of time by therapists and patient." When we
think deeply about these facts, we have to ask if it is appropriate to
continue to ignore or minimize the behavior of the majority and
devote so much time—both clinical and research—to treating and
investigating so few.

We should heed the suggestion of Bernard Bloom, who encourages clinicians and researchers to study psychotherapy in a way similar to how we study medications. We need to understand these
essential characteristics of any treatment: efficacy, or maximum
effect: threshold, or lowest possible dose that will produce a dis-
cernable effect; latency, or speed with which effects occur; potency,

or absolute amount of treatment needed to produce a desired effect; duration, or the amount of time an effect is sustained; variability, or the effectiveness of the treatment in general; and side effects, margin of safety, and negative consequences of treatment. Researchers at Northwestern and Chicago University are attempting to make these determinations concerning psychotherapy.

The Dose-Effect Relationship

Adding to the growing body of epidemiological knowledge connected with psychotherapy are a series of studies that use a dose-response methodology. These studies have examined the relationship between quantity of psychotherapy and patient improvement by calculating the linear relationship between number of sessions and percentage improvement. Data from over 2,400 patients over a thirty-year period has been scrutinized.

According to plots of the "dosage" (number of sessions) against various measures of the effectiveness of therapy,

- 10 to 18 percent of patients showed some improvement before the initial session as a function of initiating a mental health contact.

- 48 to 58 percent of patients showed improvement by the eighth session.

- 75 percent of patients showed improvement by the twenty-sixth session.

- 85 percent of patients showed improvement by the end of a year.

The authors of this study state that "8 sessions is the median effective dose of individual psychotherapy and . . . by 26 sessions, an effective dose of 75 percent is obtained."

This research clearly shows that the greatest degree of improvement in psychotherapy occurs during the early stages of therapy. There may be a point of diminishing returns, when it is appropriate to ask if the expenditures of time, energy, and money are worthwhile for the patient.

A notable finding discussed by the authors is that patients improve just by making an appointment for therapy. Does just the prospect of help bring relief? Hope may be a powerful short-term variable. This variable needs much more study.

Demographic Information

Pooling the information scattered throughout various epidemiological surveys, including the ECA and NMCUES studies, the National Health Survey Interview, and the National Survey of Access to Health Care, several additional studies describe the gender, race, age, marital status, education, income, and diagnoses of patients who made at least one visit to a mental health specialist. These findings show that those who participate in psychotherapy hardly represent the diverse spectrum of patients contained in the general population:

- Three times as many women as men are in psychotherapy.

- Men and women are equally likely to enter into more psychotherapy after an initial visit to a mental health provider, but since women are more likely to make an initial visit, two-thirds of patients in psychotherapy are women.

- Whites make up over 90 percent of psychotherapy users.

- Whites as a group are more likely than blacks to receive a variety of mental health services.

- Blacks are particularly underrepresented among long-term users of psychotherapy.

- The elderly are particularly underrepresented among long-term users of psychotherapy.

- Persons aged thirty-five to forty-nine are the most frequent age group receiving psychotherapy.

- The youngest and oldest members of society are the least likely to attend a session.

- Those who are separated or divorced are more likely to be in therapy than those who are single, married, or widowed.

- Those with at least fifteen to sixteen years of education are more likely to enter and continue in psychotherapy.

- One-half of people in psychotherapy do not meet the criteria for a DSM diagnosis.

- Only 6 to 7 percent of those with a diagnosis made a mental health visit.

- While individuals with the DSM diagnoses of depression, dysthymia, obsessive-compulsive disorder, and phobias are more likely to make an initial visit to a mental health professional, they are no more likely to enter subsequent psychotherapy than those with no diagnosis.

The authors comment that those who are in greatest need of mental health services may be the least likely to seek and receive care.

The important link between mental and physical illness, discussed earlier, is highlighted by the following findings from the surveys:

- Individuals who rated their general health as poor were two times more likely to use psychotherapy than those who rated their health as excellent.

- Those who reported health-related functional work impairments were more likely to use psychotherapy than those who did not.

These findings, coupled with research on the medical offset effect and behavioral medicine, show the need for a greater understanding of mind-body interaction.

Assimilating Epidemiological Facts

Information from many different sources shows that the epidemiological view of the psychotherapy delivery system—taking into account patient demographics, attrition curves, usage patterns, and the dose effect response—indicate that most people who enter psychotherapy become dropouts or premature terminators by long-term standards. Patients do not show patterns of use consistent with what we would expect of the prototypical long-term patient. Very brief and brief therapies are dominant. Patients vote with their feet!

What would the attrition curve look like if everyone engaged in long-term therapy? I took a straw poll among about twenty of my long-term colleagues. Here is how they answered: After an initial screening session, the attrition curve would demonstrate a sharp drop-off, showing that some people would be screened out as a function of their unsuitableness for therapy, unwillingness or inability to participate in therapy, inadequate finances, geographical moves, or external problems. After these initial disqualifications, nearly all patients would continue on for about fifty to fifty-two sessions yearly over a two- to five-year span, with most courses of therapy averaging about 250 sessions. Improvement would be slow and steady, increasing as a function of number of sessions completed. Although temporary regressions would occur, resulting in peaks and valleys on the curve, the slope of the line would show overall continuous improvement, with slow and steady progress culminating at the asymptote, corresponding with termination of treatment.

Data from national utilization, dose-response, and psychotherapy attrition studies show nothing like this imaginary distribution of long-term therapy. As noted above, regardless of the setting, the type of therapy, or the theoretical orientation of the therapist, the average number of psychotherapy visits is brief. A single session is most common. Only a minority of patients are in long-term therapy. The greatest gains occur early in treatment and diminish in intensity as treatment continues. The simple act of making a mental health appointment results in an immediate benefit for some.

Interpretations

When I asked long-term therapists to explain the discrepancy between the psychotherapy delivery system described by epidemiological studies and our imaginary long-term delivery system, they offered the following explanations:

- Just because people do not remain in long-term therapy does not mean they do not belong in long-term therapy.

- Dropouts could have been improperly screened, unsuitable candidates for long-term therapy who dropped out due to their own resistance.

- The therapists may not have been able to form a satisfactory alliance with dropouts early enough in therapy.

- Epidemiological findings should be minimized or even discounted because their significance is unclear. Since aggregate data tell us little about individual human beings, it is nearly meaningless information for the therapeutic process.

- The basic methodologies of epidemiological studies are flawed. The dependent measures are too limited; the independent measure—psychotherapy—was not clearly defined and varied too much across studies; there was no way to tell if these outpatient mental health visits were really psychotherapy.

In short, long-term therapists seldom attributed the findings from the data to any factor associated with psychotherapy; rather, they attributed the results to a deficiency on the part of either the patients or the therapists.

Short-term therapists responded differently, saying that the epidemiological data showed what they already knew to be true. The majority of patients who come for therapy get what they need early in therapy or decide therapy is not for them and find another way to meet their needs. Short-term therapy is the treatment of choice for 90 percent of people. Only a few need more, and although some may want more, it is usually not medically necessary.

The Clinician's Illusion

Why do so many therapists cling to the mythical belief that most patients in therapy are in, or should be in, long-term therapy? In the face of the facts presented above, why does the traditional view of psychotherapy as an hourly, weekly, several-year process prevail? Why do researchers stigmatize patients who do not stay in long-term therapy as dropouts?

The epidemiological researchers Cohen and Cohen provide a partial answer to these questions. They coined the term "clinician's illusion" to explain the incongruity between the beliefs of long-term therapists and the reality demonstrated by epidemiological research. Clinicians tend to attribute the characteristics and course of treatment of patients who are currently ill to the entire population of patients. They do this even when the attributes of the population are very different from those of the patients they deal with on an everyday basis. Naturally, when long-term patients dominate a clinician's caseload, a large discrepancy exists between his or her view of a disease and the truth about the duration or length of the illness. Although the clinical sample is atypical compared to the whole population, the clinician erroneously concludes that the familiar, small sample he or she treats accurately characterizes the entire population.

To clarify this point, let's look at the makeup of a successful traditional private practice.

Out of Sight, Out of Mind

Suppose that you are a therapist who has been in practice for twenty years. Over that span of time, hundreds of patients have come to your office. We now know that unless you are a rare exception the majority of all patients who came to your office most likely left before the twenty-fifth session. Only a minority, 10 percent, have remained with you in long-term work.

Let's say you have a great referral source, and one hundred new patients arrive during the first week you open your doors. (Of course, you could not actually see one hundred people; this example is just for illustrative purposes.) After twenty-five weeks, ninety of them are not in therapy, but ten remain. Let's say another one hundred referrals come along during the twenty-sixth week. Again, after twenty-five weeks ninety have terminated and only ten remain. You now have a total of twenty long-term patients. If we kept repeating this sequence, in two years your practice would be filled with long-term patients.

Psychotherapy practices begin with a majority of short-term patients and eventually become laden with longer-term patients. If no time or session limits are imposed a practice will fill up with longer-term patients, leaving only a small percentage of slots available for newcomers.

Patients who stay for only a short time recede into the background and fade from the therapist's memory. Those who stay for long-term therapy remain in the forefront of the therapist's mind.

These are the patients he or she discusses with colleagues, presents at case conferences, uses as examples for supervisee training, and perceives to be his or her "true" cases.

Therapists presume that the patients they see in long-term therapy represent the true population of psychotherapy patients. They believe a "reasonably accurate abstraction" of what they face in day to day encounters: "A therapist assumes his or her practice caseload is a representative sample of all patients. In fact, practice samples are not representative because they are duration dependent; that is, although the majority of patients are individuals with milder, more episodic disorders of shorter duration, patients experiencing severe problems of longer duration dominate the caseloads of more experienced clinicians. . . . Although the majority of psychotherapy patients stay in therapy for a relatively short time, therapists spend the majority of time with longer-term cases."

Unfortunately, the "clinician's illusion" seems to influence a great deal of the thinking of long-term therapists. Although the population of all psychotherapy patients consists largely of people engaged in short-term therapy, we have traditionally invested so much energy working with those who stay the longest that our view of therapy is skewed. We may be disregarding the successes while we study the failures.

High Users of Mental Health Services

The data from the above-mentioned studies lead us to seek the answer to a burning question: Who are these long-term patients who constitute the minority of patients yet consume 50 percent of all mental health resources? Are they a homogenous or heterogenous group? Diagnoses aside, we can say that they share some characteristics. They have some presenting problem that both they and their therapist judge to be serious and long-standing enough to require extended individual psychotherapy. They are people who seek out help, and they value human connections enough to choose seeing a psychotherapist as a means of alleviating their suffering. They or their support systems—private, public, commercial (that is, their insurance), or charitable—are monied enough to permit them to attend over twenty sessions a year.

Is their participation in psychotherapy medically necessary, or is it discretionary? What drives their exceptional pattern of use? High users fall into four basic subgroups:

- Patients with less serious mental illnesses who are undergoing insight-oriented therapy

- Patients with multiple somatic and mental complaints

- Patients with chronic mental disorders who are receiving both drug maintenance and supportive psychotherapy

- Patients with serious mental disorders who are receiving psychotherapy

Thus, there are a substantial number of patients who fit the stereotype of the high-functioning, healthy person receiving largely unneeded psychotherapy. These patients, commonly referred to as the "worried well," may fit the picture of the traditional, Freudian-style patient who seeks insights from long-term therapy to alleviate his or her neuroses. There are other high users who do not fit this stereotype, however—seriously disabled individuals with Medicare disabilities, multiple health problems, or the perception that their health status is inferior.

What drives most patients' use of psychotherapy—medical necessity or waste? Studies of medical use call them "outliers," individuals who receive a very different level or intensity of care than the norm. Why these patients are psychotherapy outliers has yet to be empirically established. Could it be due to complications, iatrogenic effects, real illness, or a desire for personal improvement? Remember, some researchers have voiced the concern that those with the greatest clinical need may be the least likely to receive care!

No one should be deprived of needed care, but should those who need care but go without it support treatment that is discretionary? Are those with the greatest need the most likely to get care under our present system? Could it be that some patients who engage in the luxury of discretionary care are doing so at the expense of the needy, who are passed over by the present system? Are the long-term models of therapy we use appropriate for those patients who most need long-term help?

We need to identify, assess, and evaluate their needs and analyze the effectiveness of the methods used to treat them. Finding out more about these patients is a top clinical priority, for reasons of quality of care and cost control.

We also must be careful when we used the value-laden term "dropout." Since there may be a variety of reasons why people leave therapy early, it is premature to accept the conclusion that leaving after a single session is indicative of failure or dissatisfaction. "Dropout" may be an accurate label for some but a misnomer for many others. More research is needed to determine if the term should be reconceptualized.

Our facts also give us a clue as to what areas we have neglected and now need to study. Although medical disabilities, poor general health, and functional impairments have not been extensively examined in relationship to psychotherapy (the Medicaid Hawaii studies are currently addressing these matters), it nevertheless remains for American psychotherapy to serve the needs of these diverse populations. We need to better explain that so many more females than males receive psychotherapy and why some minorities and the elderly are underrepresented among recipients of long-term therapy.

Implications for Clinical Work

The information in Chapter Five and in this chapter, gleaned from new research on psychotherapy, gives us much food for thought. The beliefs that long-term psychotherapy is the gold standard and that only people in long-term therapy are "really" in therapy are simply unsupported by the data. Therapists who cling to these myths have been taken in by the "clinician's illusion," a fantasy that needs to be dispelled with fact.

So what does this mean for clinical practice? If we want to be up-to-date practitioners who base our practice on scientific principles, we need to incorporate accurate research and epidemiological information into our thinking.

Short-term therapy should be the treatment of choice for the majority of patients. Yes, a small percentage of patients needs long-term treatment, but does it have to consist of weekly, hour-long sessions of psychodynamic therapy? There are more effective ways of dealing with people with long-term needs.

Short-term therapists already consider brief therapy to be the best choice unless otherwise indicated. The mental health community should no longer see brief therapy only as an emergency measure that keeps the patient in a holding pattern until long-term therapy can begin. The past negative attitude toward brief therapy is dissolving, but not as quickly as it should be. The effectiveness of short-term therapy has been demonstrated. Economic pressures to use cost-effective care are strong. Most people do not expect a personality overhaul from psychotherapy. We should assume that short-term therapy is the treatment of choice; if it does not work, the therapist can switch to a more intensive method.

Among long-term therapists, the prospect of keeping patients in therapy over prolonged periods of time is considered natural and good, but all therapists need to give serious consideration to the notion that such long-term engagements might be detrimental to their patients—and to society, since when we give care to one person, another may not receive it.

Wise clinicians will familiarize themselves with epidemiological research to keep their daily practice in line with the latest scientific knowledge and to give their patients the best and most efficient care.

We must help research, theory, and practice come together and point in a direction that leads psychotherapy to become "sociologically relevant." This goal is discussed in Chapter Seven.

Notes

p. 136, *But rapidly evolving technology:* Caper, P. (1987). The epidemiological surveillance of medical care. *American Journal of Public Health, 77*(6), 670.

p. 136, *Epidemiology is the study of:* Cohen, P., & Cohen, J. (1984). The clinician's illusion. *Archives of General Psychiatry, 41,* 1178–1182.

p. 137, *The National Medical Care Utilization and Expenditure Survey:* Taube, C., Goldman, H., Burns, B., & Kessler, L. (1988). High users of outpatient mental health services: I. Definitions and characteristics. *American Journal of Psychiatry, 145,* 19–24; Goldman, H., & Taube, C. (1988). High users of outpatient mental health services: II. Implications for practice and policy, *American Journal of Psychiatry, 145,* 24–28; Olfson, M., & Pincus, H. A. (1994, Winter). Measuring outpatient care in the United States. *Health Affairs,* pp. 173–180; Olfson, M., & Pincus, H. A. (1994). Outpatient psychotherapy in the United States: I. Volume costs and user characteristics. *American Journal of Psychiatry, 151,* 1281–1288.

p. 137, *The Epidemiological Catchment Area Study:* National Mental Health Advisory Council. (1993). *American Journal of Psychiatry, 150*(10), 1447–1463; Vessey, J. T., & Howard, K. I. (1993). Who seeks psychotherapy? *Psychotherapy, 30*(4), 546–553.

p. 137, *The Northwestern-Chicago University collaborative project:* Howard, K., Orlinsky, D. E., Saunders, S., Bankoff, E., Davidson, C., & O'Mahoney, M. (1991). Northwestern University-University of Chicago psychotherapy research program. In L. Beutler & M. Crago (Eds.), *Psychotherapy research* (pp. 65–81). Washington, DC: American Psychological Association; Phillips, L. (1991). George Washington University's international data on psychotherapy delivery systems: Modeling new approaches to the study of therapy. In L. Beutler & M. Crago (Eds.), *Psychotherapy research* (pp. 263–278). Washington, DC: American Psychological Association.

p. 139, *Lakein Phillips, a pioneer:* Phillips, L. (1985). *Psychotherapy revised: New frontiers in research and practice.* Hillsdale, NJ: Erlbaum.

p. 139, *He has determined that a characteristic curve develops:* Phillips, L. (1985). *A guide for therapists and patients to short-term psychotherapy* (p. 49). Springfield, IL: Charles C. Thomas.

p. 141, *One analyst among the handful of authors:* Bloom, B. (1992). *Planned short-term therapy* (p. 15). Boston: Allyn & Bacon.

p. 142, *Adding to the growing body of epidemiological knowledge:* Howard, K., Orlinsky, D., Saunders, S., Bankoff, E., Davidson, C., & O'Mahoney, M. (1991). Northwestern University-University of Chicago psychotherapy research program. In L. Beutler & M. Crago (Eds.), *Psychotherapy research* (pp. 65–73). Washington, DC: American Psychological Association; Howard, K., Kopta, S., Krause, M., & Orlinsky, D. (1986). The dose effect relationship in psychotherapy. *The American Psychologist, 41,* 159–164.

p. 142, *The authors of this study state that:* Howard, K., Orlinsky, D. E., Saunders, S., Bankoff, E., Davidson, C., & O'Mahoney, M. (1991). Northwestern University-University of Chicago psychotherapy research program. In L. Beutler & M. Crago (Eds.), *Psychotherapy research* (pp. 65–81). Washington, DC: American Psychological Association.

p. 143, *Pooling the information scattered:* Vessey, J., & Howard, K. (1993). Who seeks psychotherapy? *Psychotherapy, 30*(4), 546–553; Olfson, M., & Pincus, H. A. (1994). Outpatient psychotherapy in the United States: I. Volume costs and user characteristics. *American Journal of Psychiatry, 151,* 1281–1288.

p. 144, *Persons aged thirty-five to forty-nine:* Vessey, J., & Howard, K. (1993). Who seeks psychotherapy? *Psychotherapy, 30*(4), 546–553.

p. 147, *Clinicians tend to attribute:* Cohen, P., & Cohen, J. (1984). The clinician's illusion. *Archives of General Psychiatry, 41,* 1178–1182.

p. 149, *They believe a "reasonably accurate abstraction":* Vessey, J., Howard, K., Luegar, R., Kachele, H., & Mergenthaler, E. (1994). The clinician's illusion and the psychotherapy practice: An application of stochastic modeling. *Journal of Consulting and Clinical Psychology, 62*(4), 679–685.

p. 150, *High users fall into four basic subgroups:* Olfson, M., & Pincus, H. A. (1994). Outpatient psychotherapy in the United States: I. Volume costs and user characteristics. *American Journal of Psychiatry, 151,* 1281–1288.

p. 152, *Wise clinicians will familiarize themselves:* Lyketsos, C. G. (1994). Application of clinical epidemiologic methods to the clinical practice of psychiatry. *Journal of American Psychiatry, 151*(2), 299–300; Zarin, D. A., & Earls, F. (1994). Reply. *Journal of American Psychiatry, 151*(2), 300.

7

Toward a Sociology of Psychotherapy

What is honored in a country will be cultivated there.

Plato

Psychotherapy is not delivered in a vacuum; it takes place in the real world, in a multitude of settings. In our training to become psychotherapists, we are seldom groomed to think about the social and cultural aspects of our practice. My supervisors taught me well about the impact of office decor on patients, how it can serve as a projective device for patients and reveal the practitioner's personality. I knew I should be careful to make my office environment pleasant but neutral. Therefore I selected tasteful paintings, subtle colors, and warm wooden furniture. I kept my work area meticulously clean and orderly lest my patients conclude I am disorganized.

While our supervisors might tell us how to arrange our offices to enhance the therapeutic interaction between therapist and patient, we learn little about how sociocultural factors affect our patients' view of therapy. For example, while we may attend fastidiously to our immediate practice environment, we seldom talk about our sociocultural context. Within the comfortable confines of our offices, we seem to develop the impression that all psychotherapy is the same. But is it? Do patients perceive psychotherapy delivered in a state-sponsored outpatient clinic in the same way that they perceive psychotherapy delivered in a private office? Is psychotherapy delivered in a community mental health center judged to be the same as psychotherapy delivered in an HMO setting? Is it possible that the larger sociological aspects of our practice make different impressions upon our patients—impressions that might affect the outcome of therapy? It certainly is possible, yet we neglect studying these variables.

Perhaps our lack of knowledge about the role of such forces in the evolution of psychotherapy has made it easier for long-term bias to flourish. As psychotherapists we naturally focus on the needs of individual patients in individual therapy. We develop a distance from the reality that psychotherapy is now part of a larger health care system that, in turn, is part of society. We are susceptible to what I call professional tunnel vision.

Taking Providers by Surprise

Provider resistance to managed care illustrates this very point. It is because we had only a very dim sense of psychotherapy's aggregate effect on the health care system and society that so many of us found ourselves surprised, shocked, and unprepared to face the sweeping changes introduced by managed care. Had we been more aware of the "big picture," we would have known that the rise of alternative health care delivery systems was inevitable—even overdue—given the prevailing troubled economic, political, social, and spiritual landscape. But instead we seem to see managed care primarily as a threat to the survival of long-term therapy.

If we gained some perspective on the role of psychotherapy in society, we might be able to expand our tunnel vision. Although I have been critical of unfounded speculation in lieu of empirical data when it comes to psychotherapy as a medical procedure, I think that speculation can be helpful in discussing a sociological perspective on psychotherapy, simply because our information base is presently so sparse.

I am not suggesting that we take on a task as ambitious as designing a comprehensive sociology of psychotherapy in a single chapter. Rather, I suggest that we explore the sociocultural factors that may have encouraged long-term bias and discuss the dynamics of managed care, psychotherapy, and society in hopes of laying the groundwork for the future development of such a sociology.

A Sociological Perspective on Long-Term Bias

I contend that there are a number of subtle ways in which thera-pists have been conditioned to presume that long-term traditional therapy is preferable to short-term therapy. In the same way that society can through its many institutions subtly condition its citi-zens to accept certain prejudices, professions can condition their members to accept certain myths. And long-term bias has long been championed, perhaps unknowingly, by the ruling institutions and traditional customs of professional psychotherapy. Images, training, research, and language have all helped perpetuate it. It is not my intention to render a history of short-term therapy here but to provide you with selective bits and pieces of it that reinforce my hypothesis.

Images

The current generation of Americans has been continuously bom-barded with words and images that support the underlying assump-tion that long-term therapy is the standard against which all other forms of therapy ought to be compared. The choice of words and images used by clinicians, researchers, and academics reveal their bias toward long-term therapy.

In the public's mind, the stereotypical image of "being in therapy" is that of a patient "on the couch." Together, patient and therapist embark upon an arduous, extended, nearly mystical excursion into the interior recesses of the patient's psyche. Any attempt to impose time constraints on a journey this mysterious and intense would be considered sacrilegious.

In our culture, the image of the ideal therapist is one of a Freud-like patriarch sitting in his large, overstuffed wing chair and lording over his female patient. She is on the couch, in a supine position, reclining passively and obediently, waiting for her resistance to be broken down. The upright figure of the analyst, deep in thought, radiates the presence of an astute and powerful mind that is removed, objective, and, above all, analytic! The patient, in the long run, defers to the therapist's expertise. It is not only the public who holds this image of psychotherapy; this archetypal scene is deeply rooted in the consciousness and firmly planted in the imaginations of neophyte therapists. Internalizing this Freudian model of psychotherapy, trainees aspire to take on the role of "Wise Man of the West," complete with its trappings of prestige, elevated social status, and high income. In this deluxe version of psychotherapy, the therapist does not skimp on time, interpretations, or fees!

On the whole, the images associated with long-term work are generally more appealing and gratifying than those connected with short-term work. Long-term therapy is associated with reflections on sex and aggression; the world of fantasy, wish fulfillment, and dreams; male privilege; primitive notions of unlimited resources; and a wealth of time and ideas. The therapeutic situation supplies both the patient and the therapist with a feast of great abundance, from which intellectual and emotional sustenance can be devoured with great gusto.

On the other hand, short-term therapy is tied to impressions that are far less gratifying. Since its inception, brief work has been associated with painful, hard-core reality; limits and limitations; and efficiency, practicality, and restricted resources. If long-term therapy is an abundant feast, then short-term therapy is the fast food of mental health treatment.

The invention of short-term therapy has been associated with tragic events and a lack of resources in the face of overwhelming need. I contend that these associations reside in the professional collective unconscious and partly account for therapists' reluctance to embrace short-term therapy and their willingness to accept the consequent economic losses.

The origins of short-term therapy in the United States are linked with World War II, with disabled, battle-fatigued soldiers rendered incapable of fighting and in direct need of psychological help. Since both time and manpower were scarce commodities during the war, it was not possible to engage in long-term therapy with these men. Estimating that nearly 45 percent of the war's first 1.5 million medical discharges were the result of psychiatric problems, the military lavishly supported the development of psychological interventions that would get soldiers back on their feet as quickly as possible. Thus, brief therapy was blessed and maintained by the military. Naturally, priority was given to those soldiers expected to return to duty. There was an incentive for delivering a quick fix. If a soldier could be treated for battle fatigue and his symptoms resolved, he could be returned to duty. So psychotherapists worked to cure their patients quickly as the military awaited their return to duty.

To the best of my knowledge, there has never been a thorough, public, or open professional discussion of the dilemmas inherent in this wartime situation. The therapist was faced with a true conflict of interest—the competing needs of the patient, the military, and society. The country was relying on these soldiers for protection. The soldiers placed their trust in the therapist-patient relationship. When the therapist relieved patients of their debilitating symptoms, it meant a return to danger, perhaps serious injury or even death.

What kind of image is attached to the therapist when treatment success means a patient again becomes fodder for the battlefield? Thus the origins of brief therapy are partly associated with blood, guilt, and ethical dilemmas.

A second historic image associated with the growth of short-term therapy is the tragic fire at the Coconut Grove Nightclub in 1943. Many people were killed in the fire, and a substantial number of survivors suffered severe and debilitating symptoms. In order to furnish emotional and psychological support to the many who needed it, Erick Lindeman created crisis intervention. The impression of this technique is one of limited time, insufficient resources, and damage control for the survivors. The demand was overwhelming; there were not enough resources available to offer victims the "pure gold of analysis," so brief methods, or Band-Aids, were used until the real thing was available.

A Break from Tradition

A third important historical image of short-term psychotherapy arises from the community mental health movement of the 1960s. Many citizens in that era questioned the values of the establishment and the authority of traditional institutions. A good number of them disdained paying high prices for compassion in the form of private psychotherapy. As a result, free clinics sprang up, often manned by volunteers and paraprofessionals. Deinstitutionalization and the Community Mental Health Act spurred the creation and growth of numerous community mental health centers. Seeking mental health services began to lose its stigma. Psychological theories about helping and therapy began to expand. The humanists presented a whole new view of the therapeutic relationship—that warmth, empathy, and unconditional positive regard, not transference, were the essential ingredients of therapy. Existentialists added a spiritual dimension to psychotherapy. More people from the general population of working-class Americans demanded to be helped by mental health professionals and to participate in therapy.

A revolution was occurring in mental health care; increased emphasis was placed upon psychosocial factors in the community context, and the psychiatrist's therapeutic responsibility to the total population was stressed publicly for the first time. Government funding was available to develop therapeutic techniques to treat "the collectivity." The community was the patient. Of course, such an expansive mission meant there was a need for a greater number of psychiatrists and medical personnel. But there were not enough psychiatrists to go around, so others had to fill in. On the whole, the community health movement meant a gain for the people, and it was the first time that the status of long-term therapy was challenged. Traditional psychoanalytic therapists were threatened with losing their unique power, prestige, and status.

During this period, talk of a psychiatrist "shortage" and "supervision" of those other professionals who took up the slack it created served to protect the image of long-term psychotherapy and psychiatrists as superior. The "shortage of psychiatrists" is an image that permeates the literature on the community mental health movement. It became permissible to use other mental health professionals to treat the mentally ill because it was not possible to achieve the ideal doctor-patient ratio. Although there was no shortage of psychiatrists in the large urban areas or in private practice, the shortage was acute in community psychiatry.

This shortage meant that psychiatrists would have to work in teams with other professionals and even with qualified laypersons. This was permissible as long as these individuals stayed in ancillary roles and were adequately supervised by psychiatrists. And to meet the increasing demand, more and more people joined the ranks of the helping professions. Despite the psychoanalytic psychiatric community's attempt to protect their turf by referring to an overall psychiatrist "shortage," the image of the therapist diversified. The therapist was no longer limited to the realm of the Freudian psychiatrist-psychoanalyst. Therapists could now be social workers, psychologists, alcohol counselors—even paraprofessionals. Some research has indicated that paraprofessionals achieved the same results as experienced therapists.

As psychiatric elitism began to decline, long-term psychiatrists fought back. When other mental health professionals tried to break free of psychiatrists' oversight, the psychiatric community managed to portray them as professionals who possessed basic clinical skills but lacked rigorous medical training. Psychoanalysts in private practice were touted as the "best" mental health professional.

Allowing paraprofessionals into clinical settings under the supervision of psychiatrists did not work out as well as the psychiatric profession had thought it would. Unfortunate complications resulted. The number of college graduates pursuing a career in mental health care increased dramatically, flooding the market. Furthermore, many of these new professionals did not remain in community work but chose to begin their own private practice. As a result, the rivalry between psychiatrists and nonmedical practitioners deepened. Nonmedical practitioners believed they had the right to practice psychotherapy independently, without interference from psychiatrists.

In the end, psychiatry was not able to preserve its dominance over the practice of psychotherapy. Long-term therapy was no longer the only type of therapy practiced. But psychiatry still clung to its illusion of superiority by rationalizing that a lack of properly trained personnel and scarce financial resources were the reasons why everyone could not participate in long-term therapy.

By the 1970s, behaviorism, cognitive therapy, and humanist existentialism added to the diversity of therapists. The image of the behaviorist—B. F. Skinner in his white coat with his white rats and pigeons and his child in her giant Skinner box—sprang into the public's awareness. The image of the humanist-existential therapist was embodied in Carl Rogers, exuding unconditional positive regard for his patients, and Fritz Perls, the man from Esalon, unfettered in the world of Gestalt encounter groups.

Despite this increased diversity, the image of the Freudian analyst was still held in the highest esteem, but it did begin to diminish. Nontraditional mental health professionals still had less prestige and lower status than the Freudian doctor, who stressed his position as the supervisor of all other mental health professionals.

Language

Words and images are the building blocks with which we construct our understanding of the world. Language reflects and perpetuates our values and evokes images and feelings in our minds, both conscious and unconscious. Language shapes and conditions our belief systems. Language, both verbal and nonverbal, also provides the mental framework with which we view the psychotherapeutic relationship, the psychotherapist, and the patient.

Nonverbal images of the Freudian master aside, the written and spoken word have also perpetuated the myth of the superiority of long-term therapies. It is no coincidence that the language of long-term therapy is labyrinthine, flowery, and obscure. This complex rhetoric adds to the mystery of psychoanalysis. Theodore Reik calls this professional vocabulary "psychoanalese." He discusses how psychiatrists developed technical terms for well-known symptoms, clinical cases, and certain typical situations and emotional states in order to communicate with one another effectively and efficiently. An analyst himself, Reik comments on how this professional language composed of obscure Greek and Latin, purportedly a tool for uncovering unconscious processes, serves to underscore the belief that long-term therapy is superior:

> You open a new analytic book and you read "The impulse to coprophagia, which certainly has an erogenous source (representing an attempt to stimulate the erogenous zone of the mouth with the same pleasurable substance that previously stimulated the erogenous zone of the rectum), simultaneously represents an attempt to reestablish the threatened narcissistic equilibrium; that

which has been eliminated must be re-introjected." Such a sentence parades before the reader like an armored division. Believe me, there is less in it than meets the eye. You read page after page of formalizing, verbalizing sentences, but the dry terms refuse to come to life. What emerges is not an insight into human nature, but into the jargon of specialists which, as Justice Holmes once remarked, "implies a kind of snobism."

The language of most short-term therapy is far less cryptic. Terms such as *baseline, cognitive restructuring,* and *interpersonal therapy* are far less enigmatic than the mixture of Greek and Latin common in psychoanalytic discourse.

Even "short-term" connotes therapy whose normal, expected course has been abbreviated. Naturally, short-term therapists describe their work in positive terms. But long-term therapists use rhetoric that connotes an air of reserve and even condescension. They use metaphors that clearly place brief work in an inferior position to long-term work. Long-term therapists equate short-term therapy with the temporary amelioration of symptoms—a Band-Aid that covers over a festering wound without cleaning it out. If the poisons left behind become more deeply ingrained in the system, they believe, the infection could ultimately result in the demise of the entire organism.

This bias is present in the language used to describe the behavior of both research subjects and patients who stay in therapy for a short time. As stated previously, there may be a variety of reasons why people leave therapy after only a few sessions. Labeling these persons as premature terminators, treatment failures, or dropouts clearly implies that one session—or less than a long-term stint—is not psychotherapy.

But why isn't it? How did we as mental health professionals arrive at such a conclusion, and how did it come to be generally accepted, without question, in the literature? This is an example of long-term bias.

Training

Few if any students of psychotherapy are taught to "think epidemi-ologically." Students are given in-depth instruction in how to inter-act with and treat individual patients, but they are taught little to nothing about the behavior of the broader populations they will be dealing with and even less about the psychotherapy delivery system.

Our perspectives on psychotherapy are deeply affected by what master therapists teach their pupils. Graduate students aspire to be supervised by seasoned clinicians who have years of private practice experience. As discussed in Chapter Five, these veteran clinicians are most susceptible to the clinician's illusion, or the belief that most patients in therapy are in long-term therapy. These highly sought after role models shape their pupils' attitudes, expectations, and future behavior.

The model most commonly endorsed by psychotherapy super-visors remains psychodynamic treatment. The notions that it is good to keep patients in psychotherapy for relatively long periods and that a patient must attend a specific number of sessions in order to "really" be in therapy and benefit from it is passed down from supervisor to student.

So the notion of the superiority of long-term therapy over short-term therapy continues to be reinforced, although not to the degree it was in the past. It is beginning to lose its grip on the field. The dominance of long-term therapy has recently been challenged more intensely than ever before. Why has this challenge intensi-fied? Of course, changing sociocultural and economic conditions are factors. If long-term bias was sustained partly as a result of sociological forces, I say these outside forces can also play a role in its decline.

Major Concerns of Different Groups

The pressure is on to understand how outside forces—payers, insur-ers, and public demand—are interacting with internal forces within the mental health care community. Those who pay for psychotherapy are demanding a change from inefficient practices to cost-effective yet caring approaches. Various external factors shape these calls for change. Social policy dictates a need for specific products. Research, writing, and professional activities that are "politically correct" gain support. What is financed is what survives. All this has translated into an increased emphasis on short-term psychotherapy. Consequently, activities that support short-term work are increasingly held in high regard.

What pattern of interrelationships among patients, providers, and payers has made the growth of managed care possible? What are today's health care dynamics? First, patients, providers, and payers each have their own interests, concerns, and needs; these are sometimes compatible, sometimes clashing, and sometimes complementary. We can begin by identifying the needs, wants, and concerns of each group.

Patients

What do patients want? They want universal, comprehensive, secure, fair, high-quality, efficient, and affordable mental health care. Patient motivations for therapy include

- A severe mental illness; the inability to function without help

- A temporary disability or crisis

- Dependency; wanting someone to take over

- A need for a substitute for religion

- A desire for personal growth; healthy self-interest

- Narcissism

Patients want access to therapies that help them handle their emotional problems, obtain advice, promote personal growth, enrich their psychological well-being, and even acquire spiritual wisdom. In short, they want not only medically necessary services but also psychotherapy that is an avenue to the hidden positive forces that operate within themselves and society. They want access, affordability, quality care, and quantity care, as well as fulfillment of their spiritual self and economic potential.

Despite these grandiose expectations, according to Gallup polls patients are worried that they will not be able to afford health care, that they will not be able to get it when they need it, that their employers will stop providing their health care insurance, and that their wages will not be increased because health care costs are so high.

Professionals

Professionals want to care for their patients, earn a better-than-average income, and enjoy the secondary gains of prestige and autonomy that come with working in the helping professions. Of course, there is much variation among providers' motivations for becoming a therapist. Ranging from the altruistic to the self-serving, these motivations include

- Altruism or a desire to help others

- A substitute for a religious vocation (a secular priesthood)

- Involvement in the creative transformation of others

- A need to provide succor and nurturance

- Prestige and status

- Power and control over others

- Economic self-interest

- An intent to swindle people (for an aberrant few)

Providers are concerned about maintaining their autonomy and protecting their professional status and income. They want recognition of the importance of the work they perform as well as fulfillment of their compassionate and spiritual self. They worry that they will be called upon to demonstrate the effectiveness of their treatments.

Payers

What do payers want? A motley group consisting of patients, governments, insurers, and employers, payers want their insureds to have access to high-quality, cost-effective, medically necessary mental health care. They also want the care they pay for to represent the best possible return on their investment. While all payers have common goals and concerns, they also play a number of different roles. For example, insurance companies want to satisfy their customers or policyholders, but they also want to make a profit! They worry about "moral hazard"—if the benefits they offer are too generous, too much discretionary care will bankrupt them. Employers want healthy employees, to enhance productivity. The government wants to function in the best interests of citizens and to enhance public health. Individuals want the best care for the fewest dollars. Customers want more care, but insurance companies want less care.

Patient-Provider-Payer Interactions

Tension exists within the government-patient-payer dynamic. Those who want socialized medicine fight with those who want corporate medicine. For some it is important to maintain good relationships with various special interest groups (including citizens), whose needs may conflict with those of patients (for example, doctors, drug companies, insurance conglomerates). Not only do each of these groups have their own needs, wants, and concerns, each group has its own perceptions of itself and of other groups. These are colored by the group's needs, wants, and concerns.

So an endless array of possible permutations and combinations of interactions exists among patients, providers, and payers. Additionally, the perceptions and alliances of these groups shift over time and in response to necessity and convenience. Interactions among them caused many of the problems that precipitated the current health care crisis. But the same interactive triangle possesses potential solutions to those problems. If these groups had been able to form constructive alliances, work out their differences, and arrive at win-win solutions, managed care most likely would not have emerged.

The mental health system is faced with a number of problems that we all need to solve constructively. We need to improve the system by working together to control the accessibility, quality, and cost of our mental health care services. We can begin by trying to find out how the following sociological conditions are affecting the evolution of modern psychotherapy.

The Importance of Psychotherapy in American Society

Psychotherapy has become an influential American institution. We now know that it is part of our social fabric. Over the past fifty years, this personal, private, confidential enterprise has provided services that are vital and indispensable to our current way of life. Considering the fact that modern psychotherapy was not even invented until the second half of the nineteenth century, its growth has been amazingly rapid and pervasive. Its domain of influence has expanded into political and legal institutions, health care, economics, morality, philosophy, family structures, and work environments.

The Growth of Psychological and Social Problems

A look at the DSM-IV diagnoses reveals that more and more social-psychological problems are being identified as valid subjects of psychotherapy. If we consider V codes (minor mental health conditions) and adjustment disorders to be "problems in living," then 30.2 percent of mental health visits pertain to difficulties with a social as well as psychological cause. The reasons for outpatient visits in 1988 were as follows:

- 24.8 percent were for depression

- 17.7 percent were for V codes

- 14.2 percent were for anxiety disorders

- 12.5 percent were for adjustment disorders

- 8.5 percent were for childhood disorders and mental retardation

- 6.5 percent were for schizophrenia

- 6.1 percent were for alcohol or substance abuse

- 5.0 percent were for bipolar disorder

- 4.8 were for other disorders

Furthermore, if we consider medications as a form of therapy intended to change uncomfortable states and deal with very specific types of problems, mental health treatment is even more acceptable in our society than ever before as a way of dealing with very specific types of problems in living. Of the millions of psychotropic medications purchased by consumers in a recent year,

- 56.7 percent were anxiolytics, or sedative hypnotics

- 29.4 percent were antidepressants

- 13.7 percent were antipsychotics

- 2.6 percent were stimulants

- 2.0 percent were lithium

(The total exceeds 100 percent because preparations that include more than one type of medication are counted under each subtype.)

Psychotherapy Literature

A walk through any bookstore reveals the faith people have in the helping professions. The shelves are well stocked with a huge variety of titles, on topics ranging from Freudian psychoanalysis to New Age spirituality. The sales of psychotherapy, self-help, and pop psychology books topped a billion dollars in 1994, testifying to the value Americans place on seeking guidance in our emotional lives.

Unfortunately, it is difficult to discriminate between pop therapies and legitimate therapies. While the trendy codependency literature shares space with empirically based books about cognitive therapy, it is difficult for the public to gauge which books contain information about medically sound and necessary treatment and which contain folklore and unproven assumptions masked as treatment. Such faddish therapy advises women that they love too much or too little and tells men they suffer from a fear of commitment and that they need to get in touch with their feelings. Many books offer unsubstantiated advice and flimsy logic about the right and wrong way to behave in our relationships with friends, family, spouses, and business.

Pop therapies containing a kernel of valid psychotherapeutic theory strongly shape Americans' self-images and mores. Pop psychology has influenced our beliefs about how families ought to be structured, stabilized, organized, regarded, reconstructed in our memories, and responded and related to. As serious professionals, we have all had to deal with the repercussions of how trendy psychotherapies have influenced our patients' beliefs and behaviors.

Many new patients inform me that they want to rid themselves of their "codependency" or to understand how coming from one of the 96 percent of families that are extremely dysfunctional has affected them. The incest survivor movement is still a strong influence on many patients. Although the directives of self-help gurus have come under attack from the mental health profession, the reputation of psychotherapy has suffered through guilt by association. Misguided therapists have validated false memories, resulting in irrevocably damaged families who maintain a cynical bitterness toward one another for years. Women have been made to feel that their desire for interdependency is a sick need for codependency.

Stories that were previously reserved for the sanctity of the therapeutic relationship are now played out publicly, even on TV. For example, the entire nation is privy to the plight of Marc Pendergrast, a father accused of incest by his two daughters. His case was widely publicized on TV and in the tabloid press. In his own defense he has indicted his daughters' therapists, who used nonscientific treatment approaches that allegedly resulted in false memory syndrome. His book, *Victims of Memory*, ends with an emotional outpouring in a highly personal letter to his estranged daughters.

Talk show hosts such as Oprah and Sally Jesse Raphael are now purveyors of pop psychoeducation. It is not unusual to hear guests discuss their phobias, anxieties, eating disorders, or other psychological disorders and then have their therapists appear on stage and advise them—and the American public—on how to solve their problems. More and more people are finding it acceptable to reveal their innermost secrets in public, and more and more essentially normal behaviors are considered "psychological problems."

Economic Impact

Who pays the annual U.S. mental health care bill of approximately $4.2 billion? The payers are as follows:

- 45.4 percent is paid by patients, out of pocket.

- 26.1 percent is paid by private insurance.

- 16.5 percent is paid by Medicaid.

- 2.7 percent is paid by Medicare.

- 9.3 percent is paid by others.

These figures constitute a conservative estimate based on reported national statistics. We have no way of knowing how many episodes of psychotherapy are not counted in national data bases because patients do not want any trace of their contact recorded or because the therapy is conducted by nonlicensed therapists who do not participate in mainstream medical reporting.

The economic impact of psychotherapy is even greater if we factor in the fifteen million persons who annually purchase a psychotropic medication, for a total cost of $1.6 billion, or 7.1 percent of all outpatient drug expenditures. These drugs are paid for as follows:

- 56.7 percent are paid for out of pocket

- 27.6 percent are paid for by private insurance

- 10.3 percent are paid for by Medicaid

- 5.4 percent are paid for by others

Payers are worried—what else will they have to pay for? Could the expansion of mental health services keep escalating, with no way to control them? A look at the expansion of psychotherapists only adds to their concerns.

Increasing Numbers of Therapists

The number of Americans embracing the helping professions as a career is virtually exploding! Stuart Kirk and Herb Kutchins, authors of *The Selling of DSM*, say that we are medicalizing deviance and that mental health care is now a growth industry. Every year, thousands more mental health providers are licensed. Kirk and Kutchins point out that from 1975 to 1990 there was an increase in the number of psychiatrists from 26,000 to 36,000, an increase in clinical psychologists from 15,000 to 42,000, and an increase in clinical social workers from 15,000 to 80,000, for a total of 102,000 new practitioners in just these three professions. In addition, marriage and family counselors increased from 6,000 to 40,000 in this period. (There is some overlap here, however, as psychiatrists, psychologists, and social workers can also function as family counselors.)

Today there are 149,000 members of the American Psychological Association, with 70,000 at the doctoral level and 79,000 at the master's level. In 1995, membership in the American Psychiatric Association reached 40,000, which represents 70 percent of the total 52,000 psychiatrists in the United States. In 1988, the National Association of Social Workers had 116,296 members, both bachelor's-level and master's-level social workers. By 1995 that membership had grown to 152,000. Approximately 100,000 are master's-level practitioners. Numerous clergy, chemical dependency counselors, nurses, and other psychotherapists also practice. The growth of the mental health professions continues.

Psychotherapy and Society: What's Going On?

Something is going on here, but what? Just for a moment, pretend you are a sociologist. How do you make sense out of this emerging mental health subculture? If you were a consultant asked to help solve the health care crisis—or at least the mental health care crisis—how would you proceed, given these conditions? It is becoming quite apparent that psychotherapy is a big business!

Payers' Questions

Payers have tried to better understand providers by asking them to answer the following questions. The answers the payers received were often not to their liking, however.

Question: Why have the number of psychotherapies and the number of problems and conditions for which psychotherapy is sought reached an all-time high?

Answer: Mental health professionals have not reached consensus on this issue. Some say the expansion is legitimate and due to increased sensitivity, improved methods of detection, and better mental health care in general. Critics say the expansion is a result of people's wanting to earn an easy living helping others or entering the field for mercenary reasons.

Question: Why do people use psychotherapy? The reasons seem to run the gamut from the need to manage serious mental illness to a search for existential meaning to the acquisition of some pop image. *Answer:* Psychotherapy is an essential treatment that should be included in any health care benefit package. Psychotherapeutic interventions produce happier, better individuals, which, in turn, produces a happier, better society.

Question: How can we discriminate between necessary care, discretionary care, and abuse? Can clinical practice parameters be developed for mental health treatments like the standards, guidelines, and algorithms developed by medical doctors for medical treatments? Can standards for length of treatment be developed? For example, it is possible to estimate how many hospital days will be necessary for a case of appendicitis; can an amount of time be estimated for a treatment for depression? *Answer:* Discriminating between discretionary care and necessary care is difficult. It's best to leave this to the experts. Furthermore, mental health professionals balk at the prospect of finding objective, measurable, external means of demonstrating the effectiveness of the care they offer. It is too difficult a task. Sacred confidentiality is a barrier to such activities, but patients worry that information about their treatment may fall into the wrong hands or be misused. Many therapists continue to insist that long-term psychotherapy is an absolutely essential treatment and want a more generous long-term benefit.

Question: Can we distinguish between pop therapy quacks and legitimate professionals?

Answer: Pop psychotherapy is growing in popularity among consumers and within the media, so it is sometimes difficult for the consumer to differentiate between effective and ineffective therapy and competent and incompetent therapists. If only select professions and professionals are allowed to practice, it would solve the problem. Different professions are constantly lobbying for more power.

Question: Can standards of fair payment for sessions of psychotherapy be determined, as has been done for general medical treatments? Most of the time (though not always) the same medical treatment brings in the same fee, as determined by the Diagnostic Review Group (DRG) for inpatient procedures and the Resource-Based Relative Value Scale (RBRVS) for outpatient procedures. Why does the provider's profession rather than the procedure determine the fee? In other words, why do psychologists get so much more than social workers for a session of therapy?
Answer: Like everyone else, psychotherapists fight for the highest pay possible. Different disciplines require different knowledge bases and training. The more highly educated professionals should receive more money.

Question: Why is there interdisciplinary conflict among mental health professionals? This conflict does not seem to be based on improving the quality of care; rather, it seems to be centered around turf wars and therapists' desire to secure greater income and promote their professional well-being, not that of their patients. Mental health professionals do not seem to be interested in policing their ranks to protect the public from quacks practicing pop psychotherapy.
Answer: Different disciplines require different knowledge bases and training. The more highly educated are better able to perform psychotherapy, although there is no empirical evidence to prove this.

Question: Research shows that a provider's clinical behavior can be affected by the profit motive. Public scandals have tarnished the image of therapists, showing that some professionals are clearly not above engaging in criminal swindles. Shouldn't there be outside forces regulating payments?

Answer: No. Trust your professionals. They need autonomy.

Confidence and public trust in the authority of mental health professionals has clearly eroded. Discouraged, payers have begun to resent these professionals. Objective, measurable information about psychotherapy remains elusive. Reasonable questions are not getting reasonable answers. Mental health professionals appear to be a self-serving lot, especially those with the attitude that nonprofessionals should not question their judgment.

An article in the *Family Therapy Networker* eloquently summed up the situation: "The therapeutic community has brought its current woes upon itself by its amazing failure to provide decent explanations, let alone measures of cost and outcome accountability, for its treatment methods." Therapists have been "held to almost no objectively measurable, external standards for deciding what is wrong with the client, what to do about it, how long it should take to do, when it should be considered done, and how anybody knows if it is done."

Payer suspicions that some providers are motivated by greed and act in their own best interests rather than their patients' have been confirmed. Unfortunately, as a result these suspicions have extended over the entire field of mental health. Some payers believe the health care system has become so unmanageable that the only way to deal with it is to find a consultant or institution to mediate between the forces involved in delivering care.

The Managed Care Solution

Enter managed care into this world of psychotherapy, making an already incredibly complex system even more complex. Initially, as we discussed earlier, managed care was charged with the urgent task of changing the institutions of medicine and psychotherapy to make them more responsive to people's needs. In a society that holds the American dream of unlimited abundance in high regard, managed care is also a symbol of the sad reality that resources are limited. And managed care has to mediate among the sometimes competing, sometimes compatible, and sometimes complementary social forces involved in health care.

From its very inception, the promoters of managed care have had an eye for waste. Imbued with the stamp of approval from payers—with "right and might" on their side—they began their crusade to uncover excess, cut costs, and increase quality. In their quest to solve the health care crisis, they have seized the window of opportunity providers left wide open by allowing the conditions described above to develop and continue.

Among the earliest accomplishments of managed care were the following:

- Decreasing unnecessary hospitalizations

- Decreasing the number of days per hospital stay

- Demanding documented treatment plans

- Demanding that medical necessity be demonstrated

- Monitoring patient progress

- Measuring treatment outcomes

- Instituting case review procedures

The Impact of Managed Care on Psychotherapy

It was not long before managed care and many mental health providers developed an adversarial relationship. I consider this a national tragedy, since the relationship could have been a collaborative one. But the fact that managed care gained a foothold in the health system opened the door for the new age of corporate medicine.

Paul Starr, a well-known medical sociologist, says that the demise of small private practice began when a desire for "efficient, business-like management of health care . . . contributed to the collapse of barriers that traditionally prevented corporate control of health services," allowing the for-profit sector to compete for the available profits in health care. Managed care entrepreneurs, seeing a profit margin waiting to be exploited in mental health care, thus began the process of a corporate takeover of mental health care.

Again, not having a sociological view of psychotherapy means not having sociological wisdom to help us cope with these changes. Presently, millions of Americans receive their mental health care through some form of managed care. To appreciate the enormity of the numbers involved, consider the memberships of the largest managed behavioral health care companies in early 1995. Human Affairs Internationals has 14,500,000 enrollees; Medco has 14,100,000; Value Behavioral Health Care has 13,159,000; Green Spring has 10,089,000. Others who have less than ten million but more than two million include Health Management Strategies, United Behavioral Systems, First Mental Health, MCC Behavioral Care, US Behavioral Care, Foundation Psychcare, Family Enterprises, and Managed Health Network. These large corporations know that mental health care is big business, and they are trying to corner the market.

If managed care functioned only as a mediator, taking a nominal fee for its work, it could be an effective regulator of health care. Instead, managed care has also become a heavy consumer of health care dollars, commandeering a big share of the pool of limited resources. Thus the corporatization of health care, originally touted as a solution to the nation's health care problems, is now part of the problem. Those who compete for health care resources—patients, payers, and providers—have no choice but to fight over the same limited pie. How will these resources be shared among the various parties involved? The corporation is beginning to take a giant's share.

What will happen next? We need to think globally about the situation. A sociological view can be helpful. We can use sociological information, like good social scientists, to understand, explain, predict, and even gain some modicum of control over the system we are observing. By understanding the dynamics of what is transpiring, we can act constructively to effect change.

An important component of a contemporary "sociology of psychotherapy" would be a description and analysis of how psychotherapy, managed care, and society act reciprocally upon one another, as illustrated in Figure 7.1.

In this complex health care environment, it will be difficult for these divergent forces to come together and interact in a way that will be productive for all concerned. But the task is not impossible. We must understand the interaction depicted in Figure 7.1 in order to make wise policy decisions that will lead us to an improved mental health system.

If we want to have control over the evolution of psychotherapy, actively shape its future, make wise policy decisions, and promote effective interactions that bring mutual benefit to all, then we need to grasp "the big picture," not only within the field of psychotherapy but also from without. We need to understand psychotherapy from a sociological perspective.

Figure 7.1. Interaction of society, managed care, and psychotherapy.

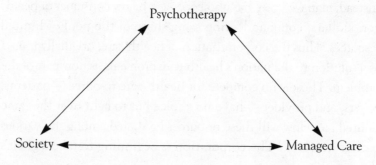

Notes

p. 159, *In the same way:* Cushman, P. (1992). Psychotherapy to 1992: A historically situated interpretation. In D. Freidheim, (Ed.), *History of psychotherapy* (p. 21). Washington, DC: American Psychological Association.

p. 161, *The origins of short-term therapy:* Koss, M., & Butcher, J. (1990). Research on brief psychotherapy. In A. E. Bergen & S. L. Garfield (Eds.), *Handbook of psychotherapy research* (pp. 627–670). New York: Wiley; Cushman, P. (1992). Psychotherapy to 1992: A historically situated interpretation. In D. Freidheim (Ed.), *History of psychotherapy* (p. 21). Washington, DC: American Psychological Association.

p. 161, *Estimating that nearly 45 percent:* VandenBos, G. R., Cummings, N. A., & DeLeon, P. (1992). A century of psychotherapy: Economic and environmental influences. In D. Freidheim (Ed.), *History of psychotherapy* (pp. 65–102). Washington, DC: American Psychological Association.

p. 162, *A third important historical image:* Koss, M., & Butcher, J. (1990). Research on brief psychotherapy. In A. E. Bergen & S. L. Garfield (Eds.), *Handbook of psychotherapy research* (pp. 627–670). New York: Wiley; Bloom, B. L. (1984). *Community mental health: A general introduction* (2nd ed.). Monterey, CA: Brooks Cole; Bloom, B. L. (1990). Managing mental health services: Some comments for the overdue debate in psychology. *Community Mental Health Journal, 26,* 107–124.

p. 163, *Government funding was available:* Rubins, J. (1971). The community mental health movement in the United States today, circa 1970. Part I. *American Journal of Psychoanalysis, 31*(1), 69–79.

p. 163, *The "shortage of psychiatrists":* Rubins, J. (1971). The community mental health movement in the United States today, circa 1970: Part II. *American Journal of Psychoanalysis, 31*(2), 165–173.

p. 164, *Allowing paraprofessionals into clinical settings:* Rubins, J. (1971). The community mental health movement in the United States today, circa 1970: Part I. *American Journal of Psychoanalysis, 31*(1), 69–79; Rubins, J. (1971). The community mental health movement in the United States today, circa 1970: Part II. *American Journal of Psychoanalysis, 31*(2), 165–173.

p. 164, *By the 1970s, behaviorism:* Cushman, P. (1992). Psychotherapy to 1992: A historically situated interpretation. In D. Freidheim (Ed.), *History of psychotherapy* (p. 23). Washington, DC: American Psychological Association.

p. 165, *An analyst himself, Reik comments:* Reik, T. (1977). *Listening with the third ear* (pp. 442–443). New York: Jove Books.

p. 168, *What do patients want?* Firsheim, J. (1995, April). Picture alternative medicine in the mainstream. *Business and Health*, pp. 29–33.

p. 168, *Patients want access:* Navarro, V. (1993). *Dangerous to your health: Capitalism in health care.* New York: Monthly Review Press.

p. 170, *Providers are concerned:* ibid.

p. 170, *What do payers want?* ibid.

p. 171, *Considering the fact:* VandenBos, G., Cummings, N. A., DeLeon, P. (1992). A century of psychotherapy: Economic and environmental influences. In D. Freidheim (Ed.), *History of psychotherapy* (pp. 65–97). Washington, DC: American Psychological Association.

p. 172, *The reasons for outpatient visits in 1988:* Olfson, M., & Pincus, H. (1994). Measuring outpatient mental health care in the United States. *Health Affairs*, pp. 172–180.

p. 174, *For example, the entire nation:* Pendergrast, M. (1995). *Victims of memory.* Hinesburg, VT: Upper Access.

p. 175, *Stuart Kirk and Herb Kutchins:* Kirk, S., & Kutchins, H. (1992). *The selling of the DSM.* New York: Aldine De Gruyter.

p. 179, *An article in the* Family Therapy Networker: Wylie, M. S. (1994, March–April). Endangered species. *The Family Therapy Networker*, pp. 20–27, 30–33.

p. 181, *Paul Starr, a well-known medical sociologist:* Starr, P. (1982). *The social transformation of American medicine.* New York: Basic Books.

Part III

....

What Do We Need To Do?

8

Individual or Societal Ethic?

*The health of the people is really the foundation upon
which all their happiness and all their power as a state
depend.*

Benjamin Disraeli

*We should do everything that is reasonably beneficial,
not everything possible.*

Larry Churchill

Once upon a time there was a well, named Willie, who was
filled to the brim with clear, sparkling water. Underground
rivers and streams fed Willie. They, in turn, were nourished by
abundant rain that came from the clouds in the sky. Willie's water
was so bountiful that it often overflowed onto the ground, providing nourishment for nearby lush foliage and enchanting flowers.

One day Willie saw a group of people in the woods. Strolling up
to his edge, they asked if they could drink some of his water. Willie,
a very generous and giving well, smiled radiantly and replied enthu-
siastically, "Oh, yes, please, have as much as you want. Drink until
you can't drink any more. My water is delicious—and magic! Not
only will it quench your thirst, but if you feel sad, you will become
cheerful!"

The friends drank. Soon they felt lighthearted, had better insight, were better able to cope, and understood more. Their attitudes were positive.

They visited Willie every day, and eventually they moved to the forest so they could have as much water as frequently as they wanted. Willie, who was happiest when he made others happy, was delighted to help.

As word of the healing water spread, more and more people came to drink. More and more people moved into the woods.

"The more, the merrier," said Willie as he freely gave of his waters.

But one day Willie noticed that his water had stopped overflowing. It no longer reached his rim. The flowers and the foliage around him were thinning. People had to stretch further and further to reach his water.

Willie called the clouds and the sky and the underground rivers and streams together and told them he wanted to be full to the brim again.

The underground river said, "I am working as hard as I can, but so much water is being used it is impossible to keep the level as it was."

The underground spring told Willie, "Every day I have to leap a little higher to get the water to you. I am getting tired."

Willie turned to the sky and clouds, asking them to send rain. But the sky and clouds replied, "We cannot give you more without disturbing the rhythm of the entire woods. We would upset the insects and the birds and all the other creatures of the forest."

Saddened by this reality, Willie asked, "What should I do? I don't want to deprive anyone of my healing waters."

Clouds and sky and spring and stream all told Willie in unison, "These human beings must learn to share their water! These humans have it in their power to be intelligent and compassionate. Willie, you must tell them to face the challenge! They must find a way to solve their problem."

Willie felt uncomfortable. He loved being generous and felt privileged to be in the business of giving. Saying no and setting limits was hard for him.

The next morning, the original group who founded the town arrived for their morning drink. Willie said to them, "We are faced with a predicament. You must find a way to manage my water, or I will run dry. When only a few of you used it, there was plenty. Now, many want its benefits. You must remedy the problem. I can continue to supply what you demand, but that would mean that very soon there will not be enough for everyone. Or I can give much to a select few. Or you can find a way to share so that everyone can have some. The big question is, Who gets my water? Should everyone who wants it have it, or will just some receive it? If so, who? You must make the choice."

How Should Psychotherapy Be Distributed?

Willie is not alone in his worries. He faces a dilemma that is hardly unique today. At the heart of his concern is whether an individual or a group ethic should govern how his healing waters will be dispersed.

The question of whether a social or an individual ethic should prevail in how we distribute psychotherapy is at the heart of the wide array of concerns and controversies we have discussed thus far. But there are even more fundamental questions that we must address: Is psychotherapy a right or a privilege? Should it be distributed according to need, want, ability to pay, or some other criteria?

Finding the best way to distribute psychotherapy and other mental health benefits in the face of limited resources is a dilemma whose answer lies in the realm of ethics and bioethics. Ethics is the study of morals. Medical ethicist Edward Pelligrino points out that "bioethics is the interdisciplinary study of problems created by medical values and progress" and it "holds more hope for a better grounding of principles, rules, virtues, and moral psychology than any other field." The new relationships among corporate medicine, patients, providers, and payers makes it crucial to revise many of our outdated ethics.

Professional Codes

Each of the mental health profession's codes of ethics already pledges its members to work for the common good. Each includes a basic principle pertaining to social responsibility. For example, the ethical standards of the American Psychological Association state that psychologists must be aware of scientific responsibilities to the community where they work. They must strive toward mitigating human suffering and support laws and social policies that serve the interests of their patients and the public. The code of the American Psychiatric Association emphasizes the psychiatrist's fiduciary responsibility to individual patients but says little about stewardship of resources. The code of the National Association of Social Workers discusses the ethics of institutions but provides little in the way of concrete guidelines about how to achieve distributive justice.

So even though the codes of ethics of the various mental health disciplines give lip service to promoting social justice, they are more strongly oriented toward protecting the individual, especially within the bounds of the therapist-patient relationship, and they contain few specific directives or definite ideas about how to promote the social welfare. Our profession—and our society—simply do not have well-articulated, coherent policies about how to justly allocate health care, let alone mental health care.

As a result, we ration care by default. Finances serve as the real ration master. As K. Davis and D. Rowland point out, "without health insurance coverage or ready cash . . . individuals can be turned away." This is true even in emergencies, let alone for early or preventive care. Ironically, it is not always the very poor who cannot afford psychotherapy, since they often have Medicaid, but the working poor with no insurance or insurance with no mental health coverage or prohibitive copayments that prevent them from obtaining needed care.

According to our own self-imposed professional codes, we must promote a societal ethic. But, how? In order to explore these issues more fully, I will first define and describe the individual and societal ethic.

The Individual-Oriented Ethic

The individual-oriented ethic, or micro ethic, centers around two basic principles pertaining to the level of care a patient receives. The first is patient-centered beneficence, meaning that the provider's actions should benefit the patient. The second is patient autonomy, meaning that the patient's right to determine his or her course of treatment should be respected.

Traditionally, when we think of medical ethics we think of the doctor's allegiance to the individual. Ethical dilemmas are usually posed about such exotic dilemmas as which of several eligible individuals should receive an organ transplant, when should life supports be removed, and whether assisted suicide is moral.

So, too, in behavioral health care has ethics traditionally centered around individual rights. As discussed earlier, most ethical concerns and discussions in mental health care involve dilemmas about patient confidentiality, release of information, informed consent, precertification, utilization review, patient abandonment, dual relationships, conflicts of interest, sexual misadventures, and practicing out of one's areas of expertise.

When motivated by the individual ethic, providers protect the needs of their own patients over the nebulous needs of society. Little consideration is shown for the needs of the aggregate patient population. The reasoning behind this is that if each and every provider looks out for all of his or her own patients, in the long run "everything will work out for everybody." When acting from an individual ethic, mental health professionals generally assume that more is better—the more psychotherapy a therapist can get for each of his or her own patients, the better. Thus open-ended, long-term therapy is the gold standard of the individual ethic.

The Societal Ethic

The societal ethic, or macro ethic, also centers around two principles pertaining to level of patient care. The first is full beneficence, meaning that resources are used to do the most good. The second is justice, meaning that resources should be distributed in such a way that everyone has an equal opportunity to obtain health care.

From the perspective of the societal ethic, the individual good must be tempered by the common good. The overriding concern is to make the distribution of psychotherapy fair so everyone who is entitled to it has equal access. Providers who subscribe to a societal ethic assume that it is better to give some therapy to everyone than to give abundant therapy to a few. The underlying premise of the societal ethic is that maximizing care for each and every patient will increase consumption of limited services beyond what can be supplied and drive up costs beyond what people are willing and able to pay. So overuse and unnecessary use hurt everyone, because they deprive people of the opportunity to procure necessary care. A second concern is that if some patients consume large amounts of resources but receive only a minimal benefit while others who are denied resources would actually benefit more, there is an aggregate cost to society. Thus the most parsimonious, least intrusive, briefest therapy is the gold standard of the societal ethic.

Balancing the Individual-Oriented and Societal Ethics

Is it possible to strike a balance between the individual-oriented and the societal ethic? How deeply must any mental health profession be committed to advancing a societal ethic? After all, we are *professional* psychotherapists, ordinary people who earn our living by helping others, not saints or missionaries!

How much should we care if one person's psychoanalysis, paid for by insurance, costs a total of a quarter of a million dollars while hundreds of homeless schizophrenics receive no therapy at all? Is it our collective concern if one dysthymic patient has an insurance policy that pays for a few years of uncovering therapy while a poor patient can't even find a provider who accepts Medicaid and must wait several weeks to get treatment for major depression?

It is interesting that the health professions have raised their consciousness about the collective effects of unsatisfactory benefits within managed care plans. For example, mental health professional organizations have made it a matter of critical concern to protect patients who have been, in their opinion, shortchanged by not receiving the optimal number of therapy sessions, such as a woman who is awarded only ten sessions after she discovers she was molested as a child.

Traditionally, psychotherapists have not been trained to think in terms of a societal ethic. Why? It is easy to shove social problems to the back of our mind when we can satisfy our altruistic urges and gain immediate contentment guiding an individual to increased self-knowledge. The gratification that comes from sitting with our individual patients and watching them evolve allows us to avoid being in direct touch with the pain of the psychotic squatting on the floor of Grand Central, wrapped in plastic garbage bags tied with string; or the mother working two waitress jobs to make ends meet, frightened by her impulses to hurt her children, who has no insurance and lacks the know-how to access an already overburdened public mental health system; or the blue-collar father who is unable to make sense of his teenage daughter's suicide and cannot bring himself to inflict more stress on his family by incurring the financial hardship of a 50 percent copayment for individual therapy.

The Dual Role of Therapists

The degree to which we are concerned about social issues depends on how we conceptualize our role as therapists and our relationship to society. The mental health care community has not reached consensus about how much emphasis we should place on the societal versus the individual ethic. Most professional organizations devote some part of their organizational structure to promoting the common good and encourage their members to incorporate some pro bono work into their private practice. For example, the American Psychological Association's Public Interest Directorate promotes social causes such as gay rights, anti-sexism, and the welfare of the chronically mental ill. But most of the organized energy of practicing professionals has been focused on promoting an environment friendly to private practice and individual therapy (especially now, in an era of managed care).

Some believe that for a doctor to serve a dual role as gatekeeper and provider represents a conflict of interest. They ask how a provider can make wise rationing decisions when the custom of protecting the individual patient has been so firmly implanted in his or her psyche. Therapists tend to err in the direction of overcommitting resources to the individual patient. Also, providers are hardly economic experts, and they typically do not possess adequate accurate information to make the best choices.

Others believe that providers should play a role in determining how health care is allocated and that over the years simple custom has driven a wedge between the ethics of individual care and the ethics of justice. However, there is no real reason not to devise sensible guidelines that permit providers to play dual roles and be advocates for their patients and for society. If this tradition were institutionalized as part of our health care culture, few would really object.

In actuality, therapists already make rationing decisions in their own minds when they determine a patient can't be helped and terminate his or her therapy. Patients themselves should make the ultimate decision regarding whether or not they want to make a sacrifice for the good of society. After all, patients are members of society. Soldiers go into battle and die for the social good. Shouldn't a patient in need of an experimental or expensive bone marrow transplant that has a tiny chance of saving him at great medical cost be given the chance to decline if he knows that the resultant savings will be used to give others better care? Shouldn't psychotherapy patients be given a similar choice?

I personally have worked with terminally ill patients who have made just such decisions. One patient, suffering from leukemia, decided not to have more treatments, first and foremost because she was tired of fighting, but second because she did not feel that the heroic efforts doctors were willing to use to extend her life a few more months were worth it. Of course, the patient needs to be fully informed about the double agency of the provider. Providers must consider the welfare of both the individual patient and of society; when the interests of a patient and those of society are pitted against each other, the provider is placed in a conflict situation. When a circumstance of dual agency arises, patient and provider should discuss the issues of fairness relevant to the patient's situation. In reality, it is society's role to distribute health care justly. But those in the trenches must do the actual work of rationing care.

Regardless of whether we favor playing the advocate for the individual only or for both the individual and society, there is no doubt that along with the special privileges afforded medical practitioners by society comes a special responsibility to help society solve the problems related to distributing health care in a fair and equitable manner.

Because our work as mental health professionals is classified as medical, we are supported by societal institutions in a different way than is the CEO of Microsoft. Payment for our work has not followed the usual market trends. Third parties support our profession. Up until recently, we have not been on the same economic playing field as the mechanic that fixes our car. The medical professions are not subjected to the marketplace rules of supply and demand. To compensate society for this preferential treatment, we must find a way to put high standards of professional conduct into practice. And as the cost of the care we provide increases and the privileges we enjoy multiply our advantage, so does our social responsibility increase.

How can we as mental health professionals shift some of our energy from single-minded concern for the individual patient's welfare to concern for society? How can we foster social justice? How can we find a way to balance out these two ethical value systems? We can begin with the following series of steps.

The first step is to raise our own consciousness of societal needs. We can make the abstract concept of "societal good" more of a concrete reality. We can make it more real by looking at how the societal ethic affects individual people.

Needing, Wanting, Receiving: Elements of Care

If we look at individual cases in terms of whether a patient needs, wants, and receives psychotherapy, we will begin to see the interconnectedness between the system and the individual. So, let's look at a few basic types of patients.

Wants Much, Needs Much, Gets Much

Martha is a twenty-eight-year-old woman who suffered her first schizophrenic episode when she was twenty. Hospitalized twelve times, she must take Mellaril daily or she hears voices. Martha met her present therapist two years ago and immediately "clicked" with her. She is able to comply with treatment. As long as she sees her therapist once a week (more frequently in times of crisis) and attends bimonthly group therapy, she is able to maintain herself outside the hospital and live a decent life-style.

Martha is a patient who wants much therapy, needs much, and actually gets what she needs and wants. The match between need, want, and receive is "ideal" for the patient, the therapist, and society, provided there are enough resources to go around. High-quality, necessary care is used to help sick or disabled people achieve as much normality as possible.

Wants Much, Needs None, Gets Much

Mary is a thirty-two-year-old married female with some college education. She is covered by indemnity insurance. She wants psychotherapy because she believes she needs someone to talk to. She has attended weekly therapy for over three years. Her issues in therapy change depending upon her mood. She thinks therapy is a great help and sees herself continuing for another three or four years. Her therapist is satisfied with her progress and enjoys watching her grow emotionally.

Mary is a member of the "worried well," the stereotypical patient that so many payers themselves worry about. These are the kinds of patients who receive discretionary care. She wants much therapy and receives much therapy. In reality, it is not medically necessary.

Mary is also the kind of patient that therapists love to work with. She is young, attractive, intelligent, verbal, successful, and financially stable, and she carries comprehensive insurance. Her copayments do not stress her budget. Therapists, of course, find interactions with such patients to be easy and profitable.

Wants Much, Needs Much, Gets None

Joan is a thirty-two-year-old female who did not complete high school. She is hoping to get her GED someday. Her three children, ages two, nine, and twelve, are unsupported by their fathers. Struggling with how to be a good mother to them, she works two jobs.

She is depressed at times and wonders how she will manage to go on. She thinks about suicide at least five times a day, but she won't go through with it because she does not want her children to be orphans. She would like to talk with someone about how to survive in this world and how to find a suitable mate that will not take advantage of her. She began therapy at a community mental health center, but because her car broke down so often, she canceled so many appointments they finally told her they would not give her another. Her sessions were painfully slow, and she seldom knew what to say.

This patient needs and wants therapy but does not get any. The reasons are primarily financial. Her seeming lack of motivation is another complication that gets in the way of her obtaining good care. She is the kind of patient that many therapists dread working with. Part of her problem is related to her socioeconomic condition and social deprivation. Therapists are often at a loss as to how to intervene. These patients often fall through the cracks.

Wants None, Needs None, Gets None

John is stable and has no desire for psychological assistance. He believes that if he ever needed to seek help, he would. He has good mental health coverage through his employer.

This match between the individual's needs and wants and what he receives obviously represents an ideal situation, whether there are enough resources to go around or not.

Wants None, Needs None, Gets Much

George attends psychotherapy because his wife prodded him into it. His long-term therapist tells him that he has many issues that are troubling him at an unconscious level. The therapist insists that he belongs in long-term therapy in order to gain insight into unresolved childhood conflicts he is denying. George wants no treatment. In terms of medical necessity he needs little to none, as he suffers no functional impairment. But because of his wife's insistence and his therapist's belief that therapy is necessary because it will help him change his character structure, George stays in therapy and feels he cannot get out. He begins to wonder if there is something radically wrong with him. Even after two years, his therapist insists that he has a number of Oedipal issues that need to be resolved and interprets his desire to leave as resistance to dealing with these deep-seated conflicts.

George's discretionary use of health care resources are more for the benefit of his therapist and his wife than for himself. He is a type of patient that suffers from the iatrogenic effects of unnecessary treatment. His treatment not only hurts him but also harms society. Precious resources are being wasted, and someone else who goes without could benefit.

Wants None, Needs Much, Gets None

John refuses all forms of help. He is suspicious of all who talk with him. He is paranoid schizophrenic and lacks insight into his condition. He is homeless, stays to himself, and receives no assistance from the health care system. Since he has managed not to break any laws, he has never come in contact with authorities. He remains isolated and receives no help at all.

John represents the most vulnerable of all individuals in need of mental health care in our society. His type is growing in number.

· ·

Wants None, Needs Much, Gets Much

Ralph is a depressive with an alcohol problem. He does not see any need to receive mental health counseling or attend any self-help groups. He does not want to stop drinking but is under such pressure from his family that he sneaks drinks when they are not around. When he does not get treatment, he becomes angry and depressed. His family forces him to go to a psychologist weekly and to a psychiatrist monthly for medications.

· ·

Ralph is also a very vulnerable patient who needs mental health care to stay in the world and out of institutions. The difference between the quality of life and level of productivity Ralph enjoys and John's experience is Ralph's family support network and the insurance benefits that cover his care.

What Should We Do?

Step 1

The first step is to make the abstract concrete by classifying patients according to the care they want, need, and receive (as we have just done). This will help us identify potential and established inequities. Table 8.1 summarizes the basic combinations of needing, wanting, and receiving psychotherapy and gives a name to the groups they represent.

Of course, many more permutations and combinations of needing, wanting, and receiving care are possible. Some patients receive much care when they need some; others receive some care when they need much, and so on. The point here is to give ourselves a framework for talking about a social ethic of psychotherapy.

Table 8.1. Potential combinations of wanting, needing, and receiving psychotherapy.

Want	Need	Get	Category
Much	Much	Much	Optimal condition
Much	None	Much	"Worried well"
Much	Much	None	Aware, needy, deprived
Much	None	None	Not needy, frustrated
None	None	None	Optimal condition
None	None	Much	Involuntary, iatrogenic
None	Much	None	Unaware, needy, deprived
None	Much	Much	Involuntary, needy

Step 2

Now we can examine the relationship between wanting, needing, and receiving care in relation to patient-centered beneficence versus full beneficence or justice and overuse or underuse. Identifying these potential problem areas will allow us to consider the societal ethic.

The two overtreated groups are the worried well, who receive discretionary care, and involuntary patients, who do not want or need psychotherapy but get much (iatrogenic) treatment. Is this overuse at the expense of those who need psychotherapy but do not get it? Underuse is found among members of the "unaware, needy, deprived" group and the "involuntary needy." Of course, we cannot say with absolute certainty that maximizing George and Mary's care actually does deprive Joan and John of their fair share of psychotherapy. After all, there are numerous factors that enter into the vagaries of distribution, such as geography, provider availability, and so on. But we must keep in mind that whatever we do to the group, we do to the individual, since the individual is part of the group.

The individual and society come into conflict when an individual uses a disproportionate amount of health care without paying for it. Others are harmed, either financially or in the form of poor health, since they either have to pay for care out of pocket or are deprived of care altogether. If a person is unable to pay and psychotherapy is essential, it is the role of a compassionate society to take care of that individual.

Step 3

We can create a public data base to accumulate meaningful information about overutilization and underutilization. At present we do not have information about how many patients fit into these categories and how they affect one another in the aggregate. We simply do not have enough economic and outcome data, but this direction of inquiry can only prove fruitful if we are going to formulate a rational ethic for distributing psychotherapy and health care resources.

Step 4

We need to come to grips with the issue of whether health care, and therefore psychotherapy, is a right. Psychotherapy is part of the health care system, and thus it follows the same principles of distribution. If health care is a right, then anyone who needs it should have it. If health care is a privilege and an economic entity, then the marketplace should determine its distribution. Like the rest of American health care, psychotherapy is in the odd position of being neither a right nor a commodity totally determined by marketplace forces.

American society must commit itself to a moral position on health and mental health care. Necessary psychotherapy must be included within a comprehensive, universal health benefit. Until we do this "right thing," our mental health care system will remain in its present state of confusion and uncertainty, and we will continue to argue about these issues. We will continue to fight the brushfires as the entire forest burns.

Step 5

We must decide if therapists should play a dual role as protector of both society and individual patients. What happens if these roles conflict? Can we devise a sensible code to help us achieve a fair apportionment of psychotherapy and yet maintain the integrity of the individual ethic? If doctors act as agents of society, can a patient trust that they will act in his best interest? Of course this is possible. Just as it is possible to provide universal coverage to all members of a staff model HMO, provided it is managed efficiently and effectively, we can also manage to care for our entire population, if that is really our primary goal. We could set up a system for ethical decision making by establishing panels and boards of providers and patients and by getting input from those responsible for resolving ethical dilemmas.

Step 6

Since a surprisingly large segment of the population has *no* access to mental health care, how much energy should we invest in promoting fair and equitable distribution of psychotherapy among those who do have access? For example, does it make sense to mount huge lobbying efforts to protect those who already have a basic benefit package—even if it is through managed care—while doing little for those who have no benefits at all? How much effort should we spend protecting those who have some benefits, when we are neglecting the quiet needy who have minimal social power and even less money than the insured? We need to increase our compassion and fight for the rights of those who have no health care.

I would like to see more mental health professionals form and support groups similar to Physicians for a National Health Program, a coalition of physicians working toward the goal of covering "all Americans under a single comprehensive public insurance program without copayments or deductibles and with free choice of provider." Groups such as these have come forward with national health program proposals, complete with budgets, that make sense and appear to be workable.

Step 7

The original prepaid and early managed care companies—which had socialistic underpinnings—had the right idea, as we will see in

Chapter Nine. Managed care should decrease its for-profit orientation and increase its not-for-profit commitments. Savings should take the form of lower fees and cost savings should be turned back to patients in the form of lowered premiums! More people could then have more benefits.

Making a profit should not be as important as taking care of patients and managing the resources of the system so that all patients are well served. Such an ethic would require a major change in providers' and insurers' expectations concerning the "profitability" of health care.

Step 8

Patient and payer participation in decision making should be encouraged. Medical ethics should not be seen as the sole property of medical professionals. Patients should be part of the decision-making process regarding resource allocation. They should be aware of the payer's point of view and of their range of options, possible outcomes, and success rates. A number of bioethicists have proposed that patient groups should participate in medical-ethical decision making, perhaps as mini community mental health councils that meet with professionals to help them decide on resource allocation issues, such as how to justly distribute benefits, ration services, and use any savings. Such arrangements would increase the likelihood that justice is done.

Patients can be very sensitive to a social ethic. If they think everyone is working for the greater good and not their own self-interest, they can be a strong asset. I think back to the many patients in my HMO who would say, "Well doctor, I guess I can stop coming now. Although I enjoy talking to you in these sessions, I am much better now, and someone who felt like I did a month ago can better use your services than me!"

Step 9

Just as drug companies try to develop medications with the greatest social value, so too can mental health professionals concentrate on developing and using models of psychotherapy that will bear the most fruit and do the most good for the most people. Caution should be used in recommending open-ended approaches, and a reevaluation of long-term care should be undertaken.

Models That Help the Most People

Using cost-effective and humanitarian models of psychotherapy will promote a social ethic among psychotherapists. We need to rethink what characteristics we value in a model of psychotherapy. It may even be useful to classify models on the dimensions of "population ethic" and "individual ethic." It is only right that society should endorse values that promote a sense of universal altruism.

As far as long-term care is concerned, there are always going to be some people who will need it. But long-term care does not necessarily mean traditional long-term therapy. If society were to try to satisfy goals as ambitious as those of long-term therapy, how could every individual who wants or need it obtain it? There is simply not enough to go around. If everyone who entered psychotherapy went into long-term therapy, the cost would be enormous. Eventually the well would run dry.

We should not confuse brief therapy with therapy that cannot continue over a long period of time. Brief therapy can consist of intermittent therapy (discussed in the introduction). Developing models of therapy that promote a social ethic would be admirable. In a broad sense, the values of long-term therapy discussed in earlier chapters are more harmonious with the individual ethic and less compatible with a social ethic. The values of brief therapy are more conducive to a societal ethic.

Let's look at models of psychotherapy with values that are compatible with a societal ethic. Models that promote necessary and essential but cost-effective care. All of these models were developed in managed care settings or have been successfully used there. Although they are not all grounded in empirical data, many managed care settings are compiling outcomes data on their results.

Intermittent Brief Therapy Throughout the Life Cycle

A model of great importance for the future of psychotherapy is Intermittent Brief Psychotherapy Throughout the Life Cycle, devised by Nicholas Cummings, former CEO of Biodyne. This model could be a prototype for modern psychotherapy. It is like an umbrella under which other models of psychotherapy can be organized and integrated.

In Intermittent Psychotherapy Throughout the Life Cycle, the therapist's role is similar to that of a family doctor. Psychotherapy consists of a series of intermittent encounters designed to help the patient adjust to life's inevitable recurring crises and situations. Once the patient has received sufficient help, he or she stops seeing the therapist for regular sessions and returns only when necessary.

This model provides a framework for conducting "long-term psychotherapy in a short-term setting." In other words, patients get long-term care but not traditional long-term therapy. The notion that psychotherapy "cures" mental health problems, a tenet of traditional long-term psychotherapy, reinforces the view that all psychological problems are illnesses that successful therapy can rid the patient of. The intermittent model of psychotherapy does not subscribe to this view. Therapists do not keep patients in treatment until every conflict in the recess of the unconscious has been analyzed. Termination is not a difficult and painful process but merely a natural step that puts the patient on the path to independence.

This simple but comprehensive model is based on a life-span view of human development. It sees life as a series of typical and predictable developmental tasks and junctures. When patients encounter difficulties negotiating developmental milestones (for example, entering school or adulthood, becoming a parent, divorcing, confronting a midlife crisis, entering old age, and, ultimately, facing death) they may need assistance from a psychological family doctor. Therapy is indicated if and only if the individual needs help to learn more effective and adaptive ways of dealing with perceived threats. Once the patient masters the necessary tasks, she leaves therapy, to return only if more help is needed in adjusting to life situations.

Intermittent Group Therapy

Carl Zimet devised the Developmental Task and Crisis Group Therapy Model. Based on the same assumptions as Intermittent Individual Therapy, it expands the tenets of developmental stage theory and crisis intervention to a group therapy format. Persons who are struggling with similar life issues can join together and focus on resolving specific developmental tasks. Sharing age- and stage-related issues with similar persons reduces feelings of isolation and helps group members get through significant transitions throughout their life span.

Single Session Therapy

The briefest of the brief therapies is single session therapy. Its proponents do not claim that most psychological problems can be resolved in one session of therapy but that the therapist should make use of reality. Since so many patients present for only a single session, as our epidemiological data shows, it is best for the patient if the therapist acts as if every session is the only one. The first session makes a lasting impression on the patient and also sets the stage for future therapy. Single session therapists use the following techniques: identify the focal problem; formulate comments in ten words or less; be active; make interpretations tentatively; encourage the expression of affect; keep track of time; keep factual questions to a minimum; do not be overly concerned about the precipitating event; do not overestimate or underestimate the patient's ability; use psychoeducation; mobilize social supports; start a problem-solving process; and build in a follow-up plan. The therapist chooses the nature of the focus—intrapsychic, characterological, interpersonal, or systemic—and then selects appropriate interventions from among educational, behavioral, psychodynamic, systemic, experiential, and medical techniques.

Interpersonal-Developmental-Existential Therapy

Developed by Simon Budman and Alan Gurman at Harvard Community Health Care, the Interpersonal-Developmental-Existential (I-D-E) model of psychotherapy leads the therapist to conceptualize the client's problems as "core issues." The major themes under which clients' problems are categorized include interpersonal and existential losses, developmental lags, specific symptoms or habit disorder, interpersonal complaints, and personality disorders.

In order to arrive at an appropriate I-D-E focus for a particular patient, the therapist seeks information such as the following:

- Why is the patient seeking therapy?

- At what stage of development is the patient?

- What are the pertinent life-cycle issues facing the patient?

- Are any significant anniversaries taking place?

- What kinds of social support systems does the patient have?

- Are any chemical dependency problems present?

- Are any outside forces exerting pressure on the individual to come in for therapy?

- What have been the patient's responses to prior treatment?

- Does the patient want limited symptom relief, or other types of change?

The therapist uses eclectic methods to help the patient reach his goals, such as psychodynamic, behavioral, and hypnotic interventions; individual, group, and marital treatment formats; and between-session homework assignments, as needed.

Possibility Therapy

According to Steve Friedman and Margot Fangor, possibility therapy encourages the patient to use her own resources to identify and reach a well-specified goal. Adapting a wellness model deemphasizes pathology and diagnosis. Therapists use the following guiding principles in this model:

- Think small.

- Complicated situations do not require complicated solutions.

- Take the patient's resources seriously.

- Collaborate to create a context for change.

- Choose small, well-defined goals.

- Do just one thing differently.

- The patient contains the seeds of the solution.

- Change is inevitable.

- Help the patient form a supportive network.

- Maintain an optimistic stance about change.

Simple interventions are used first. The therapist centers on solutions, maintains a focus on the initial request, uses possibility language, stresses the patient's resources and strengths, reframes difficulties in developmental contexts, keeps up and communicates a sense of humor, and maintains an attitude that shows that the therapist is aware of the benign absurdity of life.

Pathogenic Belief Model

James Donovan, also from Harvard Community Health Care, developed the Pathogenic Belief Model of therapy. He asserts that a crippling self-belief, which stems from a long-standing attempt to solve unresolvable conflicts, perpetuates a negative pattern of interpersonal relationships. While this defense was useful for survival in childhood, it produces bad feelings in adulthood. The therapist helps the patient reframe the pathogenic belief and develop more productive self-constructions.

The three phases of therapy in this model are searching for the pathogenic belief, reversing the past trauma, and reframing the belief. No judgmental or confrontational events occur during this empathy-building process. Reframing the pathogenic belief, the key to successful treatment, is accomplished through the therapist's offering his or her self as an alternative object, increased self-awareness on the part of the patient, and support by the nontraumatic therapist-patient interactions. A successful outcome means the patient is able to suspend his or her unconscious guilt and is freer to conduct the business of life. The model is based on psychodynamic assumptions that fit into the structure of short-term work.

Models of Therapy for Specific Populations

Other effective models of brief therapy have been designed for specific presenting problems and populations.

Personality Disorders

Kurt Strosahl describes a group cognitive-behavioral treatment model used at Group Health Cooperative. The therapist teaches the patient to identify, challenge, and correct distorted beliefs that result in a dysfunctional life-style. A partial list of what members can learn in the model's fourteen group sessions include

- How to challenge the causes of dysfunctional behavior

- A basic cognitive model to help patients make changes in their thinking

- Behavioral skills to increase interpersonal effectiveness and conflict resolution

- Relapse prevention techniques and change mainte- nance skills.

Nearly 80 percent of patients using this method achieve at last one therapeutic objective. Thus, concrete, feasible, and practical guide- lines help patients achieve their goals.

Adolescents

Jerry Adams uses a model of therapy for adolescents and their fam- ilies in which the patient is allowed up to six visits to solve any crisis. Therapy mobilizes family members' coping responses, encour- aging them to find social supports to sustain any changes they make. Issues dealt with include parenting, stepparenting, attention deficit disorders, separation and divorce, chronic medical or psychosocial illness, enuresis, and encopresis.

The Chronic Mental Patient

Lou DeStefano and Karen Henault describe creative, flexible meth- ods of treating the chronic patient used at Community Health Care Plan of New Haven, Connecticut. If keeping seriously disturbed individuals in the community and out of long-term hospitals can be counted as a successful outcome, then they have treated a number of chronic patients quite effectively. They use rapid assessment, intermittent therapy, pharmacotherapy, and family and social involvement in treatment. Infrequent individual therapy, support- ive group therapy, and collaboration among mental health profes- sionals, medical providers, and family and community support systems produce a treatment environment that keeps seriously dis- turbed individuals integrated in the community.

Depression and Anxiety Disorders

Professionals know that persons suffering from depression and anx- iety disorders can be treated with a number of effective short-term models. The effectiveness of Aaron Beck's Cognitive Therapy of Depression and Anxiety and Klerman's Interpersonal Therapy (IPT) have undebatable empirical support.

Pediatrics

At the request of pediatricians in their managed care setting, Barbara Hermann and Mary Cofresi devised a pediatric mental health consultation model to help families who were in need of care but reluctant to pursue it. These families avoided care either because they feared a social stigma, were unable to afford the copayments, or could not obtain transportation. They were offered a consultation with a mental health provider. After dealing with the presenting problems, the mental health consultant met with the patient, the pediatrician, and other nonmedical providers. A two-session follow-up was then conducted. The patient could be referred for mental health treatment, referred to community services, or told no further intervention was needed. Outcome measures performed by the project originators showed that patient and pediatrician satisfaction was high.

The Elderly

Patricia Robinson offers a program at Group Health Cooperative of Puget Sound that integrates medical and behavioral care for the elderly. Outcome data from several such programs show that they have successfully facilitated changes in patients in the areas of medical compliance, networking, and decrease of subjective distress levels. A therapy group for elderly, depressed women was conducted at a New Haven staff model health maintenance organization. The group, held every other week, served as a source of support for aging women confronted with various diseases and family crises.

The Transtheoretical Model of Change

In search of effective methods for helping a large variety of people with a large variety of problems, some therapists and researchers have tried to integrate the effective techniques of various major models of psychotherapy and find the common denominators among them that could provide practical answers for clinicians.

James O. Prochaska, studying how people change, invented the Transtheoretical Model of Change. He says change happens in the following stages:

- Precontemplation, in which the individual does little to overcome his or her problem and is often labeled "resistant"

- Contemplation, in which the individual increases his or her cognitive, affective, and evaluative functioning about the problem

- Preparation, in which the individual shows a readiness to change and develops an action plan for how he or she will proceed

- Action, in which the individual acts from a sense of self-liberation

- Maintenance, in which the individual builds on each process to sustain change.

A therapist must recognize which stage of change the patient is in when he or she enters therapy, in order select the most appropriate intervention and maximize therapeutic gain. Clinicians can choose which interventions are most effective with confidence because research actually guides practice. Change is common to all types of therapies. Understanding such universal variables is a way to unite the common elements of psychotherapy and devise cost-effective care.

Using Intermittent Therapy and the Process of Change

The following case illustrates how a therapist can use the Intermittent Psychotherapy Throughout the Life Cycle and Stages of

Change models to guide, support, and significantly influence a patient throughout her life cycle.

Monique and Dr. Levy

When Dr. Levy first met Monique she was an adolescent, brought to therapy by her parents. Monique was failing in school and had become very withdrawn. The therapist intervened, using both individual and family therapy to help Monique deal with the stress associated with her parents' overprotectiveness. Monique formed a trusting relationship with Dr. Levy, and she learned to use new coping techniques.

Monique came in for ten weekly individual sessions. Dr. Levy chose to use James Donovan's model of "pathogenic belief," since Monique seemed receptive to this kind of therapeutic intervention and it seemed that her self-image needed improvement at an early age. Dr. Levy referred Monique to a therapy group composed of other adolescents with similar problems. Monique attended group weekly for twelve sessions. While Monique was in the group, Dr. Levy continued individual therapy with her once every three to four weeks. Within six months, Monique's problems had improved. Dr. Levy and she agreed that they no longer needed to meet in regular sessions. Monique knew she could return if she felt the need or desire to do so. Until she graduated from high school, Monique did reappear every two to three months to grapple with pathogenic beliefs.

Six years later, Monique married and had a child. She and her husband experienced severe marital discord. They consulted with Dr. Levy, who used cognitive behavior therapy to help the couple communicate better. Four years later, Monique found herself in major depression. She returned to her psychological family doctor, Dr. Levy, and he intervened with methods from Aaron Beck's cognitive therapy, IPT, and pharmacotherapy.

Some five years later, when Monique was forty-five, she again visited Dr. Levy (now sixty-five) and asked for help in mourning her father's death. Dr. Levy used Simon Budman and Alan Gurman's model, focusing on the loss. When her individual grief work was done, she entered a grief support group, where she gained even greater understanding. Much improved, Monique stopped seeing Dr. Levy, adding, "I'll call you if I need to. Thanks, Doc!"

When Monique turned forty-eight she saw Dr. Levy again. She wanted to change but she was not sure how to. Dr. Levy saw that she was in a stage of precontemplation and told her to call back when she knew what she wanted to change. After a few months, Monique arrived for a new appointment. She had decided to enroll in a doctoral program of studies.

When Monique turned fifty-two she wrote to Dr. Levy, "I've longed to be able to talk to you—but I just haven't been able to see my way clear for a trip at this time. After thinking about it, I decided to drop you a letter filling you in on this past year."

Monique asked Dr. Levy for advice about completing her dissertation. Just a short note and a few phone contacts put her back on track!

· ·

By envisioning psychotherapy as an intermittent event that occurs throughout the life cycle, Dr. Levy was free to use any permutation and combination of therapy models that were helpful to his patient. He was free to give Monique necessary and sufficient mental health care at crucial developmental points in her life or at times of increased stress, problems, crisis, or exacerbations of symptoms. In these types of models are contained the core characteristics of efficiency and efficacy that can help us support a societal ethic.

In 1988 I coined the phrase "HMO therapy." I pointed out that psychotherapy conducted at HMOs seemed to be evolving a treatment philosophy compatible with a social ethic because it held to certain core characteristics. Since then this list has grown. It deserves mention here.

Principles of HMO Psychotherapy

The first five traits are characteristic of all forms of short-term therapy and were mentioned earlier. The remaining characteristics were fostered by the values of the nonprofit, staff model HMO.

1. *Focused assessment*. Rapid, accurate assessment of patient needs in the here and now is an important component of HMO psychotherapy. The therapist accepts what the patient says at face value and does not interpret its meaning at a level that delays taking immediate helpful action. The clinician is not bogged down in theoretical constructs but must respond to the demands of real people in the real world and evaluate what interventions are "necessary and sufficient" in order to develop and execute an effective treatment plan.

2. *Pragmatic therapeutic alliance*. Since managed care therapists know that the therapeutic relationship accounts for a good percentage of change in therapy, a strong therapeutic alliance is rapidly established. The reality of limited time and resources are incorporated into their work. The therapist encourages autonomy and independence rather than transference and dependence. In this teamlike alliance, elements of consumerism are openly acknowledged. Patient satisfaction is considered an important ingredient of treatment success.

3. *Active, positive therapist*. The therapist's role is active, with an emphasis on fostering positivity and strength in the client. Structuring therapeutic contacts, the therapist recommends alternative interventions for the patient. The therapist involves significant others in the therapy process as needed. The therapist is authoritative but not authoritarian. His or her role might be described as that of an "expert consultant"; this demystifies the therapist's role in the patient's life.

4. *Clearly defined goals and responsibilities*. The responsibilities of patient and therapist are clearly articulated. A contract for spe-

cific, achievable goals is negotiated. The scheduling of sessions and the duration of treatment are agreed upon by the therapist and patient. The patient's responsibilities include, at a minimum, bringing relevant material to the sessions, completing extrasession assignments, and implementing behavioral change outside of therapeutic meetings. The therapist clearly defines his or her role in the life of the patient and acts as a mental health consultant and adviser, ready to offer the most current empirically based information and treatments for the patient.

5. *Developmental orientation*. People are seen from a life-span, developmental perspective, and the therapist realizes that people are most likely to seek out psychotherapy at points in their lives when they are experiencing increased levels of stress.

6. *Psychological family doctor or primary care orientation*. Once the psychotherapeutic relationship is established in an initial session, the psychotherapeutic dyad is seen as a continuous, intermittent interaction between the therapist and patient, one that can extend throughout the patient's life cycle. The psychotherapist sees himself in a role similar to that of a family doctor. The patient is treated in brief episodes as necessary over a long period.

7. *Medical-nonmedical provider collaboration*. The nonmedical mental health provider needs to relate to multiple types of medical providers. Two areas the nonmedical provider must be familiar with in order to provide effective psychotherapeutic interventions are behavioral medicine and psychopharmacology. The integration of behavioral and biomedical science has led to an increased need to apply behavior-modification methods to enhance prevention, diagnosis, treatment, and rehabilitation. Mental health professionals are now frequently asked to use psychotherapeutic interventions to help the medical patient comply with treatment, adjust to his or her medical condition, and cope with disability and death. As mental health care becomes better integrated into general health care, behavioral techniques that alleviate health-related problems will play an even more significant role in producing effective psychotherapy. Also,

communication with both primary care physicians and psychiatrists is essential to the integration of psychopharmacology and psychotherapy. Whether the therapist works in a staff model setting, where it is easy to interact with primary care physicians, or in a PPO, where contact is less accessible, communication between the medical doctor and the therapist can only enhance the patient's treatment.

8.   *Need and crisis intervention preparedness.* Prompt handling of emergencies is absolutely essential. The therapist knows that early access to psychotherapy can avoid exacerbated clinical problems and decrease the risk of overintensive therapeutic involvement.

9.   *Parsimonious and flexible use of interventions.* The therapist's first choice of interventions are those that are least extensive, least expensive, and least intrusive. Group therapy, psychoeducation, community resources, family intervention, and self-help groups are valued forms of treatment; they are not perceived to be merely ancillary aids to individual therapy. The therapist respects and recommends alternative treatment approaches. Self-help groups are seen as significant resources. The schedule of therapy—its frequency, length, and timing—are as cost-effective as possible.

10.   *Awareness of the need for review and evaluation.* The therapist is very willing to participate in quality assurance reviews and also initiates his or her own system of outcome research or participates in global management information systems. He or she recognizes that quality, cost, and utilization management are linked. Since the therapist is committed to delivering cost-effective therapy, data and feedback about practice habits are not viewed as a threat and are welcomed. The development of adequate management information systems to assess the outcomes of therapy is considered an integral part of the therapist's practice. Therapists believe that they need to have outcome measurements, and they use the data to document their own performance and the appropriateness of their procedures.

11.   *Outpatient treatment orientation.* Because it is seen as maximally intrusive, inpatient treatment is regarded as the course of last

resort. Every effort is made to maintain the patient in an outpatient capacity. The therapist strongly believes that a less restrictive environment is preferable to one that is overly intrusive.

12. *Knowledge of current research.* The managed care therapist must remain current on relevant psychotherapy research. Although practical limitations do not allow the therapist to be familiar with all the information available, his breadth of knowledge is deep enough to help him select the most effective therapeutic interventions based on empirical research.

Societal or Individual-Oriented Ethic?

It is difficult to balance individual and social needs to effect a fair distribution of psychotherapy. We suffer from a lack of accurate data and information about the clinical and economic outcomes of psychotherapy. But that does not mean we cannot start and make real progress right now! We have enough information to point us in the right direction. As Edward Pelligrino, the medical ethicist, says, health professionals should "become familiar with shifts in contemporary moral philosophy if they are to maintain a hand in restructuring the ethics of their profession. A continuing dialogue with moral philosophers is requisite to assure that clinicians do not lose the benefits of a rigorous and critical analysis of their ethical decisions."

As mental health professionals, we must decide how to promote a societal ethic. To draw on the resources of Willie the well, we will paraphrase his words: "We are faced with a predicament. We must find a way to manage psychotherapy, or we will run out of resources. We must choose how to remedy the problem. We can continue to supply upon demand. That means there may not be enough for everyone—which is true today. We can continue to give therapy to some. Or we can find a way to share it so that everyone can have some. The big question we must answer is, Who gets psychotherapy? Should everyone who wants it get it, or will just some receive it? If so, who? You must make the choice."

To help to solve the problem, Chapter Nine looks back in history at health care professionals who can serve as role models today. We will see how the history of managed care actually reflects the struggles of innovators grappling with the identical issues we are dealing with today. They achieved workable solutions; perhaps we can too.

Notes

p. 189, *Medical ethicist Edward Pelligrino points out:* Pelligrino, E. (1993). The metamorphosis of medical ethics. *Journal of the American Medical Association, 269*(9), 1158–1161.

p. 190, *As K. Davis and D. Rowland point out:* Davis, K., & Rowland, D. (1983). Health and society. *Milbank Quarterly, 61*(2), 21–49.

p. 192, *The societal ethic:* Veatch, R. (1990). DRGs and the ethical reallocation of resources. In N. F. McKenzie (Ed.), *The crisis in health care* (pp. 187–208). New York: Meridian; Meyer, C. (1993). The doctor as gatekeeper. *HMO Practice,. 7*(1), 12–14.

p. 203, *I would like to see:* Grumbach, K., Bodenheimer, T., Himmelstein, D. U., & Woolhandler, S. (1991). Liberal benefits, conservative spending. *Journal of the American Medical Association, 265*(19), 2549.

p. 206, *A model of great importance:* Cummings, N. (1991). Intermittent therapy throughout the life cycle. In C. S. Austad & W. H. Berman (Eds.), *Psychotherapy in managed health care: The optimal use of time and resources* (pp. 35–46). Washington, DC: American Psychological Association.

p. 207, *Carl Zimet devised:* Zimet, C. (1991). Developmental task and crisis groups: The application of group psychotherapy to maturational processes. *Psychotherapy, Research, and Practice, 16,* 2–8.

p. 207, *The briefest of the brief therapies:* Hoyt, M. F., Talmon, M., & Rosenbaum, R. (1990). Planned single session psychotherapy: An analysis of patient self-reports. In S. Budman, M. F. Hoyt, & S. Friedman (Eds.), *Casebook of brief psychotherapies*. New York: Guilford; Talmon, M. (1990). *Single session therapy*. San Francisco: Jossey-Bass.

p. 208, *Developed by Simon Budman:* Budman, S. H., & Gurman, A. S. (1988). *The theory and practice of brief psychotherapy.* New York: Guilford.

p. 209, *According to Steve Friedman and Margot Fangor:* Friedman, S., & Fangor, M. T. (1991). *Expanding therapeutic possibilities: Getting results in brief therapy.* Lexington, MA: Lexington Books.

p. 209, *James Donovan, also from Harvard Community Health Care:* Donovan, J. (1987). Brief dynamic psychotherapy: Toward a more comprehensive model. *Psychiatry, 50,* 167–183.

p. 210, *Kurt Strosahl describes:* Strosahl, K. (1991). Cognitive and behavioral treatment of the personality-disordered patient. In C. S. Austad & W. H. Berman (Eds.), *Psychotherapy in managed health care: The optimal use of time and resources* (pp. 185–202). Washington, DC: American Psychological Association.

p. 211, *Jerry Adams uses a model:* Adams, J. (1991). Family crisis intervention and psychosocial care for children and adolescents. In C. S. Austad & W. H. Berman (Eds.), *Psychotherapy in managed health care: The optimal use of time and resources* (pp. 111–126). Washington, DC: American Psychological Association.

p. 211, *Lou DeStefano and Karen Henault describe:* DeStefano, L., & Henault, K. (1991). The treatment of chronically mentally and emotionally disabled patients. In C. S. Austad & W. H. Berman (Eds.), *Psychotherapy in managed health care: The optimal use of time and resources* (pp. 138–152). Washington, DC: American Psychological Association.

p. 211, *Professionals know that persons suffering from depression:* Schulberg, H., & Scott, C. P. (1991). Depression in primary care: Treating depression with interpersonal psychotherapy. In C. S. Austad & W. H. Berman (Eds.), *Psychotherapy in managed health care: The optimal use of time and resources* (pp. 153–171). Washington, DC: American Psychological Association.

p. 212, *At the request of pediatricians in their managed care setting:* Hermann, B., & Cofresi, A. (1994, January 11). *The pediatric population.* Paper presented at the Group Health Institute of America, Miami Beach, Florida.

p. 212, *Patricia Robinson offers a program:* Robinson, P. (1994, January 11). *The elderly.* Paper presented at the Group Health Institute of America, Miami Beach, Florida.

p. 215, *In 1988 I coined the phrase:* Austad, C. S. (1993). Health care reform, managed mental health care, and short-term psychotherapy. In L. VandeCreek, S. Knapp, & T. L. Jackson (Eds.), *Innovations in clinical practice* (pp. 241–256). Sarasota, FL: Professionals Resource Press; Austad, C. S., & Hoyt, M. (1992). The managed care movement and the future of psychotherapy. *Psychotherapy,* 29(1), 109–118; Austad, C. S., Kisch, J., & DeStefano, L. (1989). The health maintenance organization: II. Implications for psychotherapy. *Psychotherapy,* 25(3), 449–454; Austad, C. S., & Berman, W. (1991). HMO psychotherapy. In C. S. Austad & W. H. Berman (Eds.), *Psychotherapy in managed health care: The optimal use of time and resources* (pp. 5–19). Washington, DC: American Psychological Association; Sederer, L. I., & St. Clair, L. (1990). Quality assurance and managed mental health care. *Psychiatric Clinics of North America, 13*(1), 89–97; Truscott, A. M. (1992). Cost and quality—Are they compatible? *HMO Practice,* 6(2), 3–10.

p. 219, *It is difficult to balance individual and social needs:* McGuire, D. (1990). [Foreword]. In N. F. McKenzie (Ed.), *The crisis in health care* (pp. 11–18). New York: Meridian; Meyer, C. (1993). The doctor as gatekeeper. *HMO Practice,* 7(1), 12–14; Luft, H. (1993). Health maintenance organizations and the rationing of health care. In N. F. McKenzie (Ed.), *The crisis in health care* (pp. 70–100). New York: Meridian.

p. 219, *As Edward Pelligrino, the medical ethicist:* Pelligrino, E. (1993). The metamorphosis of medical ethics. *Journal of the American Medical Association, 269*(9), 1158–1161.

9

Lessons from History

Every job is a self-portrait of the person who did it.
                                        Anonymous

You may not have been responsible for your heritage,
but you are responsible for your future.
                                        Anonymous

This and the following chapter highlight the leaders and clinicians who developed the staff model health maintenance organization (HMO) and made it what it is today. These health delivery
systems provide comprehensive medical care to diverse populations
of patients with a staff of salaried providers. In this chapter we will
look back in history to see how managed care came to be and what
it could have accomplished had its socialistic roots been nurtured.
We will look at its early heros, often considered radicals, who were
opposed by the defenders of the status quo. In Chapter Ten we will
sample the wisdom of mental health professionals working in contemporary HMOs.

An understanding of the origins of managed care will prevent
us from reinventing the wheel and help us gain perspective on what

---

Epigraphs from *An Apple A Day*, Great Quotations, Inc.

could have been and still could be. By examining the historical, social, and cultural elements that played a role in the development of managed mental health care, we can begin to eke out parts of our "sociology of psychotherapy." Familiarizing ourselves with the experience of staff model HMOs can stimulate our thinking about how to attain a social ethic of health care. To do so, we must study not just behavioral health care but the general health care system. Mental health benefits are a relatively new addition to managed care, included only since the 1970s in most HMO benefit packages. However, to understand the HMO concept, we must go back to a point in time when health care did not even include psychotherapy.

We begin our short and selective history by discussing the two components that were necessary for the development of contemporary managed care: group practice and prepaid plans, or a set package of health care services provided by a practitioner for a preestablished fee.

Group Practice

Group practices, formal associations of three or more physicians or other health care professionals, originated with Dr. William W. Mayo and his two sons, Charles and William, Jr., who set up the Mayo Clinic in Rochester, Minnesota, in 1887. They later added more doctors to became a multispecialty practice.

By 1925, approximately 1,500 physicians worked in about 150 private medical groups in the United States. The heaviest concentration of group practice clinics was west of the Mississippi, as a result of colonization by the physicians trained at the Mayo clinic. In a 1931 study of private medical groups, nearly all of the fifty-five clinics examined had at least one physician who had a prior association with the Mayo Clinic. During the same period the Mayo Clinic increased to a group of 386 physicians representing all specialties. From 1930 to 1960 the trend toward developing private group practices slowed, and by 1960 only 5.2 percent of the nation's physicians were in group practice. By 1975 it was 17.1 percent, and by 1980, 25 percent of all active physicians worked in a private group practice. This number is now growing again, since the demand for integrated health services—small groups of providers who join forces with one another or a health care facility to create an integrated provider network—is increasing.

Why group practice? There are distinct advantages for providers to practicing in a group rather than solo, and there are even more advantages for patients. According to John Nelson, author of *The History and Spirit of the HMO Movement*, these advantages include

- The accumulated experience and wisdom of a team of physicians with separate skills and a common philosophy. Group members pool their skills for the benefit of the patient and have mutual responsibility both for their patients and for each other.

- The ability to share ancillary staff members, equipment, and office space—making each physician's practice more cost-effective.

- A master file of information containing the medical records of each patient, available to all the providers in the group. This file also provides a wealth of data for the research investigator.

- A natural construct for peer review and quality assurance.

- An environment of intellectual rapport, stimulation, and professional collegiality.

- Increased patient trust and satisfaction as a result of the opportunity to select a provider from a group whose qualifications and ongoing competence are reviewed by professional peers.

The advantages of group practice are the same today as they were when the Mayos started it. And they are again being supported as excellent vehicles for developing modern integrated care systems.

The Prepaid Concept

Prepaid medical care existed as far back as the American colonies. George Washington paid a contract surgeon to oversee the health of his plantation workers, and his colonial army was also served by contract physicians.

By the end of the eighteenth century it was apparent that medical services were needed for merchant seamen harboring epidemic diseases. In 1798, at the urging of the Boston Marine Society, an act of Congress established the U.S. Marine Hospital Service. This act provided for small monthly deductions—20 cents per month—from the wages of seamen, who were then covered for the cost of health services provided by the Marine Hospital Service. From 1884 until 1905 these hospitals were supported by a tonnage tax. Since 1905 they have been supported by direct federal appropriations. This structure represents one of the oldest ongoing systems of prepaid medical care.

The large-scale development of prepaid systems came about mainly with the industrialization of the West during the nineteenth century. Lacking medical care in remote areas of the Pacific Northwest, railroad, mining, and lumber companies wanted to treat their own employees on-site. Doctors were salaried, a practice akin to the contracting of physicians during the Revolutionary War.

Early Prepaid Group Practice

The first example of a prepaid group practice was probably the Western Clinic in Tacoma, Washington. At that time, Tacoma was the lumber capital of the world. Dr. Thomas Curran and Dr. James Yocum opened a practice in 1906 in response to the mills' and their employees' seeking medical services through prepaid contracts. Around 1910 they entered into the first fee-for-service contract with the lumber industry, at a cost of 50 cents per member per month. At the same time, another Tacoma doctor, named Bridge, contracted with other employee groups. The Bridge Company eventually evolved into a chain of about twenty clinics throughout Washington and Oregon.

Tacoma can also claim the first recorded organized resistance to the concept of prepaid medical care. By 1917, private practice doctors organized the Pierce County Medical Service Bureau. Its job, theoretically, was to screen all medical contracts to preserve some professional control and offer more consumer choice. In reality the bureau worked to limit competition from the prepaid groups and employee-sponsored programs. This and other medical service bureaus became the predecessors of the local county medical societies, who would later oppose HMOs at virtually every stage of their development.

Health care changed considerably during the Great Depression. Hospitals had to turn from philanthropists' donations to patient fees for survival. In 1929 a great transformation began, however, when Baylor Hospital of Dallas, Texas, agreed to provide hospital care for 1,250 teachers with a prepaid premium. This action represented the founding of Blue Cross and traditional indemnity insurance as we know it today.

Patients saw other options becoming available. In the small, isolated farming community of Elk Creek, Oklahoma, Dr. Michael Shadid, a Syrian immigrant who cared about the relationship between poverty and illness, combined the ideas of prepaid health care and group practice. Dr. Shadid quickly became known as "the crusading doctor," or "a doctor for the people." In 1929 he talked with farmers about the high cost of medical care and created plans for a nonprofit, cooperative, community health care association. Unable to get local physicians to support his plan, he sold shares in the construction of Community Hospital for $50 each. Each shareholder was entitled to comprehensive medical care in the hospital as well as home visits for a $1 copayment and 10 cents per mile. Other doctors in the region were greatly distressed by Dr. Shadid's activities. Responding in anger and fear, they expelled Shadid from the county medical society and afterward from the state medical organization and the American Medical Association (AMA) as well. He was even threatened with suspension of his license. Any doctors applying for licensure to the state of Oklahoma who revealed that they planned to work at Community Hospital had an unusually difficult time passing the examination.

Despite this opposition Dr. Shadid's project grew, until in 1934 the Community Hospital became the Farmers Union Cooperative Association. It took Shadid twenty years, but his antitrust suit against the county and state medical societies was eventually settled out of court. Completely vindicated, he and his associates were awarded $300,000. The controversy gained national attention and widespread interest. Shadid toured the country. Other consumer groups jumped on the bandwagon. By 1950 over one hundred rural cooperatives existed, based on Shadid's ideas.

Dr. Donald Ross and Dr. Clifford Loos were approached simultaneously in 1929 by employees of the Los Angeles Water and Power Department. Subsequently they established the Ross-Loos Clinic, a prepaid program with employee premiums for a family contract of $1.50 per month. By 1935 the plan enrolled nearly thirty-eight thousand employees and dependents, drawing on a cross-section of governmental, educational, and industrial workers.

Both Donald Ross and Clifford Loos were expelled from the Los Angeles County Medical Society for running their prepaid group. In 1937, eighteen Ross-Loos Clinic staff physicians were refused membership in the society and as a result could not obtain staff appointments to accredited hospitals. Once again, "professional" regulations against consumer control, prepaid fees, and regular salaries for physicians were enacted. Both Drs. Ross and Loos appealed to the AMA and were later reinstated. Across the country, other medical societies reacted in similar ways to the formation of any prepaid health plan, but in case after case the courts protected the group practitioners from further harassment.

In 1932 the AMA issued a statement strongly opposing prepaid medical plans; this is what led to the blossoming of Blue Cross indemnity insurance. Organized medicine perceived health insurance as the lesser of two evils and supported it only because of a combination of public pressure and self-interest.

Kaiser-Permanente Health Plan

In 1933 an enterprising young surgeon, Sidney R. Garfield, worked in the Mojave Desert for the company that had contracted to build an aqueduct from the Colorado River to Los Angeles. The Industrial Indemnity Exchange offered Garfield 17 percent of the existing employees' insurance premium to treat injured workers on-site instead of transporting them to Los Angeles for surgery. Garfield also convinced the construction company to prepay him 5 cents a day per employee to cover their job-related medical needs. Garfield hired four other doctors and set up four small field hospitals, which were dragged along on skids as construction progressed.

The aqueduct was finished in 1938, just as Henry Kaiser signed the contracts to finish Grand Coulee Dam in Washington State. Kaiser was connected to the construction company building the Los Angeles aqueduct. Kaiser was impressed with the system Garfield had instituted in California, and the worker's union wasn't satisfied with the fee-for-service medical care in the Washington area. These factors led Edgar Kaiser (Henry's son) to support Dr. Garfield in creating a medical group and treatment facility at the new construction site. The group was paid 7 cents per day for the men and their wives and 25 cents per week for the children.

As the dam neared completion in 1941, the United States entered World War II. Kaiser Industries built shipyards in Richmond, California; Portland, Oregon; and Vancouver, Washington; and

steel mills in Fontana, California. The company employed a quarter of a million people at its peak. Kaiser requested that Sydney
Garfield organize the clinics and hospitals providing prepaid comprehensive care to the company's workers and their dependents.

When the war ended, the shipyards closed and the number of
employees dwindled. The Kaiser Permanente Health Plan opened
its membership to the general public. It was an immediate success,
with enrollments by the mid 1950s exceeding that of the war years.
Kaiser has now been available to the public for over fifty years and
serves 6.6 million people with plans in sixteen states. The plan
employs 9,200 doctors, who provide forty million outpatient visits
to Kaiser enrollees. It is the largest HMO in the United States. People have willingly chosen to receive their health care from Kaiser
as well as from other HMOs across the country.

The growth of prepaid health care was much slower in the East.
The first nonprofit HMO on the East Coast, Group Health Association, began in 1937 in Washington, D.C. It eventually developed
into an organization covering 150,000 people. Its membership consists of 55 percent commercial or corporate group employees, 40 percent federal employees, and about 5 percent individual, direct
subscribers.

Consumer-Initiated Plans

The New York City government provided another impetus for the
development of prepaid medical care. Mayor Fiorella La Guardia
wanted to establish a health care system for the employees of New
York City, and he believed a prepaid group model would work well.
Laws were changed, medical societies were placated, administrative
structures were established, and medical groups developed. In 1944
the Health Insurance Plan of Greater New York had group clinics
scattered throughout the metropolitan New York area.

A planning committee of consumers based in Seattle, Washington, spurred on by an appearance by Michael Shadid, set up the

Group Health Cooperative. The planning committee organized four hundred families, which paid $100 apiece to establish a clinic for themselves. In 1947 they purchased the assets of the Seattle Medical Securities Clinic and contracted with its physicians for care.

The local county medical society strenuously objected to the formation of the Group Health Cooperative. A court battle ensued, which the medical society lost. In 1957, a lengthy war with the King County Medical Society established a legal precedent that outlined the rights of both consumers and organizations in developing prepaid medical practices.

During the 1940s and 1950s other prepaid group practices developed throughout the country, particularly in areas where unions were strong and advocated good health care for their members. The Teamsters in St. Louis, the United Mine Workers in Appalachia, and the United Auto Workers in Detroit all established prepaid practice programs.

An ultimate role reversal took place when the Group Health Mutual Insurance Company, serving rural Minnesota and Wisconsin, made plans to introduce what it termed a direct service program. In 1956, while building its new headquarters, the company added a clinical facility. And so began Group Health Plan, today the largest HMO in the Minneapolis–St. Paul area, where the contemporary HMO movement was to begin.

Instead of just trying to defeat the prepaid concept, some physicians took a more constructive stance. A movement began within fee-for-service medicine to preserve "free enterprize" through a system of foundations for medical care. These were also prepaid plans, in which fee-for-service physicians were loosely bound in an agreement to accept fixed fee schedules, peer review, and the risk of financial loss.

One of the first of these plans was the San Joaquin Foundation for Medical Care, established in Stockton, California, in 1954 when the boilermakers union in the San Joaquin Valley was negotiating with Kaiser-Permanente to bring a prepaid plan into the area. The brother of the union president, Dr. Donald Harrington, decided to compete with the Kaiser plan. He established a group of physicians, independent of the medical society, who agreed to work for a set fee while also offering prepaid services to groups of subscribers. This represented a new form of HMO, the independent practice association, which is the most common model of HMO being developed today.

By 1970, prepaid medical group practices enjoyed legal acceptance and member satisfaction, but their use remained limited. No such plans were available for the majority of Americans. In fact, most Americans would not have known what an HMO or a prepaid group plan was, let alone how to find, join, or use one. It is a tragedy that American health care lost a golden opportunity to give all of its citizens universal health care through the growth of such comprehensive medical plans.

Mental Health Care in HMOs

Prepaid mental health care is relatively new in the history of the HMO movement. Most prototype HMOs did not include any mental health benefits. In its earlier days, Kaiser made mental health services available on a reduced-fee fee-for-service basis. The Health Insurance Plan of Greater New York provided mental health diagnosis and consultation as part of its general benefit package.

In the 1960s, however, new HMOs began to include mental health care on an optional basis in response to the influence of large contractor groups such as Medicare, Medicaid, Federal Employees Health Benefit Program, and various union groups. By the late 1960s a few plans did include mental health care as a part of their basic benefit package, notably Community Health Care Plan in Connecticut, Columbia Medical Plan in Maryland, and Harvard Community Health Plan in Massachusetts. And from 1971 to 1973 there were several critical developments for mental health care in HMOs. These changes were largely due to the efforts of one man.

Paul Ellwood and the Advent of HMOs

Dr. Paul Ellwood, director of the American Rehabilitation Institute, concluded that fee-for-service medicine created "perverse incentives" that rewarded providers for treating illness and canceled out rewards when patients were healed. Ellwood wanted to restructure health care in a way that would provide incentives to promote prevention and rehabilitation.

In seeking to create a more functional system, Dr. Ellwood decided not to reinvent the wheel. He found that high-quality health care already existed in the form of the group practices founded by those earlier leaders who had wanted to provide medicine for the people. Groups such as Kaiser had survived and flourished and were providing good care to large populations at reasonable costs.

In 1969, Paul Ellwood, seeking to convince the government to promote the growth of such HMOs, had the good fortune to find an administration in search of a national health policy. When President Nixon took office, he did not have a well-thought-out health care program in his platform. Formulation of the administration's health care policy was delayed by a grueling six-month battle with the AMA, which objected to the appointment of Dr. John Knowles as the assistant secretary of Health, Education and Welfare. He was eventually rejected, and Dr. Roger Ebert was named instead.

This delay proved advantageous to Paul Ellwood's promotion of HMOs, however. Public concern about inflated health care costs and government concerns over Medicare and Medicaid expenditures were rising. Having fallen behind in creating a health care strategy, the administration was open to accepting a policy that had been thought out in advance. The AMA was not able to fight another political battle, since it had used up much energy opposing Knowles. Lawyers, M.B.A.'s, and other nonphysicians who were not biased against prepaid group practice plans assumed the power to determine health policy in the leaderless Health and

Scientific Affairs branch of the Department of Health, Education and Welfare.

The Democrats, who favored national health insurance, supported the HMO concept and were willing to provide support. Nixon's health care policy aids were progressive nonphysicians from California who were familiar with Kaiser and the San Joaquin Foundation for Medical Care. Their ready acceptance of the concept of prepaid care gave Paul Ellwood a wonderful opportunity to advance his agenda. He persuaded the administration that a nationwide system of group practices linked by a fiscal strategy of prepayment was the most efficient answer to the nation's health care problems and a way to reverse existing perverse incentives. To avoid the traditional negative response to prepaid group practice, he coined the term "Health Maintenance Organization," or HMO.

HMOs grew rapidly over the next few years. In 1971, Nixon told Congress that HMOs were the keystone of his national health policy. During this time, $26 million in redirected government funds were allocated in support of 155 HMO projects. The goal was to create 1,700 programs, making an HMO option available to 90 percent of the population. The Health Maintenance Act of 1973 was passed, but by the time it got through the House and Senate it was riddled with stipulations, provisions, and limitations that restricted HMO development. However, $325 million over five years was authorized for grants, contracts, and loan guarantees to help HMOs get organized, and another $40 million was authorized for studies of the quality of care they provided. Federal law overrode statutes in states that impeded the development of HMOs.

HMOs were mandated to provide mental health care. Under the law, HMOs had to offer a benefit package of outpatient mental health care not to exceed twenty visits, outpatient evaluation and crisis intervention services, and medical treatment and referral services for alcoholism or drug abuse. Among members of the mental health community, particularly those invested and attached to the philosophy of long-term therapy, anti-HMO feelings ran strong.

Much resistance to mental health care delivered within this prepaid system was evident. In particular, proponents of long-term therapy strenuously objected to what they considered to be a meager benefit package of twenty sessions. Such objections seem ironic today in light of the common HMO practice of "carving out" mental health and chemical dependency benefits from the general medical benefit.

From 1973 to 1981 the federal government provided over $350 million for the support and development of 115 HMOs. President Carter's ten-year plan was initiated, with the goal of establishing 450 new HMOs with a membership of twenty million. By 1988 a total of 659 HMOs served over 37 million Americans.

Federal qualification requirements were relaxed over the next few years. A 1976 amendment to the 1973 HMO Act provided greater administrative flexibility, increasing the opportunities for interested groups to become federally qualified. HMOs could contract with individual health care professionals who didn't qualify as independent practice associations (IPAs) or medical groups, and they were allowed to use the clinical expertise of "other health care personnel," including nurse practitioners and clinical psychologists. Other managed care practice arrangements emerged, including the preferred provider organization (PPO). PPOs involve contracts between insurers and providers by which the provider discounts his or her fee in exchange for guaranteed referrals. IPAs, contracting with providers to work in group practices and compensating them on a per capita, fee-for-service basis, flourished under the new laws.

But in addition to subsidizing the original HMO movement, further amendments welcomed the inclusion of for-profit corporations. HMOs had originally been nonprofit organizations that controlled medical costs for the good of the overall membership. A nonprofit organization is one that is "'organized and operated exclusively for religious, charitable, scientific, testing for public safety, literary or educational purposes.' The provision of medical care has been determined by the courts and IRS to qualify as a 'charitable' purpose." Furthermore, a nonprofit corporation has members rather than shareholders, is not in the business of making a profit, and gives its members reasonable control and participation in the business.

For-profit corporations had not played a major part in the HMO movement up to this time. For-profit health care, in comparison to nonprofit, is "far less cumbersome to administer, easy to create, has no complex filings with the IRS and is flexible in structuring both ownership and financial aspects." However, it exists to give back a profit to its owners and shareholders.

Over time, then, Nixon's health care policy and the HMO movement were ultimately separated from the idea of creating a national health care system. The rediscovering, reshaping, and re-formulating of the HMO movement into today's managed care environment shows how the spirit of the movement has changed.

Current Trends in Behavioral Health Care

So what are the new trends we must face? It is beyond the scope of this chapter to give a detailed description of the state of affairs in behavioral health care. The point to stress is that managed care has departed a great distance from its early roots. While its original leaders wanted to provide comprehensive medical care to their membership, the structures they built were rejected by the system. Today acts of love are transformed into profiteering.

So why didn't we listen to those who had us on the right track in the first place? Why did preserving a fee-for-service system take priority over establishing universal coverage? Herein lies an important point. Had the mental health community been open to working within these ethical and socially responsible guidelines and systems and had it not used up so much energy opposing all HMOs, perhaps we would not be in the crisis in which we find ourselves today. But many of the old guard misinformed their contemporaries, telling them that HMOs and other forms of managed care were simply passing fads that would go away—or needed to be actively opposed. This was a mistake. Now we are moving away from the dream of health care for all citizens.

Present Problems

The future of mental health care is uncertain as we move away from universal coverage rather than embrace it. In *Dangerous to Your Health: Capitalism in Health Care*, Vincente Navarro, professor of health policy, sociology, and policy studies at Johns Hopkins, writes that 82 percent of Americans want major and profound change in our health care system, despite the fact that we are constantly being told that we have the best health care system in the world. Backing up his arguments with solid facts and figures, he demonstrates that a great deal of money is being made in the house of medicine, where the wealth of so few is based upon the suffering of so many. He contends that our system is more responsive to the greed of those who control health care than it is to satisfying people's needs. The system is deteriorating, and our mode of funding is becoming more regressive.

In a recent *New York Times* article, Paul Starr, sociology professor and noted historian of health care at Princeton, expresses similar beliefs. He sees "reverse reform" in the making. The Clinton plan was formulated by the Jackson Hole Group, a think tank in Jackson Hole, Wyoming, that brings together leaders in health care to discuss health care policy. Headed by Dr. Paul Ellwood, the Jackson Hole Group is the home of managed competition. The idea was to use managed care and methods as a means to hold down costs so that the resultant savings could be used to pay for universal coverage. Ironically, the trend has moved in the opposite direction, toward dismantling the part of the health care system that takes care of the poor and the elderly. Some want to cap Medicare expenditures and uncap provider charges. Some want to give the elderly a fixed amount of money (or a voucher), which might not allow them to get the same amount of coverage they now receive as an entitlement. Some want to cut costs by retracting rights to coverage and replacing Medicaid with block grants to the states. This would mean it would no longer be a federal entitlement.

Converting Medicare into a voucher system and Medicaid into

block grants would abolish the legal rights to medical benefits that some poor and elderly now have. Not only would such a policy eventually give the states 30 percent less money by 2002; the many poor who receive Medicaid through welfare would lose their health coverage when they lost relief. Paul Starr adds that the overwhelming paradox is that "many people who opposed reform because they believed it would restrict their choices now face a system that is becoming far more restrictive."

Meanwhile, declining employer coverage has increased the number of uninsured to a whopping 41 million today! Dr. Navarro points out that if Medicaid had not expanded in the 1980s, we would have 50 million uninsured today. Employers have cut their own expenses by "cost shifting"—making their employees pay a larger part of the bill. Furthermore, employment-based health insurance is on the decline.

From around 1980 to 1992, the number of citizens not covered by insurance has increased by 22 percent, out-of-pocket payments have increased by 42 percent, administrative costs have quadrupled, and the price of health care has increased while benefits decreased for most people. At the same time that many citizens faced these forfeitures, the incomes of physicians and the profits of pharmaceutical companies have increased. Dr. Navarro reports that while the average doctor earned $89,900 in 1981, in 1992 he earned $164,300. Over the past ten years, the profits of the top twenty drug companies increased 15 percent per year, as compared to the 3.2 percent increase seen in the Fortune 500 companies. In 1992 the salary of the top executives of the twenty-six most important health care corporations was eighty-five times greater than the salary of the average nurse. The CEO of Hospital Corporation of America was the highest-paid person in the United States, making $127 million in one year!

And the prospects in the near future for extending coverage to those 41 million uninsured seem dim—despite the fact that numerous polls clearly show that for American citizens, health care reform is a high priority, and despite the fact that the people voted for the Health Security Act, a prominent attempt at reform, when they voted for Bill Clinton.

So, the problems in our health care system run much deeper than just those associated with managed care, for managed care is simply one tool used by those who are directing the system.

Before we mental health professionals can ensure that psychotherapy is delivered according to a fair societal ethic, general health care must also be delivered equitably. The survival of good mental health care is at great risk in an environment where people must fight for basic health care. As deep cuts are made to essential public health programs, people will prioritize what they spend their money on. And when they must make bare-bones choices, caring for diabetes will take priority over relieving feelings of anxiety or depression. Of course, the two are connected; but in a behavioral health care system where professionals have spent more time thinking about psychodynamics than educating people about the link between physical illness and emotional states, psychotherapy will first and foremost be seen as a luxury, not a necessity.

Hopes for the Future

Does it have to be this way? Do we have to be the only major industrialized country without a national health care program? Our look back at history shows that there are ways to solve our problems. If we were to deliver psychotherapy within the context of a prepaid group practice in a staff model setting, we would be able to render sufficient mental health care to most people who needed it. The requirements of the small proportion of people who need extended care would have to be studied, and a commitment would have to be made to finding a way to satisfy their needs.

Compassionate medical heroes have attempted to change the face of the system and have met opposition from defenders of the status quo every step of the way. Hopefully mental health providers will not suffer the same indignities, although some HMO therapists have met with hostile opposition.

So as the great experiment in health care reform evolves, yesterday's prepaid group health plans bear only a vague resemblance to today's big business of managed care. Paul Starr put it very poetically when he said, "A remarkable change has taken place. Prepaid group practice was originally associated with the cooperative movement and dismissed as a utopian, slightly subversive idea. The conservative, cost-minded critics of medical care have now adopted it as a more effective form of management. They have substituted a rhetoric of rationalization and competition for the older rhetoric of cooperation and mutual protection. The socialized medicine of one era has become the corporate reform of the next."

Today the buzzwords for good-quality health and mental health care are "access," "comprehensive range of services," "coordination and integration of services," "group practices," and "cost management," all highly sought after characteristics promoted by the health care heroes during the early days of the HMOs. Can the big health care corporations develop a compassion for the citizens of this country? Can the profit motive take a backseat to a social ethic?

Some say yes, that quality care matters to the large managed care firms. Anthony Broskowski of Prudential Insurance has said that managed care began as a way for the insurer and employer to contain costs. The next generation of managed care added access and use to the equation, and the third generation is now adding quality and outcomes to the mix. The coming generation will add personal and community health status to the equation. We will have to wait and see. Only time will tell.

John Nelson, former CEO of Community Health Care Plan in New Haven, Connecticut, and author of "The History and Spirit of the HMO Movement" (from which this chapter draws heavily), eloquently summed up the issues involved: "This historical review raises serious concerns about the evolution towards the social- and business-linked health care delivery systems of today. The cham-

pions of nonprofit HMOs and hospitals are pitted against the advocates of for-profit managed health care. The outcome of this conflict is in doubt. That HMO which was born of the principles of the
Public Health Service, the Mayo Brothers medical group practice
and the prepayment concepts of Drs. Shadid, Ross, Loos, Garfield,
and Harrington is in direct philosophical conflict with the contemporary HMO structures created by venture capitalism. Who will
inherit this legacy?"

In Chapter Ten we will examine the reactions of frontline clinicians delivering behavioral health care in staff model HMOs across
the country. From them we can learn that it is possible to deliver
good psychotherapy in the HMO setting.

Notes

p. 223, *"Every job is a self-portrait"*: *Great quotations.* (1967). Glendale Heights,
IL: Quing Court, p. 72.

p. 223, *"You may not have been responsible"*: ibid.

p. 224, *Group practices, formal associations:* Talbott, J. (1985). The fate of the
public psychiatric system. *Hospital and Community Psychiatry, 36*(1), 46–50.

p. 225, *This number is now growing again:* Dacso, S. T., & Dacso, C. (1995).
Managed care answer book. New York: Aspen.

p. 225, *Why group practice?* Bennett, M. J. (1988). The greening of the HMO:
Implications for prepaid psychiatry. *American Journal of Psychiatry, 145*(12),
1544–1549. Esselstyn, C. (1964, February 20). *Group health: A better way to good
health care.* Address to the executive council of the AFL-CIO, Washington, DC,
pp. 4–12.

p. 225, *According to John Nelson:* Nelson, J. A. (1987). The history and spirit of
the HMO movement. *HMO Practice, 1*(2), 75–85.

p. 226, *Prepaid medical care:* ibid. Starr, P. (1982). *The social transformation of
American medicine.* New York: Basic Books.

p. 230, *The first nonprofit HMO:* DeLeon, P., VandenBos, G. R., & Bulatao, E. Q. (1991). Managed mental health care: A history of the Federal Policy Initiative. *Professional Psychology: Research and Practice, 22*(1), 15–25.

p. 232, *By 1970, prepaid medical group practices:* Davis, M. M. (1937). *Public medical services: A survey of tax-supported medical care in the United States* (p. 81). Chicago: University of Chicago Press.

p. 232, *Prepaid mental health care:* Ettel, T. D. *The history of psychology's involvement in the HMO industry (1973–1990).* Ann Arbor, MI: University Microfilms.

p. 233, *Dr. Paul Ellwood, director:* Starr, P. (1982). *The social transformation of American medicine.* New York: Basic Books.

p. 234, *HMOs were mandated to:* DeLeon, P., VandenBos, G. R., & Bulatao, E. Q. (1991). Managed mental health care: A history of the Federal Policy Initiative. *Professional Psychology: Research and Practice, 22*(1), 15–25.

p. 235, *A 1976 amendment:* ibid.

p. 235, *IPAs, contracting with providers:* Dacso, S. T., & Dacso, C. C. (1995). *Managed care answer book* (p. GL-18). New York: Aspen.

p. 235, *A nonprofit organization:* ibid., pp. 4–36 to 4–39.

p. 236, *For-profit health care, in comparison to nonprofit:* ibid., p. 4–38.

p. 237, *In Dangerous to:* Navarro, V. (1993). *Dangerous to your health: Capitalism in health care* (pp. 10–11). New York: Monthly Review Press.

p. 237, *In a recent:* Starr, P. (1995, September 3). Look who is talking health care reform now. *New York Times Magazine.* p. 43.

p. 238, *Dr. Navarro points out:* Navarro, V. (1993). *Dangerous to your health: Capitalism in health care* (pp. 10–11). New York: Monthly Review Press.

p. 240, *So as the great experiment in health care reform evolves:* Mayer, T. R., Mayer, G., & Gloria, R. N. (1985). Occasional notes. *New England Journal of Medicine, 312*(9), 590–594.

p. 240, *Paul Starr put it very poetically:* Starr, P. (1982). *The social transformation of American medicine*. New York: Basic Books.

p. 240, *Today the buzzwords for good-quality health and mental health care:* Open minds. (1995, April). *Trends in Behavioral Health Financing*. Gettysburg, PA: Author.

p. 240, *Anthony Broskowski of Prudential Insurance:* Broskowski, T. (1995). The evolution of health care: Implications for the training and careers of psychologists. *Professional Psychology: Research and Practice, 26*(2), 156–162.

p. 240, *John Nelson, former CEO:* Nelson, J. A. (1987). The history and spirit of the HMO movement. *HMO Practice, 1*(2), 84.

. . . .

10

Stories of Successful Adaptation to Managed Care Practice

There are many truths of which the full meaning
can't be realized until personal experience has brought
it home!

John Stuart Mill

The wisdom of the wise and the experience of the ages
are perpetuated by quotations.

Benjamin Disraeli

This chapter is devoted to psychotherapists who work in HMOs and have successfully adapted their practice style to that environment. Over the past six years I have interviewed and surveyed a number of mental health professionals who have fit their practice into managed care settings. I chose to study HMO staff model clinicians for several reasons.

First, the legacy of the health care leaders of the past is today's staff model nonprofit HMO, an organization that employs providers to deliver health care to all its members and compensates them primarily by means of a salary. All premiums and revenues accrue to the HMO. These environments capture the concept of what it is like to treat a population of patients. I believe that the staff model managed care setting is a prototype for an ideal integrated managed care setting that can benefit many. Staff model therapists have learned to work within the framework of a benefit package of around twenty yearly sessions and deliver high-quality but cost-effective mental health care.

Second, since such HMOs have a goal of caring for the needs of entire clinical populations, their therapists will be more likely to see therapy from an epidemiological perspective. Regardless of whether we move in the direction of staff model HMOs or IPAs, we will probably have some form of capitated prepaid care, so we need to look at our patients as a population or a collectivity.

A third reason is that the process of "backward integration" has begun. Carving out mental health care has given large corporations the opportunity to corner the behavioral health care market. Now that these companies have "set up house," the integration of mental health care with general health care will dictate that providers work in group practices. The characteristics and issues intrinsic to staff model managed care are likely to be important in integrated group practices in the near future. So the experience of staff model clinicians is relevant to tomorrow's practice settings.

Finally, change has its enemies as well as its friends. Asking its allies how they managed to change is a sure way to learn. Listening to the words of those who have shifted successfully from a traditional view of therapy to an HMO perspective is a learning experience. They have lifted the veil of the clinician's illusion. By attuning ourselves to the processes by which these therapists transformed themselves, we can speed up our own metamorphosis.

This discussion focuses on three questions I asked these therapists: How has the managed care setting affected your practice style? How does a benefit package of twenty sessions per year affect psychotherapy? How has performing psychotherapy in the HMO setting changed your inner self? My impression is that the change from traditional to short-term approaches involves problem-solving opportunities and methods of adaptation that are remarkably consistent across all HMO settings.

The reader will note that the responses to these questions are quite positive. Overall, they are very optimistic. In all fairness, I must stress that this special sample is composed of clinicians who have successfully acclimated to an HMO setting and are content enough with it to have remained there over an extended period. We won't hear from clinicians who, not willing or able to make the transformation, left the HMO.

The Providers

The information presented here is based on the responses of 294 mental health professionals (master's-level social workers, psychologists, psychiatrist nurses, and other master's-level therapists) with an average age of 42.5 years, an average of 5.4 years of managed care experience, and an average of 6.7 years of prior clinical experience.

For my initial study I tape-recorded in-depth interviews with therapists from ten different staff or group model managed care companies. After transcribing these interviews I mailed questionnaires to staff and group model facilities across the United States that offered a mental health outpatient benefit of twenty sessions yearly, as prescribed by the HMO Act of 1973. In this way I ensured that all the therapists in the study had undergone similar experiences and had struggled with having to adapt to similar practice parameters.

The Evolution of Provider Practice Styles

These staff model psychotherapists told me that when they entered into their respective managed care practices they found themselves in a state of culture shock. Most "happened" into their new setting, knowing little about the history, philosophy, or organization of any form of managed care. They began questioning the value of their graduate training as well as the usefulness of traditional therapy models. They learned "on the job" and sought out opportunities for professional learning seminars in short-term therapy and managed care. They coped by using models of therapy that fit into the managed care environment, adjusting familiar models to fit their new setting, or creating new models or techniques. They tended to shed long-term psychodynamic orientations and adopt more eclectic or nontraditional problem-solving, solution-oriented models.

I asked the therapists to rank order the models they had used at three different points—in supervised clinical work, at the time they started working in a staff model managed care setting, and the present time. Table 10.1 summarizes their responses. The rankings demonstrate a trend toward using traditional models less and using eclectic or brief, solution-focused methods and problem-solving methods more.

Some of the therapists described a strenuous environment that contributed to burnout—too heavy a caseload, too few supportive interactions with administrators or colleagues, and on-call responsibilities. A too-heavy caseload is a very different complaint from what we hear from therapists in non-staff-model managed care networks who lack sufficient referrals or worry about being left out of provider networkers. On the whole, the HMO therapists believed that the effectiveness and quality of the care they provided was high, despite their heavy caseload.

Table 10.1. Changes in therapist theoretical orientations.

Orientation	Supervised	Start	Now
		Percentage of Therapists	
Psychodynamic	46.5	28.5	17.6
Cognitive/behavioral	13.2	17.4	24.1
Humanistic	9.8	4.4	4.4
Eclectic	18.0	29.2	35.3
Solution/Problem solving	9.1	13.6	18.7

Specific Components That Changed

In response to the question of how their practice styles evolved, providers discussed a number of specific changes. (To be included on this list, an item had to be spontaneously mentioned by at least 10 percent of the therapists surveyed.) The changes included the following:

- Increased use of short-term therapy models and developed a stronger belief in the effectiveness of short-term therapy

- Converted to a new therapy model or orientation

- Became quicker or more efficient at conducting therapy

- Believed more in the importance of decreasing patient dependency and increasing patient responsibility

- Increased crisis management skills

- Used intermittent scheduling of psychotherapy

- Developed increased skills and greater confidence in practice abilities

- Increased use of problem-, solution-, and goal-directed therapy

- Became more active and directive

- Developed an increased awareness of the importance of psychotropic drugs in treatment plans

One social worker who had left a psychoanalytic child practice discussed his feelings about entering into the HMO with no preparation: "I felt myself scrambling. . . . The volume of work and the pace was very different from what I had been doing—working in a long-term setting with a stabilized caseload of ten patients per year. Since I came from a training and work background of long-term therapy . . . my practice style had to . . . change radically."

Two psychologists spoke about questioning the value of the long-term orientation they had developed in their private practice: "I began to question the value of weekly long-term therapy. . . . I wondered whether it was a waste of time and money and not necessary for some people who were receiving it. . . . It certainly feeds into the patient's dependency needs. . . . I think there are times when patients enjoy and get something that feels good out of seeing a therapist on a weekly basis for a long period of time, but I don't know anymore if that is real therapy."

"When I started I was long-term oriented . . . less active, more passive . . . and I had great expectations of what therapy can and ought to do. . . . After working here for a short time, I felt my long-term techniques were . . . intrusive. Now I . . . am a firm believer in the idea that—deep inside—the patient knows what is good for the patient. . . . And now I am a firm believer in letting the patient guide their way through therapy."

A social worker who had been in the HMO for eight years struggled with the fact that in other settings it was often a relief when patients did not return, but in the HMO, a patient's discontinuing therapy did not mean that he or she simply went away. If the terminated patient experienced mental health problems, the HMO providers still had to take care of the patient's needs: "I remember a couple of patients did not come back. . . . I thought . . . what did I do wrong, what's happening here? I don't operate that way anymore. . . . I'm relieved when people don't want to stick around." Of course, this therapist added that when a patient did not come back to one particular therapist, he or she could return to another HMO therapist, who would then have to deal with the patient's issues. "When I first came here a number of people were looking at Mann's model [a brief-therapy model in which patients receive twelve and only twelve sessions]. But [Mann's] notion that people just disappear forever after termination is not realistic. Here in the HMO, the idea does not hold true. Patients appear in new forms after a while . . . after they are terminated. They come back intermittently and . . . we must take care of them."

One very seasoned social worker became devoted to problem-solving psychotherapy because it fit easily into the HMO structure: "When I first started doing therapy I was trained in existential psychoanalysis. . . . I wanted to find a way to work with patients more briefly . . . and achieve a worthwhile goal. . . . Rather than use the long-term, what I call . . . noncommittal, always passive approach that I was taught . . . I became interested in the competencies of the people . . . and building on these rather than spending years and years looking at deficiencies and trying to figure out what in the world to do about them.

"So I began looking for . . . therapies that would work. . . . I experimented with using one-way mirrors, working in teams, working interactively between the teams and the client, and . . . I studied what is most important in the interaction between client and therapist—not just what's going on with the client . . . and how you, the therapist, can influence change. . . . And I did this with patients who had drug and alcohol problems on an outpatient basis, with very serious problems. And I did this working with families, individuals, and couples.

"I . . . was open to taking in as many as 350 new clients the first year that I was here . . . and I wasn't in the least bit burned out. I was energized. And I keep track. I'm a very scientific-minded person."

A doctoral-level social worker, previously a devout long-term psychodynamic therapist, experienced a newfound delight in the HMO work setting. While the change was difficult at first, he saw results that he liked: "I started going through the motions of seeing people short term. . . . I thought, 'This is how one does brief therapy . . . by keeping it brief.'. . . That was . . . my starting point. . . .

"But my evolution has been an internal process. . . . I now have a level of flexibility that is very syntonic. The assumptions that

inform my work are very different now than when I first started. . . .
I don't think of brief treatment . . . in terms of a time element [any-
more] but in terms of the attitude of the therapist. . . . I don't need
to see people weekly. I can start treatment and set somebody in
motion and send them on their way for three weeks, knowing the
therapy is continuing without me. . . . I believe that time really
helps and that I don't need to be there to see the patient change.
A long-term therapist feels like they have to be there and . . . watch
the change and . . . see the patient work it through. . . . I feel much
more comfortable with doing small pieces of work. I work hard on
the question, 'Why now? Why is this person seeking help now?'

"Now, I *feel* myself to be a brief therapist . . . like clothes that I
put on when I started that really didn't fit just right. It feels like the
cloths fit now. . . . My style . . . was stiff at first. Now I am more
eclectic, more creative. I . . . pick and choose . . . certain hypothe-
ses, and if they don't work I'll throw them out the window. . . . I'm
less overprotective of my patients. I now think the long-term model
. . . generates overprotectiveness and dependency."

How the Benefit Package Affects Providers' Style

I asked providers to express their opinion about whether or not the
benefit package (remember, these HMOs all provided twenty sessions per year) was adequate to handle the needs of their patients.
To my surprise, the majority of therapists (76 percent) thought
twenty sessions was adequate to treat most of their patients. Very
few (less than 5 percent) thought it was not enough, and 12 percent were uncertain.

The perceptions of these therapists are in agreement with the
realities of clinical practice discussed in Chapter Four. Only a small
percentage of patients continue in therapy beyond twenty-six sessions. Since most patients do not stay beyond four to six sessions,
of course most clinical needs can be covered within the confines
of this benefit!

The majority of therapists (84 percent) thought that the twenty-session limit definitely affected their style in these ways:

- It forced them to use brief therapy.

- It encouraged them to convert to a new therapy model or orientation.

- It caused them to work quicker, more efficiently, and harder and to seize the moment.

- It encouraged them to stress messages of decreased dependency and increased responsibility.

- They deemphasized pathology.

- They increased their use of crisis management techniques to keep their patients out of the hospital.

- It forced them to use intermittent scheduling.

- They made greater use of community resources.

- They made greater use of self-help groups.

- It forced them to discriminate between patients who will and will not benefit from treatment.

- It provided freedom from fees' affecting therapy.

- It increased their awareness of limited time and resources.

- It encouraged them to see the patient as a consumer.

A psychologist with only two and a half years of experience in the HMO setting said, "I think it affects my thinking about therapy in that I am in no way, shape, or form biased by finances. And I think that even in the best of all [worlds, finances] can't help but be a conscious or unconscious factor in the therapy. It [would make] no difference to my living if all my patients were to move or terminate."

A nurse from the same HMO stated, "I see people here as consumers. They sign up for a service. Hopefully they're educated about what they're getting.

"They have a choice as to whether they want to sign up for this health plan. I also think it enables a group of people who under other circumstances might not be able to have access to mental health care. . . . As long as it has been made clear to the person what kind of benefits they have, the responsibility is on them as to how they are going to utilize it."

A minority of therapists (16 percent) felt they had no need to change when they began working in managed care, since the models of therapy they used fit directly into the managed care setting and required little change.

For example, here are the words of a young social worker who had worked in managed care for only a year and a half. She adhered to a family therapy approach: "I'm a family therapist with a systems point of view, so I see myself as a coach or a helper in the therapeutic process. I am not the sole important force in someone's life. So [managed care] fits well with my model of treatment. . . . I feel that people on the whole should be doing most of their work outside the session. And unless someone is in crisis . . . I'm comfortable seeing someone every other week. . . . I think that the model that you come from is very important in terms of how you fit . . . [into managed care]."

On the negative side, two therapists, both from different settings, worried about the minority of patients whose necessary long-term work was not covered. These therapists tended to feel demoralized: "I passively discourage people from starting therapy. . . . I say to them, 'Why don't you see how it goes for a week or so. . . If you feel you want to come back, give me a call.' I give them a card. . . . Many people are ambivalent about starting anyway. . . . I don't do this if they absolutely need to be seen."

"Twenty sessions is good for 95 percent of the people I see

and . . . the other 5 percent are the most difficult cases, and that's going to be a problem for some of them."

Two other therapists were disgruntled because their autonomy had been challenged. For example, one psychologist who had been in practice for fifteen years felt that she wanted to practice elsewhere. Her disappointment is reflected in her words: "It affects me in every way imaginable. Sometimes patients come in feeling entitled to twenty sessions, and you may not feel they need to be here at all, but . . . they insist. . . . 'I got my benefit, I want my twenty sessions.' . . . [It's] unpleasant to see their sense of entitlement.

"It also dictates how we do therapy . . . for different groups of patients . . . certain people . . . are not going to stick, and maybe they just need a session or two . . . to be told they are not crazy or just . . . to vent. Or they may not need anything at all. . . . For those people I don't think the benefit affects therapy very much."

Another stated that she very much wanted to go back into private practice: "For the people . . . who . . . could benefit from—I'm not even talking long-term therapy—eight months or a year . . . there is nothing to do with those people.

"In private practice, the session limit would be determined by the therapy relationship. What happens here, it gets determined externally. . . . The plan they bought is twenty sessions. . . . It also makes me . . . careful about who I start to see. We get some borderline, narcissistically disturbed people, and I think it is a . . . disservice to [them to] meet for a limited time. . . . And I think it borders on malpractice to meet with them and then abandon them after twenty sessions. That's a big question. . . . Would it hurt this person to meet for [only] twenty sessions? . . . There are certainly some people who have real intense issues around abandonment and loss and who [have fragile egos] to begin with."

These interviews suggest that the benefit package of twenty sessions appears to be acceptable to most therapists if they believe that short-term therapy is effective or if they have the authority to exceed the maximum benefit in certain cases.

Personal Changes

When asked to describe if and how performing psychotherapy in a managed care setting had affected them as human beings, 98 percent of therapists listed positive changes and 28 percent of therapists reported negative changes. (The numbers do not add up to 100 percent because many therapists listed more than one change.) The changes are as follows:

Negative Changes

• Became more cynical (unhappy, withdrawn, lonely, stressed, disillusioned)

• Felt tired and as if their internal resources were taxed

• Felt less caring, patient, idealistic

Positive Changes

• Grew professionally

• Became wiser and more mature

• Became more patient, humorous, resourceful, fulfilled, empathic

• Increased confidence and strength

• Became better able to set limits on their time and prioritize

• Broadened their views and acquired greater acceptance of different models of therapy

• Increased recognition of patients' resilience

A psychologist who worked at two different staff model HMOs and loved both settings said, "When I count the number of patients that I have seen and the number of problems and life experiences about which I've heard . . . I'm a wiser and more mature individual. . . . I'm confident about my skills as a therapist because I am now able to work with a variety of different kinds of problems."

A master's-level nurse clinician stated, "I think there has been some positive changes and some detrimental changes too. On the positive side, . . . the professional growth and training has been excellent. I have seen many patients from many diagnostic groups and gotten much more knowledge and information about psychotropic medication and . . . internal medicine.

"On the negative side . . . the demands of the HMO, as far as workload . . . has a cost on [therapists'] personal life. . . . Many times I come home and I'm just too exhausted . . . to participate in family life or to really want to do anything."

A psychologist who worked for several managed care companies felt that therapy in HMOs was democratic, benefiting people in all walks of life, not just the elite who can pay for services out of pocket:

"I . . . was seeing about two hundred or three hundred different people a year. . . . That's very exciting . . . in terms of getting in touch with the kinds of things that trouble your neighbor next door or the person across the street or the person living in the lower-income section of your town, or employees at the telephone company versus employees of the post office and so forth. We've seen people from all these different settings . . . it's given me the opportunity to share a little more of the human experience . . . to know what it is like to be with all these different people. And to get in touch with those with whom we are living . . . who the people on the street are. . . . I think I've . . . become a more tolerant, accepting person. . . . Nothing much surprises me. I suppose that happens to most clinicians but . . . if you were in private practice and you only saw well-heeled populations with certain kinds of problems, it wouldn't be the same. I think I've become a more understanding person as a result of being in an HMO. I'd like to say that it's taught me to work under pressure better, but I still don't particularly care for pressure. . . . But I don't get rattled as much as I did."

A psychologist who works with adolescents and their families added, "I have become more willing to accept the varieties of human experience and to broaden my sense of what is normal . . . what is reasonable in human life . . . and that I don't have the answers to anything. . . . It may have given me a little more humility . . . that sometimes the thing to do is to cut someone loose and . . . let them live their life."

Another psychologist who had practiced in the HMO for five years said, "I've heard so many stories from so many people that I really understand life a lot better [from] having had these relationships. . . . I feel that I've helped a lot of people and I've left a mark in their lives. . . . Ten, fifteen years down the road a lot of these people will remember what I've said. . . . So I feel like I have helped."

A psychiatric nurse who had worked in one HMO since it opened over twenty years ago felt she had learned a great deal about people: "It's given me a great degree of tenacity . . . a great deal of confidence in my own professional skills, because . . . we were seen as being nontraditional, doing innovative things that people were highly skeptical of. . . . It has given me a great deal of self-confidence to know that for the last ten years I have been on the cutting edge of doing things innovatively."

A social worker who had worked in a community health setting prior to coming to her HMO found that "working within the HMO . . . has made me more aware of the reality of the limits of life. Working here focuses us on living within limits. The official terminology for it is 'cost containments,' but it's certainly a part of life. It's reality that there's a certain amount of money and a certain amount of resources and a certain amount of needs or expectations for it. . . . Living within those limits, whether it's . . . at an HMO or anywhere else, is important in life for all of us. In many other settings it . . . appears as though you can live without a sense of limitations. If a third-party payer is paying, if you're funded for state grants, you . . . believe you are seeing people for free, but it is one level of denial. You are pretending that it's just free and available.

But it is not just free and available. . . . Somebody pays taxes for it. . . . In terms of the therapist's view of things, that often . . . there are limits, . . . the HMO brings it closer to home—there are limits here. The reality of life is there are limits. [Working here] probably made me more keenly aware of that for myself."

Tips for Therapists in Managed Care

Finally, advice to other clinicians on how to adapt to a managed care setting flowed freely. To be a good managed care therapist,

- Develop competence in short-term therapies.

- Develop crisis management skills.

- Set boundaries and limits.

- Be flexible.

- Take care of yourself.

- Use clinical supervision.

- Investigate the models that are most useful for the kind of work you do.

- Train as much as possible when needed.

- Ask for and give peer support.

- Be a good team member.

- Sharpen your clinical assessment skills.

- Work well with members of the medical profession.

- Know your own limits.

- Develop and maintain a good sense of humor.

- Be empathic and supportive.

- Use community resources.

- Be assertive with patients, colleagues, and supervisors

- Solve problems skillfully.

- Accept criticism openly.

- Develop stamina.

- Use triage skills.

- Tolerate frustration and ambiguity.

- Develop the attitude of a generalist, of a psychological family doctor.

I end this chapter with two pieces of advice about how to not just survive but thrive in a managed care setting. First, a social worker who been practicing in her HMO for three years advised, "Throw away the theories. . . . Struggle to learn what it is that a person is telling you. Don't have all sorts of preconceived notions. . . . People use language so differently that you really have to learn to understand what they mean. . . . Consider the patient as competent—because when you start to see them as competent you . . . discover all sorts of skills that they have [that] they are not giving themselves credit for. And your work is much easier."

And finally, from a psychologist who had practiced in his HMO for over ten years: "Keep an open mind to new things. . . . Share ideas . . . even if you do not know for certain whether something's going to work or not. If it seems reasonable and . . . appropriate . . . at least give it a try. Don't hold on to . . . the old way of thinking just out of habit . . . because you think those old ideas are best. . . . [Working at the HMO] is a good opportunity to do . . . many different kinds of work and gain many different kinds of experience with a variety of patients. I think that the more flexible someone can be in terms of their thinking—and I don't mean to the point where somebody doesn't know what they are really doing—but if you really try . . . to pair an approach with the needs of a particular client, you can often help someone. . . . I think the work here is really great. I love it. I really enjoy it."

Notes

p. 245, *"There are many truths"*: Peter, L. (1977). *Peter's quotations: Ideas for our times* (p. 174). New York: Bantam.

p. 245, *"The wisdom of the wise"*: ibid (p. 473).

p. 245, *First, the legacy of*: Dacso, S. T., & Dacso, C. (1995). *Managed care answer book*. New York: Aspen.

p. 261, *The information presented here*: Austad, C. S., & Berman, W. A. (1991). *Psychotherapy in HMOs: The practice of mental health in managed health care*. Washington, DC: American Psychological Association; Austad, C. S., DeStefano, L., & Kisch, J. (1988). The health maintenance organization: II. Implications for psychotherapy. *Psychotherapy, 25*(3), 449–454; Austad, C. S. (forthcoming). Can effective psychotherapy be conducted in managed mental health care? In R. Lazarus (Ed.), *Controversies in managed mental health care*. Washington, DC: American Psychiatric Association; Austad, C. S. (1994). Managed care and psychotherapy. In Vandencreek, L., Knapp, S., & Jackson, T. L. (Eds.), *Innovations in Clinical Psychology* (pp. 241–262). Sarasota, FL: Professional Resource Press; Austad, C. S., Sherman, W. O., & Holstein, L. (1993). Psychotherapists in the HMO. *HMO Practice, 7*(3), 122–126; Austad, C. S., Sherman, W. O., Morgan, T., & Holstein, L. (1992). The psychotherapist and the managed care setting. *Professional Psychology, Research and Practice, 23*(4), 807–812; Austad, C. S., Morgan, T., & Holstein, L. (1992). Techniques in independent practice and managed health care settings: Interviews with 43 HMO psychotherapists. *Psychotherapy in Private Practice, 10*, 1–6; Austad, C. S., Henault, K., Steefel, N., & DeStefano, L. (1992). Psychotherapists in independent practice and managed health care settings: A comparison. *Psychotherapy in Private Practice, 10*, 1–6.

11

Is Long-Term Psychotherapy Unethical
in an Era of Managed Care?

Instead of stressing the bad things which I am against,
I stress the good things which I am for.

Peace Pilgrim

I sn't it time to change our thinking about the ethics of health
care? Shouldn't we end the dominance of the individual ethic
over the societal ethic? Why should we? Because we live in the
midst of a society with an unjust health care system where 41 million citizens go without basic health coverage and millions more go
without mental health care.

Isn't it also time to change our thinking about the ethics of
psychotherapy? Shouldn't we end the dominance of traditional,
long-term psychotherapy over temporal eclecticism? Why should
we? Because the indiscriminate practice of long-term psychotherapy is unethical in an era of health care reform. When long-term
psychotherapy is discretionary, when a person does not directly pay
for it out of pocket, when it comes out of a common pool such as

insurance monies and thus deprives one person of needed care in order to give another unneeded care, this is unethical. In this era of limited resources, when there is not enough psychotherapy for everyone who needs it, any unnecessary use contributes to an inequitable distribution.

David Eddy, an ethicist from Duke University, says that whenever one person uses a disproportionate amount of health care without personally paying for it, society must either cover the cost of replacing that service or deprive some other person of care. This situation causes harm to others by depriving them of either needed care or their financial assets. A societal ethic holds that it is society's obligation to care for persons in need who are unable to pay for necessary services. But a sharing ethic does not mean everyone should get as much as they want. People should get only what they need. To encourage sharing, society should support a policy whereby health care professionals do everything that is reasonable and beneficial for their patients but not everything possible.

Long-term bias was understandable when psychotherapy was in its infancy, but perpetuating its infantile and outdated guidelines is inexcusable today. Let's consider the sociological elements of psychotherapy for a moment. Traditional long-term psychotherapy emerged from a sexually repressed Victorian society, but it does not meet the needs of the fast-paced, uninhibited American culture of today. It is time for the old guard to relinquish its hold on a discipline that is now in its adolescence, freeing it so that it can evolve into adulthood and remain relevant in our contemporary health care system.

Thanks to the more refined research methods now available, we now know far too much about psychotherapy to allow ourselves to perseverate and persist in outmoded and obsolete practice. It is now impossible, foolish, and unscientific to uphold the doctrine that traditional long-term therapy should be the gold standard of behavioral health care.

We now know that a great deal of long-term psychotherapy is

unnecessary. Unfortunately, we also know that some of this un-needed treatment is performed more for provider profit than for patient beneficence. All of us are human, and we cannot help but be influenced by the profit motive. This means we must monitor our own selfish motivations and eliminate their influence on our treatment decisions.

Not all long-term therapy is discretionary. There will always be people who are engulfed by constant psychic pain and therefore genuinely need long-term mental health care. These people ought to receive the care they need. Unfortunately, those who truly need lifelong help are often not those who receive it. While the more fortunate, well-insured among us get long-term discretionary care, many truly needy people get none. One man's psychoanalysis can be another man's homelessness. But even for chronic patients, we have never empirically established that a schedule of weekly sessions (or more) of psychotherapy is the most effective way to help. Surely, in the name of a societal ethic, we can better serve greater numbers of people through the use of more progressive models (such as intermittent developmental therapy and so on).

In the best of all worlds, where everyone could have as much as they want, we might not have to consider these thorny issues or make the tough choices about how to ration psychotherapy. But in the real world of limited and diminishing resources, we must implement a plan to solve these problems.

A Program for Ethical Psychotherapy

How can we, as mental health professionals, help promote a fair share of psychotherapy for everyone? I propose a three-step program that will allow us to begin to remedy the problems discussed in this book. The activities in each step can be performed chronologically or concurrently.

First, we can begin to rectify the wrongs and undo the legacy of long-term bias, thereby improving the image and reputation of psychotherapy and helping it become as valued by all as other health care treatments. Second, we must fight to make basic health and mental health care a right instead of a privilege. Third, we must establish guidelines for creating and implementing a societal ethic of psychotherapy, enlisting the help of managed care organizations, payers, providers, and patients.

Step 1: Establish a "Right View" of Psychotherapy

Throughout this book we have seen that long-term bias has generated a number of beliefs that are not scientifically valid. Proponents of long-term psychotherapy has used the mantle of science and the status of the expert professional to perpetuate the myth of the superiority of long-term psychotherapy in the absence of empirical support. Assumptions have been made about treatment parameters (quantity of treatment, length of treatment, scheduling of sessions, and so on) without current scientific data to substantiate them and without clearly qualifying the limits of their scientific basis for the public. Relevant research findings—epidemiological as well as clinical—have been ignored and not integrated into practice. There has been a general failure to distinguish between discretionary and medically necessary psychotherapy; as a result, overtreatment has been encouraged. Furthermore, focusing on illness rather than wellness has discouraged the development of prevention techniques.

Long-term bias has taken its toll on the acceptance and advancement of psychotherapy as an essential medical resource. First, it has given psychotherapy the image of an interminable treatment. Payers are frightened away, worried that reimbursing unlimited services might bankrupt them. This is manifested in an unwillingness on the part of insurers to treat psychotherapy as an equal counterpart to general medical treatments and a policy of reimbursing psychotherapy at only half the rate of other services. Second, long-term bias has stimulated a kind of functional fixedness that has prevented therapists from freely experimenting to discover models that could distribute care more democratically.

To rectify these wrong views, we need to establish a "right view" of psychotherapy and create a new image of it in the eyes of the public and payers. We must advocate the following principles:

- Accurate, scientific information should guide the theory and practice of psychotherapy.

- Standards, guidelines, and algorithms based on empirical data should be established and adhered to.

- Temporal eclecticism should prevail so that the choice of long- versus short-term therapy should be patient- and need-driven, not provider- and theory-driven.

- An epidemiology of psychotherapy should be developed to increase our knowledge and understanding of it and to help us monitor and ensure fair and equitable use.

- A firm distinction should be made between discretionary and medically necessary psychotherapy, in the same way that we distinguish between necessary plastic surgery and elective cosmetic surgery.

- Responsive models of psychotherapy should be developed. We should consider the possibility that interminable analysis is indicative of treatment failure and that it is humane to try another form of treatment if therapy goes on too long.

- A national data base for outcomes research as well as other research should be created and available to all.

Step 2: Establish Psychotherapy as a Right

Once we have taken Step 1 and we are sure that our treatments are based on empirical data, we can move forward with confidence. But before we put a societal ethic in place, we must answer one very important question: Is health and mental health care a right or a privilege?

The compassionate answer is yes, health care ought to be an entitlement for all Americans. Yet, it is not. As Vincente Navarro has pointed out, "the United States and South Africa are the only major countries whose governments do not provide a national health program that guarantees access to health care in time of need. Health care in the United States is not a right; it is a privilege. At a time when the U.S. government declares it is the great defender of human rights around the world, it continues to ignore this basic right at home. Forty years after the United Nations passed the Declaration of Human Rights, which includes . . . the right to health care, the U.S. government does not guarantee a right that is guaranteed in most other developed countries. Why?"

To be without a health care system that is universal, accessible, comprehensive, and humanitarian amounts to national irresponsibility. Our inability to supply the basic health and behavioral health care needs of our citizens is not a problem of economics but a social-moral predicament that haunts our culture. Responsibility for health care continuously shifts. The buck is passed from payer to government to provider to insurer to patient and round and round again. It's time for the buck to stop at the only body empowered to take on the responsibility to orchestrate a comprehensive plan and enact legislation to ensure the equitable distribution of health care—our government. As long as there is one person who needs psychotherapy but cannot obtain it, we are not fulfilling the moral responsibilities of a good society.

Until health care is guaranteed and necessary psychotherapy is considered a part of that health care, we cannot ensure an equitable distribution of psychotherapy for our patients. General health care is the foundation for behavioral health care. To campaign for the right to psychotherapy for *all* citizens, then, is an essential part of establishing guaranteed psychotherapy.

Our professional organizations have tremendous power to wield if they would only focus their energy on a massive attempt to achieve universal health care reform. If we stopped fighting among ourselves; put professional status, theoretical ideologies, and turf wars aside; and joined together to achieve the common goal of promoting basic mental health care for all, we could be much closer to achieving some form of national health care reform.

While it is everyone's responsibility to create a societal ethic, as mental health professionals we should assume a leadership position to help others organize and work toward making health and behavioral health care a right, not a privilege.

Once we have taken Step 2 and established that all Americans have a right to health care, we can devise and implement a societal ethic. The path to universal coverage has many potential turns, with numerous ways to give everyone a fair share. While the specifics of how to accomplish this goal must be decided by each society, there are some basic elements that must be included in any society's health care plan.

Step 3: Devise a Societal Ethic

Since the supply of psychotherapy is finite, it requires distribution. To do so fairly requires a well-articulated, agreed-upon societal ethic. How can we arrive at such an ethic in our culture? How can we strike a balance between the individual and society to enable everyone to obtain his or her fair share of needed health care resources, including psychotherapy?

To put a working societal ethic in place, we must recognize a basic truth that many Europeans already know—all people within a health system are bound together by mutual, interlocking obligations to one another. To be successful, health care requires shared responsibility between citizens, government, and the private sector. Everyone involved in the health care system is expected to share in making it work.

Convincing a society founded on rugged individualism that the success of its health care system depends on human interconnectedness and a sense of responsibility toward others might be a struggle. Our society must move away from its fixation on its already well cultivated and protected individual ethic.

We already have some basic guidelines in place. As discussed earlier, broad directions are already in place for mental health professionals within their professional codes of ethics. The values of social responsibility tell us to strive to palliate human suffering and support laws and policies that will serve the interests of our patients and the public.

As long as it is part of our health care system, we can no longer afford to hold a vision of psychotherapy as a one-on-one activity that occurs in the isolation and privacy of the therapy room. We must see it within its ecological context and from an epidemiological perspective. Psychotherapy is an essential health care resource and an aggregate activity with cumulative effects on our health care system and society. It consists of millions of sessions conducted on a daily basis for millions of people seeking help for a wide assortment of problems. Its annual cost is in the billions of dollars. Hundreds of thousands of providers make income from psychotherapy, and some make a great deal while others make a little. The process of psychotherapy affects the relationships, attitudes, and worldviews of many.

To change our emphasis from an individual to a societal ethic, a paradigm shift is in order. Mental health professionals must rethink psychotherapy. Here is where we can draw on the perspective of the HMO therapist to help us to stretch our consciousness.

As discussed earlier, the successful HMO therapist has a well-developed societal ethic. Seeing the whole membership of the HMO as "her patient" when she works with an individual, she is ever aware of the needs of the rest of the population. Her job is not only to be an individual therapist but also to allocate resources as efficiently as possible. She also knows that the health of all the

HMO's members depends on the health of each member. The unnecessary use of psychotherapy has repercussions that affect the aggregate, the community of those in need. She incorporates a social ethic of sharing into individual therapy. What makes this possible is a salary rather than a fee-for-service payment system, which ensures that financial incentives do not prolong treatment beyond what is necessary.

Establishing and using fair and reasonable practice standards ensures that patients are not undertreated. A nonprofit staff model HMO given a government subsidy to treat the severely ill and the nonresponding patient would be one of the best ways to promote humanitarian methods to deal with patients who are neglected under our present system. I believe that our best chance for implementing a democratic societal ethic that yields universal, comprehensive, accessible, preventive, and holistic health care is through an HMO-type system that is federally subsidized so there is no incentive to limit care to increase profits.

We need to take the following steps before we decide upon specific actions to take:

- Advocate for health and behavioral health care as
  a right governed by a societal ethic. Think of psychotherapy as being similar to penicillin. If one is suffering
  from debilitating psychic pain, as in the case of major
  depression, schizophrenia, or torturous obsessions, then
  like penicillin for a dangerous infection, psychotherapy
  is not an option but a necessity and a right.

- Separate discretionary from necessary care. Necessary
  care must follow a societal ethic and be financed by
  society. Discretionary psychotherapy should follow a
  consumer ethic and should be available for purchase by
  willing consumers. Anyone can purchase a guide for his
  own personal growth, but society should not be obliged
  to pay for it.

- Explore new models and paradigms with the ability to help a large variety of people with a large variety of problems, especially the chronically mentally ill and severely disabled. Constantly assess if we are using our existing resources in a way that will benefit the most people.

- Build a sociology of psychotherapy with which we can study psychotherapy's evolution, usefulness, and effect on our culture.

What Managed Care Can Do

Just as mental health professionals can assist society by working toward the implementation of a societal ethic for psychotherapy, so should the leaders of managed care companies take positive action toward achieving the following goals:

- Adhere to a humanitarian health care ethic, not just a business ethic. Remember and incorporate the socialistic origins of nonprofit managed care—high quality, accessibility, universal care delivered in an ethical manner by ethical people. Assess if the idea of profit is truly compatible with these goals, and if not, promote an alternative system.

- Adhere to strict standards of high-quality care and attend to issues of liability, regulation, and litigation where needed.

- Do not allow the "newness" of the managed care industry—with its current lack of legal and regulatory controls, established norms, policies, procedures, rules, and regulations—to be used for windfall profiteering.

- Help patients and providers change from indemnity, fee-for-service care to managed care. Be sensitive to the impact of an immature industry; its shifting, ambiguously defined parameters have caused destabilization of the status quo and considerable pain to both patients and providers. Transitions must be made with sufficient compassion.

- Do not treat necessary psychotherapy as if it were discretionary.

Showing Kindness

In the midst of the metamorphosis of American health care, life is hard! For mental health professionals the disruption in "business as usual" is an all-too-painful reality. Intense commotion and upheaval are everywhere. The house of cards in which we lived seems to be collapsing all around us.

As the familiar disintegrates, we face a unique window of opportunity that will not be here twenty years from now. A fresh generation of health care providers will grow up in a reformed system. Wide-eyed, green therapists will eagerly anticipate their first job conducting psychotherapy within mammoth managed care corporations. As they listen to their elders from the old guard talk about the "good old days of fee-for-service, indemnity insurance, and solo practice," they will have had none of this experience themselves.

So these ethical dilemmas and issues related to managed care and psychotherapy are time-locked. By the year 2015, policies and regulations will be in place to resolve these issues. A new status quo will prevail. What that status quo will be depends upon how we respond today.

The managed care movement is a catalyst, reminding us that our health care system is riddled with inequities and compelling us to confront issues that have long been swept under the carpet. Out of every adversity comes the seed of potential benefit. Coping with chaos has forced us to come face to face with the unsettling ethical dilemmas discussed in this volume.

We are being forced to take a long, hard look at our professional selves and to ponder and reevaluate our values; our motivations; the nature of the theory, research, and practice we created; the manner in which we obtain money for our work; the social and political causes that our professional organizations endorse or neglect; and our lack of a well-developed, universally endorsed societal ethic. We must examine the merit of long-term and short-term therapy and consider who long-term therapy is serving.

Mental health professionals can be grateful to managed care in the future. There is an old Buddhist saying that enemies are to be cherished and respected, for they teach us patience. The anger we have for the enemy is most useful when it is focused in a way that brings about constructive transformation. The actions we take now will determine what new policies will prevail in the future.

Finding solutions to this complicated web of ethical dilemmas will not be easy. We need to work together—provider, payer, patient, and politician—to promote social justice and provide high-quality health and behavioral health care. We are all responsible.

We can take the words of the Dalai Lama—spiritual leader of the Tibetan people, winner of the 1985 Nobel Peace Prize, and one of the greatest social ethicists of the century—under advisement. He tells us that using the medicine of wisdom and compassion is the best way to achieve a societal ethic. Noted for finding simple solutions to complex problems, he discusses what all of us as mental professionals already know in our hearts but need to act upon now: "Showing kindness to others, we can learn to be less selfish; sharing the suffering of others, we will develop more concern for the welfare of all beings. . . . As our wisdom develops our sense of ethics naturally grows stronger."

Let us find a way to integrate these values into our thinking about psychotherapy. Once we understand that we are all interconnected, we understand that increasing the mental health of one person increases the mental health of all. A change from an individual ethic to a societal ethic will lead to a change from long-term dominance to temporal eclecticism. And this change will command greater accessibility and universality for behavioral health care. Let us develop a societal ethic of psychotherapy whereby both patients and therapists know that they should take what they need and leave the rest for others.

Notes

p. 263, *Instead of stressing:* Peace Pilgrim. (1983). Steps toward inner peace. Hemet, CA: Friends of Peace Pilgrim.

p. 268, *As Vincente Navarro has pointed out:* Navarro, V. (1993). *Dangerous to your health: Capitalism in health care* (p. 17). New York: Monthly Review Press.

p. 270, *As discussed earlier:* American Psychological Association. (1992). *American Psychological Association code of ethics.* Washington, DC: Author.

p. 274, *We can take the words of the Dalai Lama:* Gyatso, T. (1985). *Kindness, clarity, and insight* (p. 30). Ithaca, NY: Snow Lion Publications.

About Carol Shaw Austad

CAROL SHAW AUSTAD is a clinical psychologist who lives in New Britain, Connecticut. She grew up in Waterbury, Connecticut, and attended the University of Connecticut. Austad attended Carleton University in Ottawa, Ontario, where she graduated with a B.A. degree in psychology. During the five years in which she lived in Canada, she was deeply impressed with the excellent health care rendered by the Canadian system. This experience had a great impact on her thinking about national health care.

Austad received her Ph.D. degree (1982) from the University of North Texas, where she obtained excellent instruction in psychodynamic psychotherapy from a number of supervisors. From 1979 to 1982, she completed an internship at Connecticut Valley Hospital, a state institute for the chronically mentally ill. She then worked at a private psychiatric hospital for one year. Austad began her "career in managed care" at Community Health Care Plan, a staff-model health maintenance organization (HMO) in New Haven, Connecticut, in 1983. After five years as a full-time managed care psychologist, she assumed a full-time faculty position at Central Connecticut State University. Austad is presently an associate professor at the university and continues to work part-time as a clinician in the HMO.

Austad has been researching and studying the interaction between health care delivery systems, psychotherapy, and professional development for ten years. She is the coeditor of *Psychotherapy in Managed Health Care: The Optimal Use of Time and Resources* (1991, with W. Berman), as well as numerous articles on managed care and psychotherapy.

About Nicholas A. Cummings

NICHOLAS A. CUMMINGS is president of the Foundation for Behavioral Health, former president of the American Psychological Association, founding CEO of American Biodyne (now MedCo Behavior Care), founding president of the California School of Professional Psychology, past president of the National Academies of Practice in Washington, D.C., and chief psychologist (retired) of Kaiser Permanente Health Plan.

Index